YES PRIME MINISTER

*The Diaries of
the Right Hon. James Hacker*

VOLUME II

Edited by Jonathan Lynn and Antony Jay

BBC BOOKS

The BBC TV series *Yes Prime Minister* was written
by Jonathan Lynn and Antony Jay and
produced by Sydney Lotterby.
The part of *James Hacker* was
played by Paul Eddington, *Sir Humphrey
Appleby* by Nigel Hawthorne and *Bernard
Woolley* by Derek Fowlds.

Published by BBC Books
A Division of BBC Enterprises Ltd
Woodlands, 80 Wood Lane
London W12 0TT

First published 1987

© Jonathan Lynn and Antony Jay
1987

ISBN 0 563 20584 9

Typeset in 11 on 13 point Times by
Phoenix Photosetting, Chatham
Printed in England by
Mackays of Chatham Ltd

YES
PRIME
MINISTER

Contents

Editor's Note

Jim Hacker's memoirs presented unusual editorial problems. Grateful though we are for the honour of editing and transcribing his extensive tape-recordings, we were astonished to learn that, at times, he seems to have decorated and rearranged past events in order to present himself in a favourable light. Indeed, surprising though it may be to the modern reader, he seems positively confident that this goal can be achieved.

We cannot believe that any politician would rearrange past events deliberately in order to distort the historical record, and so we have had to assume that Hacker had some strange defect of mind that frequently led him to ask not 'What did I do?' but 'What is the most impressive explanation of my actions that cannot be disproved by published facts?'

The reader of political memoirs will know that most politicians' memoirs are models of fairness and accuracy, suffused with generosity of spirit, making no attempts to justify past errors. Politicians generally write of their colleagues with a warmth and admiration which is only equalled by their modest deprecation of their own contribution to government. They seldom try to pretend or suggest that every measure they proposed turned out to be successful, nor do they claim to have warned against every decision that led to disaster. Politicians are a noble breed of men, who by their dedication and selfless public service have made Britain what she is today.

Indeed, the sad task of the editors of most political memoirs is to compel the politicians, who have the deepest reluctance to comply with this demand, to inject sufficient controversy, distortion and malice into their books for the publisher to have a chance of selling the serial rights to the *Sunday Times*.

Why was Hacker different? Perhaps the most likely explanation is that elevation to high office actually made him come to see language in a different way. Politicians are simple, direct people. They are accustomed to saying what they mean in a straightforward manner.

But prolonged exposure to the Civil Service, as personified by Sir Humphrey Appleby, may have led Hacker to see language not as a window into the mind but as a curtain to draw across it.

Hacker devoted a great deal of time to talking into his cassette recorder. It would hardly be an exaggeration to say that he had a sort of love affair with it. Finally it was the only thing in the world that was willing to listen to him uncritically. And not only would it listen – it would repeat his own ideas and thoughts to him, a quality that Prime Ministers find very reassuring.

Hacker's recollections would thus be a very imperfect record of his period at Number Ten Downing Street were it not for the other documentation which has so generously been made available to us. Once again we have made copious use of the voluminous Appleby Papers, which contain Sir Humphrey's private diaries, letters and memoranda, and we would like to express our gratitude to his widow, his trustees, his executors, and the Public Record Office which has generously released all possible documents under the Thirty Year rule. We are especially grateful also to Sir Bernard Woolley GCB, formerly Hacker's Principal Private Secretary at Number Ten Downing Street and eventually Head of the Home Civil Service, who has again given us his own recollections and checked this volume for historical accuracy, a thankless task indeed. The responsibility for all errors, whether of omission or commission, remains entirely our own.

Hacker College, Oxford   Jonathan Lynn
May, 2024 AD   Antony Jay

1
Man Overboard

July 2nd

The Employment Secretary has clearly been thinking hard during Wimbledon. Straight back from the Centre Court he came to me with a fascinating proposal.

In a nutshell, his plan is to relocate many of our armed forces to the north of England. He has come to the realisation that, although we have 420,000 service personnel, only 20,000 of them are stationed in the north. Almost everything and everyone is here in the south. The navy is in Portsmouth and Plymouth. The Royal Air Force is in Bedford and East Anglia, barely north of London. The army is in Aldershot. There are virtually no troops in Britain north of the Wash. And yet – here's the rub – virtually *all* our unemployment is in the north. [*See map overleaf – Ed.*]

Dudley[1] is not concerned about the military personnel themselves. Many of them come from the north anyway. No, what he sees is that if we move two or three hundred thousand servicemen from the south to the north we will create masses of civilian jobs: clerks, suppliers, builders, vehicle maintenance . . . the possibilities are immense, limitless. Three hundred thousand extra pay packets to be spent in the shops.

There is really no good argument against this proposal, and I defy the Civil Service to provide one. [*A rash challenge – Ed.*] They should underestimate me no longer. I'm getting wise to their tricks.

[*Hacker, after eight months in Number Ten Downing Street, was clearly much more intelligently aware of the likely Civil Service response to any alteration in the status quo. Even so, he seems to suffer from overconfidence here, and left the door open for 'a good argument' against this plan. New readers may interpret this attitude as reasonable, moderate and flexible. But those students who are familiar*

---

[1] Dudley Belling, the Secretary of State for Employment.

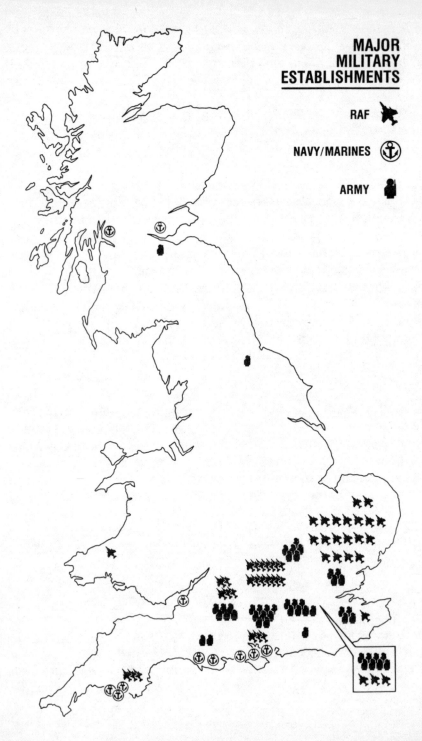

**MAJOR
MILITARY
ESTABLISHMENTS**

RAF

NAVY/MARINES

ARMY

with Hacker's earlier career will know that Sir Humphrey Appleby could conjure up very good arguments out of thin air. Hacker, unshakeably confident though he was that he was wise to Sir Humphrey's tricks, apparently forgot that he was dealing with a master magician.

As soon as the Employment Secretary's relocation proposal was circulated, an emergency meeting was convened at the MOD.[1] The minutes record total approval for the plan, with a note that minor reservations were expressed about the feasibility of certain peripheral details concerning the actual execution of the proposal. Sir Humphrey's private notes, recently released under the Thirty Year rule, tell a rather different story – Ed.]

Meeting today at the MOD with Alan[2] and Geoffrey.[3]

Geoffrey was late. Not particularly soldierly, I thought, but Alan explained that this proposal by the Employment Secretary has put the whole of the Ministry of Defence into a state of turmoil.

Alan, who's new, was taking it very badly indeed. I tried to explain to him that it was a perfectly reasonable plan, seen from the Prime Minister's point of view. Alan refused to see it from the Prime Minister's point of view, remarking bitterly that this wretched proposal emanated from the Department of Employment, and defence was none of their bloody business. I corrected him: the plan emanated from the Secretary of State for Employment – the Department itself had nothing to do with it.

Furthermore, as I could see civil war between the two Departments looming here, I indicated that all work on the proposal was done by the Employment Secretary's political advisers.

[*Sir Humphrey, a circumspect man, probably did not say that the proposal came from the Secretary of State's political advisers. He merely 'indicated' it. He would have been most concerned not to tell lies, even if he was not telling the truth. His distinguished predecessor Sir Arnold Robinson described this process as being 'economical with the truth' on one famous occasion, though he was in turn quoting Edmund Burke – Ed.*]

I pointed out to Alan that we should all stay quite calm, and that we were only dealing with a relocation proposal, not a Russian invasion. Alan said: 'I'd be less worried if it were a Russian invasion – the Ministry of Defence is prepared for that.'

We were all more than surprised to hear this. So he clarified the statement: what he meant was that the MOD knows what it would have to do to repel a Russian invasion. I was even more surprised, and asked if we *could*

[1] Ministry of Defence.
[2] Sir Alan Guthrie, the Permanent Secretary, Ministry of Defence.
[3] Field Marshal Sir Geoffrey Howard, the Chief of the Defence Staff.

11

repel it. He said no, of course not, but at least the MOD don't have to do any more *thinking* about it.

It was up to me nominally to defend the Employment Secretary's proposal, since the Prime Minister has publicly supported it, so I reiterated that, although the armed forces contain a lot of men from the north, *they* are not the ones who are unemployed now. And the Employment Secretary's scheme is designed to help those who are currently unemployed.

Alan felt that we were doing quite enough already. Many of our troops from the north *were* unemployed, that's why they joined up. This argument won't wash with the PM, who is concerned about jobs in the north, whereas the troops who have joined up in the north are spending all their money in the south where they now are.

Alan said that this was logically inevitable, since there is nothing to spend it on in the north.

Field Marshal Sir Geoffrey Howard joined us. He went straight on to the attack, informing me that this proposal must be stopped. He told me that you can't just move hundreds of thousands of men around the country like that.

I thought that's what you did with armies. It sounds a feeble argument to me. But upon closer examination it was the permanence of the move to which he objected. Quite reasonably.

He conceded that *some* servicemen could be stationed permanently in the north of England: other ranks perhaps, junior officers possibly. But he made it clear, very properly, that we really cannot ask senior officers to live permanently in the north.

I asked for a list of reasons. He obliged.

1. Their wives wouldn't stand for it.
2. No schools. [*There* were *schools in the north of England at this time, but perhaps Sir Geoffrey meant that suitable fee-paying schools were not accessible – Ed.*]
3. Harrods is not in the north.
4. Nor is Wimbledon.
5. Ditto Ascot.
6. And the Henley Regatta.
7. Not to mention the Army and Navy Club.

In short, he argued that civilisation generally would be completely remote. This sort of sacrifice is acceptable to the forces in time of war but if the move were made in these circumstances, morale would undoubtedly plummet.

I was impatient with these arguments. The matter is to be discussed in Cabinet this afternoon, and more serious arguments are required than senior officers being three hundred miles from the club, however disturbing, however true!

Geoffrey could think of nothing more serious than that. He remarked indignantly that chaps like him and me might have to move up there.

I pressed him for objective reasons against the plan. He insisted that these *were* objective reasons. I decided against showing him the dictionary, and enquired if there are any *strategic* arguments against it.

He said there were. Several. My pencil poised, I asked him to list them. He was unable to do so. He said that he hasn't had time to think about it yet, but that strategic arguments can always be found against anything. He's absolutely correct in that.

So when Alan and Geoffrey have had time to find some strategic arguments, we must ensure that if they cannot stand up to outside scrutiny we will make them top secret. This is in any case customary with all defence matters, and is the way in which we have always managed to keep the defence estimates high. We will make the strategic arguments *For The Prime Minister's Eyes Only*, which certainly means that they will not be subject to expert scrutiny.

However, the strategic arguments might not be sufficient to deflect the Prime Minister from the Employment Secretary's plan. So I proposed that, for additional safety, we play the man instead of the ball. This is always a good technique, and the man in question is – and deserves to be – the Employment Secretary, whose dreadful idea this was.

The plan we devised involves appealing to the Prime Minister's paranoia. All Prime Ministers are paranoid, this one more than most. It should be child's play to suggest to the Prime Minister that the Employment Secretary is plotting against him.

Geoffrey asked if this were true. Soldiers really are awfully simple people. The question is not whether there is a plot (which, so far as I know, there is not) but whether the Prime Minister can be made to believe there is.

Geoffrey asked if there were any chance of getting rid of him completely. At first I thought that he was referring to the PM, and I indicated that it would be an awful pity to get rid of him after all the effort we've put into getting him house-trained.

But it transpired that Geoffrey meant getting rid of the Employment Secretary. The man is dangerous. If he's moved from Employment he might get Industry – in which case he might try to sell the RAF. Or privatise the army. Or float the navy.

In view of the presence of one or two junior MOD officials at the meeting and the consequent risk of ponting,[1] I expressed appropriate horror at Field Marshal Howard's notion that humble civil servants should presume to try and remove a member of Her Majesty's Government from the Cabinet. I explained that it was out of the question, that only a Prime Minister can remove Secretaries of State.

Nonetheless, any Prime Minister would be forced to consider such drastic

[1] See Editor's note overleaf.

action if he were to suspect the loyalty of a member of his cabinet. And since only someone in an advanced state of paranoia would suspect the Employment Secretary of a plot . . . we're in with a chance.

Before the meeting broke up we ensured that the minutes reflected our enthusiasm for the Employment Secretary's proposal to relocate substantial numbers of our armed forces, at all levels, in the north of England and Scotland. [*Appleby Papers 36/17/QQX*]

[*Sir Humphrey's comment about the discretion of the junior officials reflects the growing concern about freedom of information at this time. An Assistant Secretary by the name of Ponting was one of those officials who had taken it upon himself to leak information to Members of Parliament and other totally unqualified and unsuitable individuals, in what was claimed to be the public interest. 'Ponting' became the participle from the verb 'to pont' used to describe such leaks, and many junior officials were concerned with the problem of to pont or not to pont, the alternatives being loyalty and discretion in the job or resignation from it. 'Ponting' was clearly an attractive temptation, carrying with it the improbability of conviction, the certainty of notoriety and the serialisation of one's memoirs in* The Guardian.

The day following the secret meeting at the MOD, the Employment Secretary's proposal came up for discussion in Cabinet Committee. Hacker's diary continues – Ed.]

July 4th
We discussed Dudley's proposal today in Cabinet Committee and I encountered opposition, just as I expected. Sir Humphrey was present. So were Max[1] and Dudley[2] and several others. Bernard was there too, of course.[3]

Dudley, at my prompting, asked for reactions to his paper.

Max spoke first. He was bound to be against it. 'Well, Prime Minister, I know that on the face of it this plan looks as though it might benefit the employment situation in depressed areas. But this is to be achieved, as I understand it, by relocating most of our defence establishments. I suggest that it affects the Defence Department at least as much as the Department of Employment and I need time to do a feasibility study.'

I looked around the table. Nobody else spoke.

---

[1] Sir Maxwell Hopkins, Secretary of State for Defence.
[2] Dudley Belling, Secretary of State for Employment.
[3] Bernard Woolley, the Prime Minister's Principal Private Secretary.

'Anyone else have an opinion?' I asked. 'Quickly.' Brian,[1] Eric[2] and Neil[3] all looked rather doubtful.

Brian said: 'Well, I don't really know much about it, but it sounds like a bit of an upheaval.' He's right on both counts.

Eric murmured: 'Rather expensive.'

And Neil commented carefully that it was rather a big move.

Having had my little bit of fun, I gave my opinion. 'I'm thoroughly in favour of the proposal,' I said.

'So am I,' agreed Geoffrey[4] without hesitation.

'Absolutely first-rate,' said Eric, and Neil commented that it was a brilliant scheme. Sometimes being surrounded by yes-men is rather irritating, though it certainly has its compensations. And, after all, since I'm usually right on matters of government strategy it does save a lot of time when they all agree with me right away.

I smiled at my colleagues. 'I think that the Secretary of State for Defence is in a minority of one.'

Max stood up for himself. He was grimly determined. I have to admire that, even though he can't win this one. 'Nonetheless, Prime Minister,' he said, 'I am the responsible Minister and this can't be decided till I've done my feasibility study. The defence of the realm is in question. We must have a further meeting about this, with time allotted for a full discussion.'

A reasonable request. I agreed that we would have a full discussion of it at our next meeting, in two weeks' time, after which we would put it to full Cabinet for approval.

The rest of the Committee agreed with me again. 'Hear hear! *Hear* hear!' they all grunted vociferously.

Dudley added: 'May I request, Prime Minister, that it be noted in the minutes that the Cabinet Committee was in favour of my plan, save for one member?'

I nodded at Humphrey and Bernard, who made notes. But Max refused to accept Dudley's request without comment. 'The one member', he remarked stubbornly, 'is the member whose department would have to be reorganised. It's quite a problem.'

I began to feel impatient with Max. 'May I urge the Secretary of State for Defence to remember that every problem is also an opportunity?'

[1] Brian Smithson, Secretary of State for the Environment.
[2] Eric Jeffries, the Chancellor of the Exchequer.
[3] Neil Hitchcock, Secretary of State for Transport.
[4] Geoffrey Pickles, Secretary of State for Trade and Industry.

Humphrey intervened. 'I think, Prime Minister, that the Secretary of State for Defence fears that this plan may create some insoluble opportunities.'

We all laughed. 'Very droll, Humphrey, but not so.' I dismissed them and, as they trooped out obediently, I remained behind to catch up on the details of Dudley's proposal. I hadn't had time to read much of it before the meeting.

'Er . . . Prime Minister.' I looked up. To my surprise, Sir Humphrey had remained behind. I gave him my full attention.

SIR BERNARD WOOLLEY RECALLS:[1]

Not as I recall. And I do recall this conversation very well, as I dined out on it for some months. It went rather like this. Sir Humphrey did indeed say: 'Er . . . Prime Minister.' Thus far Hacker's account is accurate but no further.

'Oh, still here, Humphrey?' said Hacker, reading.

'Yes,' said Humphrey. 'I wanted to have a word with you about the Employment Secretary's scheme.'

Hacker was now engrossed in whatever he was reading. 'Terrific scheme, isn't it?' he replied without looking up.

Humphrey did not think so. 'Well . . . the Service Chiefs weren't entirely happy with it, I gather.'

'Good,' said Hacker cheerfully, then looked up. 'What?' He hadn't heard a word.

Humphrey was getting pretty irritated. He never much cared for the proverbial brush-off unless he held the brush. 'Prime Minister,' he said testily, 'do I have your full attention?'

'Of course you do, Humphrey. I'm just reading these notes.'

'Prime Minister, there's been an earthquake in Haslemere,' remarked Humphrey, by way of a small test.

'Good, good,' murmured Hacker. Then something must have penetrated, albeit slowly, because he looked up. Sir Humphrey, well aware that the Prime Minister had the attention span of a moth, confined himself to repeating with unusual clarity of speech that the Service Chiefs didn't like the plan.

[*Hacker's diary continues – Ed.*]

Humphrey kept batting on about how the Service Chiefs didn't like the plan. Of course they didn't! One could hardly expect them to appreciate the prospect of moving their wives away from Harrods and Wimbledon.

Sir Humphrey responded snootily to this suggestion. 'Prime

---

[1] In conversation with the Editors.

Minister, that is unworthy. Their personal feelings do not enter into it. Their objections are entirely strategic.'

'Oh yes?' I leaned back in my chair and smiled benevolently. He didn't fool me. Not any more. I spoke with heavy sarcasm. 'Strategic? The Admiralty Ships Division needs a deep-water port so it obviously has to be in Bath – thirty miles inland. The Marines' job is to defend Norway so we station them in Plymouth. Armoured vehicle trials are conducted in Scotland so the military engineering establishment clearly needs to be in Surrey.'

'These are just isolated examples,' replied Humphrey unconvincingly.

'Quite,' I agreed. 'And there's another seven hundred isolated examples in this paper.' And I waved the report at him. He gazed back at me, unsmiling, cold, totally unshakeable, his piercing blue eyes fixed upon me as they stared at me down his patrician nose. I hesitated. [*And we all know what happens to he who hesitates – Ed.*]

'Why are you against it, Humphrey?' I felt I had to understand.

'I, Prime Minister? I assure you, I am not against it. I'm simply trying to furnish you with the appropriate questions. Like the question of cost.'

He has completely missed the point. 'But that's the whole beauty of it, Humphrey. It *makes* money! We sell all those expensive buildings in the south and move into cheap ones in the north. And there would be hundreds of thousands of acres of high-priced land in the Home Counties to sell too.'

'So you think the Employment Secretary has done well?'

'Yes, he's a good chap.'

To my surprise Humphrey agreed wholeheartedly. 'Oh, I do agree with you there. Absolutely brilliant. Outstanding. A superb intellect. Excellent footwork. Strong elbows. A major figure, without doubt.'

I didn't think he was *that* good. In fact, I was rather amazed that Humphrey went overboard for him like that. I said as much.

'But he is a good chap,' insisted Humphrey. 'Wouldn't you say?'

'Yes,' I said. I'd already said it.

'Yes indeed,' mused Humphrey. 'Very popular, too.'

This was news to me. 'Is he?'

'Oh yes,' Humphrey told me.

I wanted to know more. 'Not *that* popular, is he?'

Humphrey was nodding, eyebrows raised, as if slightly astonished by the extent of Dudley's popularity. 'Oh yes he is. In Whitehall. And with the parliamentary party, I understand.'

I considered this. I suppose he's right. Dudley *is* very popular with the parliamentary party.

'And with the grass roots, I'm told,' Humphrey added.

'Are you?'

He nodded. I wonder who tells him these things.

'And he seems to have quite a following in the Cabinet too.'

A following in the Cabinet? How is that possible? I'm supposed to be the only one with a following in the Cabinet. 'Tell me more.' I was curious. 'Sit down.'

Humphrey sat opposite me, but seemed unwilling to say more. 'There's nothing to tell, really. It's just that people are beginning to talk about him as the next Prime Minister.'

I was startled. 'What? What do you mean?'

'I mean,' said Humphrey carefully, 'when you decide to retire, of course.'

'But I'm not planning to retire. I only just got here.'

'Exactly,' he replied enigmatically.

I had a little think. 'Why', I asked eventually, 'should people be talking about a next Prime Minister?'

'I'm sure it's just general speculation,' he drawled casually.

It's all right for Humphrey to be sure. But I'm not sure. 'Do you think he wants to be Prime Minister?'

Suddenly Humphrey seemed to be on his guard. 'Even if he does, surely you have no reason to doubt his loyalty? He's not trying to build up a personal following or anything, is he?'

'Isn't he?'

'Is he?'

I thought about it for a few moments. 'He spends a hell of a lot of time going round the country making speeches.'

'Only as a loyal minister.' Why was Humphrey so keen to defend him? 'I'm sure he pays personal tributes to you in all of them.'

We looked at each other. And wondered. 'Does he?' I asked. I'd never thought of checking. I told Bernard to get me copies of Dudley's last six speeches. At once.

We waited in silence. And it occurred to me, once I started thinking about it, that Dudley also spends a considerable amount of time chatting up our backbenchers in the House of Commons tea room.

I mentioned this to Humphrey. He tried to reassure me. 'But you asked ministers to take more trouble to communicate with the party in the House.'

True enough. 'But he has them to dinner parties as well.'

'Oh.' Humphrey looked glum. 'Does he?'

'Yes, he does,' I replied grimly. 'This starts to get worrying.'

There seemed no more to say. Bernard returned and said that Employment had phoned to let us know that we wouldn't be able to get copies of Dudley's speeches till later today or tomorrow. I'll read them as soon as I get them. Meanwhile, I won't worry about it. It's lucky I'm not paranoid. And I'm also fortunate to have someone like Humphrey as my Cabinet Secretary, someone who doesn't shrink from letting me know the truth, even if it is a little upsetting.

July 5th

I couldn't sleep. This business with Dudley is really worrying. I told Annie[1] about it, and she said airily that she's sure there's nothing to worry about. What does *she* know?

Today, first thing, I went through copies of Dudley's six most recent speeches. As I suspected, and feared, there was nothing in them by way of a personal tribute to me. Well, virtually nothing.

I called Humphrey in for a confidential word. Like me, he could hardly believe that Dudley had said nothing suitable about me.

'Surely,' asked Humphrey, evidently puzzled, '*surely* he must have talked about the new Prime Minister bringing a new hope to Britain? *The Dawn of a New Age.* You know, that leaflet you told party headquarters to issue to all MPs and constituencies?'

I shook my head. 'Not a word.'

'That *is* odd.'

'It's more than odd,' I remarked. 'It's suspicious. Very suspicious.'

'Even so, Prime Minister, he surely isn't actively plotting against you?'

I wasn't so sure. 'Isn't he?'

'Is he?'

'How do I know he's not?'

Thoughtfully, he stroked his chin. 'You could always find out.'

'Could I?'

'The Chief Whip would be bound to know.'

Humphrey was right, of course. Why didn't I think of it? I told Bernard to send for the Chief Whip right away. And we were in luck. The Chief Whip was in his office at Number Twelve.[2] We told him to drop everything and come right over.

---

[1] Mrs Hacker, the Prime Minister's wife.

[2] No. 12 Downing Street, two doors up from the Prime Minister. A half-minute's walk away.

It was my duty to meet the Chief Whip and show him into the Cabinet Room. So when Sir Humphrey left the Prime Minister, who by now was chewing the Bokhara – figuratively, of course – I hurried out after him. I was anxious for more details of this apparent plot.

I stopped Humphrey in the lobby outside the Cabinet Room, where I could also keep my eye on the front door of Number Ten.

'Sir Humphrey,' I said, 'I'm very troubled by what I've just learned.'

He looked at me with detached amusement, and asked what that was. I explained that I felt that I'd been walking around with my eyes shut. I'd never realised that there was a Cabinet plot against the Prime Minister.

He raised his eyebrows. 'Is there?' he asked. 'How interesting.'

'You said there was,' I said.

He said: 'I said nothing, Bernard. Nothing at all.'

Rapidly, I put my brain into rewind search, and realised that he had indeed said nothing. So . . . what *had* he been saying? Something, certainly, even if it was nothing. But it couldn't have been nothing, or why was he not saying it?

I owed it to Hacker to get to the bottom of this. I decided to ask a straight question. After all, though rare, it was not entirely unknown for Humphrey to give a straight answer. 'So . . . you mean . . . do you know if there is a plot?'

'No.'

This *appeared* to be a straight answer. But no. I sought elucidation.

'No there is a plot or no there isn't?'

'Yes,' replied Humphrey obligingly.

I decided to try a new tack. 'Sir Humphrey,' I said carefully, 'what has the Employment Secretary actually done?'

'Nothing, as yet, Bernard. And we must keep it that way.'

I could see that he was referring to the plan, not the plot. Or non-plot. Then, suddenly, the penny dropped. I had been bemused as to why Sir Humphrey had been so forthcoming about the Employment Secretary's popularity. I now saw that he was playing the man and not the ball.

So I played the ball. 'Isn't the Employment Secretary's plan actually rather a good one?'

'For whom?'

'For the country.'

'Maybe. But that's hardly the point.'

'Why not?'

Humphrey stared at me, irritated. 'Bernard, when you move on from here, where do you plan to go?'

I thought it was one of his threats. Cagey, I replied that I didn't really know.

[1] In conversation with the Editors.

'How would you like to be Deputy Secretary in Charge of Defence Procurement?'

This suggestion surprised me. Dep. Sec. is pretty high. One's K^1 is guaranteed. Dep. Secs are top people, their names are in *Who's Who* and everything. Normally, if Humphrey were trying to threaten me, he'd suggest the War Graves Commission or the Vehicle Licensing Centre in Swansea. So, if he wasn't threatening, what *was* he driving at? I waited.

'You could find yourself doing that job in Sunderland. Or Berwick-on-Tweed. Or Lossiemouth.'

He *was* threatening me. I instantly saw the major drawback to the Employment Secretary's plan. I certainly wouldn't want to leave London for Sunderland or Berwick-on-Tweed. They're up north somewhere!

And I didn't even understand the reference to Lossiemouth. 'Is that a place?' I asked Humphrey.

'What did you think it was?'

'A dogfood.'

Humphrey smirked menacingly. 'If the Employment Secretary has his way you may have a three-year diet of Lossiemouth yourself. You see?'

I saw.

I also saw that the plan cannot possibly be good for the country. It is not possible for a plan to be good for the country and bad for the Civil Service – it's a contradiction in terms. But I still didn't understand why Humphrey had suggested sending for the Chief Whip to confirm a plot that didn't exist.

We were still standing in the lobby of Number Ten, a fairly public place. Humphrey looked around cautiously, to check that we were not being overheard. Then he explained something that I have never before understood.

'The Chief Whip, Bernard, is bound to hedge. He dare not categorically state that there is no plot against the Prime Minister, just in case there *is* one. Even if the Chief Whip has heard nothing, he must say that he has suspicions, to cover himself. He will also say that he has no solid evidence, and he will promise to make urgent enquiries.'

At that moment the Chief Whip himself, Jeffrey Pearson, bustled through the front door like a ship in full sail and surged along the wide corridor towards us. My eyes indicated his presence to Humphrey, who swung round and gave him a warm greeting. 'Ah, good morning, Chief Whip.'

'Good morning, Cabinet Secretary. Good morning, Bernard.'

I asked Pearson to wait in the Private Office.[2] I wanted to be sure that Sir Humphrey and I were now fully in tune.

Humphrey instructed me to go into the meeting with Jeffrey – which, in any case, I would have done – and inform Sir Humphrey of everything that was said – which I may not have done.

---

[1] Knighthood.
[2] The office of the Private Secretary, i.e. Bernard Woolley's office.

'I'm not sure I can do that. It might be confidential.'

Humphrey disagreed. 'The matter at issue concerns the defence of the realm and the stability of government.'

'But you only need to know things on a "need to know" basis.'

Humphrey became impatient. 'Bernard, I need to know everything. How else can I judge whether or not I need to know it?'

I'd never thought of that. Hitherto, I'd thought that others might have been the judge of the Cabinet Secretary's need to know. I decided to get this straight.

'So that means that you need to know things even when you don't need to know them. You need to know them not because you need to know them but because you need to know whether or not you need to know. And if you don't need to know you still need to know so that you know that there was no need to know.'

'Yes,' said Humphrey. A straight answer at last. And he thanked me for helping him clarify the position.

[*Hacker's diary continues – Ed.*]

Jeffrey Pearson, the Chief Whip, was in the Cabinet Room within ten minutes. He was evasive but during the meeting he made it perfectly clear that there is indeed some sort of leadership challenge, either led by Dudley or using Dudley as the figurehead. His problem is a lack of concrete evidence. So he can't make a move to stamp it out.

I was magnanimous. After all, one wants ambitious men in the Cabinet, one *needs* them. Just as long as they don't get *too* ambitious. . . .

I'm grateful to Humphrey for drawing my attention to it. He really is a good man and a loyal servant.

[*Jeffrey Pearson's account of this is somewhat different. We reprint this extract from his stylish memoirs* Suck It And See *– Ed.*]

I had a sudden urgent call from Number Ten. Hacker wanted to see me right away. Bernard Woolley, his Private Secretary, refused to give me a reason.

Naturally I thought I'd done something to upset him. So it was with some caution that I entered the Cabinet Room, with Woolley in attendance. The morning sun shone brightly through the windows, creating patterns of intense light and deep shade.

Hacker sat in the shadows. 'How are things going, Chief Whip?'

Naturally I was cautious, though I had nothing to hide. I told him things were going quite well really, and asked why.

'You mean, you noticed nothing?'

So I was supposed to have noticed something. What, I wondered, had I missed? I couldn't think of anything in particular, though it was a slightly difficult time with a little unrest on the back benches. But then it's always a slightly difficult time with a little unrest on the back benches. Unless, that is, it's a very difficult time with lots of unrest on the back benches.

[*A slightly difficult time with a little unrest on the back benches' was what fortune-tellers call a cold reading: something that is always true and always safe to say. A fortune-teller's cold reading might be: 'You went through a slightly difficult time round the age of thirteen.' A doctor's cold reading, if he cannot diagnose an illness, would be: 'I think it might be a good idea for you to give up smoking and lose a little weight' – Ed.*]

'Is there anything you haven't told me?' asked the Prime Minister.

I racked my brains furiously. He prompted me. 'A plot? A leadership challenge?'

I hadn't heard a thing. But I couldn't say so, because Hacker obviously had suspicions. Perhaps he even had evidence. I played safe, avoided giving a direct answer, and told him that I had no real evidence of anything.

'But you have suspicions?'

I couldn't say I hadn't . . . and anyway, I always have suspicions of one sort or another. 'It's my job to have suspicions,' I replied carefully.

'Well, what are they?'

This was tricky. 'Jim,' I replied with my frankest manner, 'it wouldn't be right for me to tell you all my suspicions, not unless or until there's something solid to go on.'

'But you know who I'm talking about?'

I had no idea. 'I think I can guess,' I said.

Hacker remained in the shadows. I couldn't quite see his eyes. He heaved a sigh. 'How far has it got?' he asked finally.

I was still searching for a clue as to the identity of the pretender. One thing I knew for sure – it hadn't got very far or I would certainly have known about it. At least, I think I certainly would.

He was waiting for reassurance. I gave it. 'Only to a very early stage. So far as I can tell.' I was still being strictly honest.

'Do you think you ought to have a word with him?' the Prime Minister wanted to know. 'Tell him I know what's going on? I don't want to lose him from the Cabinet. I just want him under control.'

I didn't see how I could possibly have a word with him until I knew who he was. 'Perhaps you should have a word with him yourself,' I replied carefully.

He shook his head. 'No. Not at this stage.'

I waited.

'Who else is involved?'

I saw my chance. 'Apart from . . .?'

The Prime Minister was getting irritable. 'Apart from Dudley, obviously.'

Dudley! Dudley? Incredible! Dudley!!

'Oh, *apart* from Dudley, it's a bit early to say. After all, Prime Minister, there may not be anything to it.'

The Prime Minister stood up. He stared at me over his reading glasses. He looked thin, tired and drawn. This job is taking a toll on him, and he's only been at it less than a year. 'Jeffrey, I'm not taking any risks,' he said quietly.

I could see that he meant business. I left the Cabinet Room, and assigned all the Whips to make some enquiries. Top priority. After all, if there is a plot I need to know its full potential.

[*Jeffrey Pearson certainly wanted and needed to reassure himself that the plot, if plot there was, could be nipped in the bud. If it could not, he would have wanted to reassure himself that it was not too late to change sides.*]

[*Two days later Sir Arnold Robinson, Appleby's predecessor as Secretary of the Cabinet, received a note from Sir Humphrey. It has been found in the archive of the Campaign for Freedom of Information, of which Sir Arnold was the President. Naturally the letter was confidential and has been kept under wraps, but the archive of the Campaign for Freedom of Information was recently made available to historians under the Thirty Year Rule – Ed.*]

Cabinet Office
July 6th

Dear Arnold,

You will have heard on the grapevine about the Employment Secretary's plan to move many of our armed forces' establishments to the north. There are three reasons why the PM is in favour of this plan:

1. It will reduce unemployment.
2. Alternatively, it will look as though he is reducing unemployment.
3. At the very least, it will look as though he is *trying* to reduce unemployment.

The reality is that he is only trying to look as if he is trying to reduce unemployment. This is because he is worried that it does not look as if he is trying to look as if he is trying to reduce unemployment.

Curiously, the P.M. has come to suspect that the plan may be the start of a leadership bid by the Employment Secretary.

This is, of course, a ridiculous notion. But the higher the office, the higher the level of political paranoia. Nonetheless, it is undoubtedly in the national interest that this plan does not proceed, and the Prime Minister's paranoia would undoubtedly be fed (and the Employment Secretary's chances of survival in high office much reduced) if a leak occurred in the press which suggested that this brilliantly imaginative plan by the Employment Secretary was being blocked by the Prime Minister.

We must devoutly hope that no such leak occurs. Have you any thoughts on this matter?

Yours ever,
Humphrey

[A reply was received from Sir Arnold Robinson at the beginning of the next week. A copy was found at the Campaign's headquarters, but we were fortunate enough to find the original among the Appleby Papers – Ed.]

July 9th

Dear Humphrey,
Thank you for your letter. A leak of the sort you suggest would almost certainly result in man overboard.

I cannot see, however, how such a leak can occur. You as Cabinet Secretary cannot be party to a leak. And although, as President of the Campaign for Freedom of Information, I have an undoubted duty to make certain facts available, I do not see in all conscience how I, as a former Cabinet Secretary, can give confidential information to the press.

Yours ever,
Arnold

[A reply was apparently sent to Sir Arnold Robinson by return – delivered by messenger – Ed.]

July 10th

Dear Arnold,
I would not dream of suggesting that you give confidential information to the press. It is confidential misinformation to which I refer.

Yours ever,
Humphrey

[Sir Arnold sent a brief and immediate reply – Ed.]

July 10th

Dear Humphrey,
I shall be happy to oblige.

Yours ever,
Arnold

[The original letters are reproduced on the following pages – Ed.]

70 WHITEHALL, LONDON SW1A 2AS

From the Secretary of the Cabinet and Head of the Home Civil Service

July 6th

Dear Arnold,

You will have heard on the grapevine about the Employment Secretary's plan to move many of our armed forces' establishments to the north. There are three reasons why the P.M. is in favour of this plan:

1. It will reduce unemployment.

2. Alternatively, it will look as though he is reducing unemployment.

3. At the very least, it will look as though he is <u>trying</u> to reduce unemployment.

The reality is that he is only trying to look as if he is trying to reduce unemployment. This is because he is worried that it does not look as if he is trying to look as if he is trying to reduce unemployment.

Curiously, the P.M. has come to suspect that the plan may

be the start of a leadership bid by the Employment Secretary.

This is, of course, a ridiculous notion. But the higher the office, the higher the level of political paranoia. Nonetheless, it is undoubtedly in the national interest that this plan does not proceed, and the Prime Minister's paranoia would undoubtedly be fed (and the Employment Secretary's chances of survival in high office much reduced) if a leak occurred in the press which suggested that this brilliantly imaginative plan by the Employment Secretary was being blocked by the Prime Minister.

We must devoutly hope that no such leak occurs. Have you any thoughts on this matter?

Yours ever

Humphrey

The Campaign for Freedom of Information

3 Endsleigh Street, London WC1H ODD
Telephone 01-278 9686

July 9th

Dear Humphrey,

Thank you for your letter. A leak of the sort you suggest would almost certainly result in man overboard.

I cannot see, however, how such a leak can occur. You as Cabinet Secretary cannot be party to a leak. And although, as President of the Campaign for Freedom of Information, I have an undoubted duty to make certain facts available, I do not see in all conscience how I, as a former cabinet secretary, can give confidential information to the press.

Yours ever,

Arnold.

70 WHITEHALL, LONDON SW1A 2AS

From the Secretary of the Cabinet and Head of the Home Civil Service

July 10th

Dear Arnold,

I would not dream of suggesting that you give confidential information to the press. It is confidential misinformation to which I refer.

Yours ever

Humphrey

The Campaign for Freedom of Information

3 Endsleigh Street, London WC1H ODD
Telephone 01-278 9686

July 10th.

Dear Humphrey,

I shall be happy to oblige.

Yours ever,

Arnold.

[*Hacker's diary continues – Ed.*]

July 11th

I am now convinced that a dirty little scheme has been hatched behind my back. It is a disloyal, ungrateful and treacherous plot, and I will not tolerate it.

I spoke to the Chief Whip. He said that he had no real evidence but he had *suspicions*. He said that he would make enquiries! He refused to tell me about them till he had something solid to go on. I regard that as proof positive.

I discussed the matter with Humphrey today. He expressed surprise that Dudley is plotting against me. 'I would have thought all your Cabinet were loyal.' Sometimes I am amazed at how trusting and naive Humphrey reveals himself to be. Loyal? How few people realise what the word loyalty means when spoken by a Cabinet Minister. It only means that his fear of losing his job is stronger than his hope of pinching mine.

'So,' said Humphrey, wide-eyed, 'you believe that the Employment Secretary has his eye on the Prime Ministerial chair?'

'Yes.' I sat back. 'But look what I've got on it.'

Humphrey didn't get my little joke and merely commented that loyalty was a fundamental requirement of collective responsibility.

Hasn't he noticed that collective responsibility has fallen out of fashion? Collective responsibility means that when we do something popular they all leak the fact that it was their idea, and when we do something unpopular they leak the fact that they were against it. This country is governed by the principle of collective irresponsibility.

'You were a Cabinet minister once.' Humphrey seemed to be admonishing me gently.

'That's different,' I reminded him. 'I was loyal.'

'You mean, you were more frightened of losing your job than . . .'

'No, Humphrey,' I interrupted him. 'I was *genuinely* loyal.'

Humphrey asked me why my colleagues want my job so much. The explanation is simple: I'm the only member of the government who can't be sent to Northern Ireland tomorrow.

'Even so,' he remarked, 'I find it hard to believe that the Employment Secretary is actively plotting against you.'

I told him it was obvious. I asked what more proof he would need. He thought for a moment.

'Well . . .' he began, 'this proposal to move Defence establishments to the north is bound to be leaked to the press, isn't it?'

'Bound to be,' I agreed. 'I'm surprised it hasn't been already.'

'Well, if it were leaked as the Employment Secretary's plan, I agree that it would confirm your suspicions. But I'm sure it will come out as a government plan.'

He's right. It's a good test. We shall see what we shall see.

July 12th

So much for Humphrey's faith in Dudley's loyalty. *The Standard* today contained the leak we were waiting for. And the proof that that disloyal swine is gunning for me.

THE LONDON EVENING STANDAR[D]

TONIGHT'S WE

THURSDAY, 12 JULY

HACKER HITS JOBLESS

by Peter Kirkston

SOURCES in Whitehall report that an imaginative plan, an initiative by Dudley Belling, the Secretary of State for Employment, to reduce unemployment in the depressed areas, has been blocked by the Prime Minister.

How dare he? How *dare* he??

It was Humphrey who showed me the newspaper. I was very angry indeed. I told Humphrey how I'd backed Dudley all along, I told him how I fought for that sodding plan of his. I told him how I gave him his first Cabinet post and how I've treated him like a son. And this, I said, is how he thanks me. I was speechless, utterly speechless.

Humphrey nodded sadly. 'How sharper than a serpent's tooth it is to have a thankless Cabinet colleague.'

What can you say? Nothing. 'It's envy,' I said. 'Dudley is consumed with envy.'

'It's one of the seven Dudley sins,' said Bernard, trying to lighten the atmosphere. I quelled him with a glance.

Humphrey, a tower of strength as always, suggested a possible course of action: that we draft my letter accepting his resignation.

But there are several disadvantages to that idea. Dudley will deny that he leaked the story, in which case I've no grounds for sacking him. And if I then sack him anyway, what are the consequences? He'd be even more dangerous on the back benches than in the Cabinet – sacked ministers don't even have to pretend to be loyal.

'So,' enquired Humphrey, 'you intend to go ahead with his plan?'

That option is also closed to me now. Once a story in the press says that I'm blocking it I can't possibly let it go ahead – it will look as though he has defeated me. Regretfully, I must abandon the plan, even though it's good. At least, I think I must.

I told Humphrey my dilemma.

'Prime Minister, you're not being indecisive, are you?'

'No,' I said. He looked at me. He knew I was. 'Yes,' I acknowledged. Then I thought: I'm damned if I'll be indecisive. 'No,' I snarled. Then I realised that I'd already answered the question all too clearly. 'I don't know,' I said weakly, putting my head in my hands. I felt deeply depressed, enervated. All my energy was sapped by the treachery and disloyalty.

He offered to help. I couldn't see how he could. But he produced some papers from a file on his lap. 'Technically I shouldn't show you this.'

'I don't see why not. I'm Prime Minister, aren't I?'

'Yes,' he explained. 'That's why I shouldn't be showing it to you. It's a Ministry of Defence draft internal paper. Top Secret. The Defence Secretary hasn't seen it yet.' He passed it over the desk. 'But as you see, it casts grave doubts on the Employment Secretary's plan.'

This was a paper I was keen to read. It is fascinating. Part One pointed out that many of the 'valuable' army buildings that Dudley quoted cannot be sold. Some are listed.[1] Some are under strict planning controls. Some don't conform to private-sector fire and safety regulations. It all showed that the cost of the move would be prohibitive.

Part Two showed that the move would create massive unemployment in the Home Counties and East Anglia, with far fewer new jobs created in the north-east than would be lost in the south.

And then, in Part Three, which I read in bed tonight, there are pages and pages of objections on grounds of military strategy.

Tomorrow I'll question Humphrey about this further.

July 13th

At a meeting with Humphrey first thing this morning I questioned him closely about the MOD paper. 'Is it quite honest and accurate?'

Humphrey was evasive. He said that everything is a matter of interpretation. And if we were to look at the conclusion of the report we would see that all of the objections to the scheme were known to the Employment Secretary before he produced his plan. He added one other rather telling point: that the whole plan may not be completely unconnected with the fact that Dudley represents a Newcastle constituency.

This had not escaped me either. [*In which case, it is strange that Hacker had never mentioned it – Ed.*].

'The public', I commented, 'has a right to know this.'

Humphrey shook his head. 'It's a top secret document.' I simply stared at him, and waited. 'On the other hand,' he continued, 'the Service Chiefs are notorious for their indiscretion.'

'Notorious,' I agreed.

'It could well find its way into the hands of an irresponsible journalist.'

---

[1] 'Listed' buildings under Section 54(9) of the 1971 Town and Country Planning Act, which was replaced by the Town and Country Planning (Listed Buildings and Buildings in Conservation Areas) Regulations of 1977, which were further amended by the 1986 Act, necessitating changes in the Town and Country Planning (Listed Buildings and Buildings in Conservation Areas) Regulations 1987 (S1 1987, No. 349), are buildings which are of special architectural or historic interest listed since 1 July 1948 (when the Town and Country Planning Act of 1947 came into operation) and compiled by the Secretary of State with reference to national criteria, classified into three grades to show their relative importance, namely Grade I, Grade II* and Grade II. It is an offence under Section 107 of the 1971 Act to alter, extend or demolish a listed building unless excepted from control by Section 56, Section 54(9) (see paragraph 73) or Section 56(1)(a) and (b), excluding buildings for ecclesiastical use (see paragraphs 103–105).

'Could it?' I asked hopefully. 'Or several irresponsible journalists?'

Humphrey felt that such an eventuality was not beyond the bounds of possibility.

I made it quite clear, however, that I could not be a party to anything like that, even though it would at least give the public the true facts. Humphrey agreed wholeheartedly that I could not be party to such a leak.

We agreed that we would defer discussion of the plan until an unspecified future date [*i.e. abandon it – Ed.*], and that meanwhile Sir Humphrey would attend to the plumbing.

After he left, Bernard, who lacks subtlety sometimes, turned to me. 'When's he going to leak it?' he asked.

I was shocked. 'Did I ask for a leak?'

'Not in so many . . .' he hesitated. 'No, Prime Minister, you didn't.'

'Indeed not, Bernard,' I replied stiffly. 'I have never leaked. I occasionally give confidential briefings to the press. That is all.'

Bernard smiled. 'That's another of those irregular verbs, isn't it? I give confidential briefings; you leak; he has been charged under Section 2a of the Official Secrets Act.'

July 18th

Everything went like clockwork – until today. Two days ago a story appeared in several newspapers, attributed to various non-attributable sources, effectively torpedoing Dudley's plan.

All the important points were covered – the fact that the MOD can't make a profit on many of the valuable buildings in the London area; the fear of huge unemployment in the south without creating enough new jobs up north; and the military and strategic arguments against the plan. At least two of them ran the story reminding readers that Dudley himself represented a constituency in the north-east.

All of this was picked up by the TV news. [*Television news in the 1980s hardly ever originated a news story – Ed.*]

But today it all came to a head. I was horrified when I saw the front page of *The Guardian* and the cartoon [*see overleaf – Ed.*].

THE GUARDIAN

Wednesday 18 July

...and Manchester

Dudley Belling alleges conspiracy

Employment secretary denies leaking

By David Tow

Dudley Belling, the Secretary of State for Employment, yesterday denied leaking the details of his plan last week, in which it was revealed that the Government was considering moving some of our military bases to centres of high unemployment.

Mr Belling also claimed that the Cabinet supports his plan, including Prime Minister Jim Hacker. But the leak has caused a succession of other leaks and done considerable damage to his credibility and to his policy. Last night he spoke angrily to reporters and demanded a public enquiry.

The day began with Cabinet Committee. Humphrey and Bernard were waiting for me in the Cabinet Room. They wished me good morning. I told them it was *not* a good morning.

They knew anyway. They'd read the papers.

'Dudley has been answering back to the press about that new leak,' I said.

'Shocking,' said Sir Humphrey.

'He says that he's leaked nothing and that someone's trying to damage him.'

'Shocking.'

'He's demanding a public enquiry!'

'Shocking!!' he murmured again, with real feeling. Bernard was strangely silent.

'You'd think he'd know better,' I went on. 'Anyway, leak enquiries never find the true source of the leak.'

'But we know the true source, Prime Minister,' intervened Bernard. 'Just between ourselves. You asked us to . . .'

I quelled him with a look. 'Bernard, you're not saying I authorised this leak, I hope?'

Bernard hesitated. 'No, I . . . that is . . . yes but . . . I mean, I remember now. Sorry.'

I had to be sure. '*What* do you remember, Bernard?'

'Um – whatever you want, Prime Minister.'

'What I want is to show the public that there are no divisions in the Cabinet.'

'But there are divisions,' said Bernard.

'I don't want to multiply them,' I explained.

'Prime Minister, if you multiply divisions you get back to where you started.' I couldn't see what he was driving at. Undeterred, he continued to explain. 'If you divide four by two you get two and then if you multiply it you get back to four again. Unless, of course, you multiply different divisions, in which case . . .'

'Thank you, Bernard,' I said firmly. He is too literal-minded for this job. And we were in a hurry. The members of Committee would be arriving any minute and we had to consider our strategy. I explained my plan.

'Humphrey, I want to keep the Employment Secretary in the Cabinet. *And* the Defence Secretary, Max. But I can't allow this row to go on any longer and I won't allow the Employment Secretary to be seen to defeat me – I can't risk it. Therefore, we must see that his plan is stopped.'

Humphrey gazed thoughtfully at his shoes for a moment, then came up with a three-point plan.

'I suggest you ask the Committee to agree to these three points: First, that they agree to accept Cabinet's collective decision. Second, that there is a cooling-off period with no further discussion. And third, that all further speeches and press statements are cleared with the Cabinet Office.'

Well, that seemed a pretty good plan to me. I instantly understood it. But when the meeting began Dudley immediately challenged the agenda.

'Excuse me, Prime Minister . . . on a point of order, I see that my plan for defence establishments' relocation is not on the agenda.'

I told him that was correct. He asked why. I explained that because of all the leaking that's been going on and the very damaging press consequences, the government looks divided.

'It is divided,' said Dudley.

He's very dense sometimes. 'That's why it mustn't look it,' I explained. I added that it's a very complex issue and that was why I was deferring consideration of it till a later date.

Dudley was baffled. 'I can't understand it. You were in favour of my plan last time.'

I couldn't allow Dudley or anyone to make such a claim, even if it were true. 'No, I wasn't,' I said. Perhaps I should have acknowledged that I *had* been in favour, even though I am now against it. But a simple denial seemed easier.

Dudley stared at me, as if I were lying. [*Hacker was lying – Ed.*]

'You were in favour of it,' he repeated. 'And so was *everyone* except the Secretary of State for Defence.'

'No they weren't,' I said, committed now.

'Yes they were!' Dudley would not let go. 'And you promised further discussion.'

This was perfectly true. I was completely stuck for a suitable reply when Humphrey stepped in. I can't remember what he said, but his gobbledegook interpretation of the minutes of the previous meeting saved the day.

But then we went on to Humphrey's three-point plan and, somehow, I don't know how, I simply can't understand why, we reached a point of no return with Dudley. What I had hoped would be a compromise scheme somehow turned into an ultimatum, and I found myself telling Dudley that he must consider his position. [*This means co-operate or resign – Ed.*]

I fear we'll lose him. I still don't quite know how this happened. Sir Humphrey seemed as baffled as I.

SIR BERNARD WOOLLEY RECALLS:[1]

That meeting was a total triumph for Sir Humphrey's strategy. All along he had been seeking to remove the Employment Secretary from the Cabinet, because he saw this as the only way to save thousands of senior officers and MOD officials from exile in the Siberia north of Birmingham.

Humphrey was not baffled at the outcome, for it had gone exactly to plan. I was not party to his scheme, but I marvelled at the brilliance of both its conception and execution.

Before the meeting he suggested the three-point plan as a compromise, knowing full well that it would be the *coup de grâce*. Hacker's claim that he instantly understood the plan was manifestly false: first, if he had understood it he would have seen the full implications and rejected it outright. Second, he was so confused that he couldn't even remember it. As the members of the Committee were entering the room Hacker was trying to remember it.

'Your three-point plan, Humphrey, remind me.'

'You ask them, Prime Minister, to agree to three points. First, that they agree to accept Cabinet's collective decision. Second, that there is a cooling-off period with no further discussion. Third, that all further speeches and press statements are cleared with the Cabinet Office.'

'Excellent,' said Hacker. 'That should do it. Point one, they cool off and . . . er, no, no further discussion without decision, or decisions without discussions and, what was the second? Collective press statements and . . . sorry, Humphrey, I don't think I've quite got it yet.'

He really was in a frightful state. He could remember nothing. He was flapping around pathetically, the proverbial headless chicken. Humphrey offered to write down the three-point plan for him, and Hacker accepted with gratitude.

Well, the agenda was immediately challenged by Dudley Belling, as Hacker correctly remembered. Dudley reminded the Prime Minister that he

[1] In conversation with the Editors.

had supported the proposal last time, and that Hacker had acceded to Dudley's request to discuss the matter again at this meeting.

Hacker was on the ropes when Sir Humphrey intervened.

'There was no such promise,' Sir Humphrey said, being economical with the truth again. 'And the Prime Minister did not support the proposal. If he had it would appear in the minutes. And it doesn't.'

Dudley was floored. 'Doesn't it?' And he glanced hurriedly through the minutes, which we had all agreed – on the nod – to sign as accurate. Careless of him not to have read them more thoroughly.

He looked up, angrier than ever. 'Sir Humphrey, why was my request for a further discussion, and the Prime Minister's reply, not minuted?'

Sir Humphrey was ready for that one. His reply was an object lesson. I recall it perfectly. 'While it is true that the minutes are indeed an authoritative record of the Committee's deliberations, it is nevertheless undeniable that a deliberate attempt at comprehensive delineation of every contribution and interpolation would necessitate an unjustifiable elaboration and wearisome extension of the documentation.'

Hacker stared at him. The Committee stared at him. The Foreign Secretary told me later that he wished he was at the UN where he'd have had the benefit of simultaneous translation. What he had said would have been crystal-clear to most people, but politicians are simple souls.

Finally Hacker said hopefully: 'Does that mean you don't recall the discussion?'

Sir Humphrey's reply was masterly. 'It is characteristic of committee discussions and decisions that every member has a vivid recollection of them and that every member's recollection differs violently from every other member's recollection. Consequently we accept the convention that the official decisions were those and only those which are officially recorded in the minutes by the officials, from which it follows with an elegant inevitability that any decision officially reached will be officially recorded in the minutes and any decision not recorded in the minutes was not officially reached even if one or more members believe that they recollect it, so in this particular case if the decision had been officially reached it would have been officially recorded by the officials in the minutes. And', he finished with triumphant simplicity, 'it isn't so it wasn't.'

There was another pause. Dudley was smouldering. 'It's a fiddle,' he snarled.

Hacker intervened firmly. 'This must stop!'

'Yes it must,' snapped Dudley, though I suspect that they were talking at cross purposes.

Hacker took charge. 'I have drawn up a three-point plan which we must all agree to. Point one . . . er, what did you say, I mean what did I say was point one, Humphrey?'

Humphrey silently unzipped his slimline document case that lay on the floor between the chairs and slid his handwritten, three-point plan a few inches along the Cabinet table till it rested in front of the Prime Minister.

'Thank you,' said Hacker. 'Point one, everyone will accept collective decisions, Dudley.'

'I'm perfectly willing to,' Dudley responded with caution. 'How are they defined?'

He was a good man. He knew the right questions to ask.

'I define them!' said the Prime Minister brusquely. 'Point two, there will be a cooling-off period on the subject of defence relocations. And point three . . .'

He hesitated. We all waited expectantly. Then he leaned towards Sir Humphrey and muttered that he couldn't quite read point three. 'Cleaning what?'

'*Clearing* all speeches . . .' whispered the Cabinet Secretary.

'Ah yes,' said the PM loudly. 'All speeches and press statements must in future be cleared with the Cabinet Office.'

On the face of it point three looked like a sensible way of preventing members of the Cabinet making embarrassingly contradictory statements. But it had one other major virtue – it put Sir Humphrey in charge of all relations with the press.

Dudley spotted it. 'I can't accept point two, we can't cool off discussion on something that hasn't been discussed yet because the officials refused or neglected to minute my request for further discussion – even though it was agreed by you, Prime Minister – and which has consequently been left off the agenda. As for your third point, I cannot in principle accept that anything I say in public must be cleared by him.' He pointed at Sir Humphrey, refusing to dignify him further by mentioning him by name. 'I have no confidence,' Dudley concluded, 'that he will clear what I want to say.'

Hacker was now committed. 'Well, that's my decision and I must ask you to accept it.'

'I don't accept it.' Dudley was implacable.

'Oh,' said Jim. He looked at Humphrey for guidance. Humphrey whispered something to him. Jim nodded sadly, and turned to his Employ-ment Secretary.

'Then, Dudley,' he pronounced solemnly, 'I must ask you to consider your position.'

Everyone present knew that Dudley's career was over.

[*Hacker's diary continues – Ed.*]

July 19th

I was sitting in my study this morning, hoping for the best but expecting the worst. Bernard knocked and entered.

'I have news for you, Prime Minister.'

41

I looked at him. But I could tell nothing from his face. I waited.

'Do you want the bad news first?' he asked.

I perked up. 'You mean, there's bad news and good news.'

'No, Prime Minister – there's bad news and worse news.'

It was all very predictable. Dudley has resigned. He sent the usual letter, rather more curt than usual. Bernard gave me a draft letter of acceptance to sign. Humphrey and the Press Office were working on a draft press statement for me.

I wanted to have words with Humphrey. I told Bernard to fetch him. But first Bernard told me the worse news: apparently Dudley has made a resignation speech on the steps of the Department of Employment, accusing me of being dictatorial and running a Presidential style of government.

At first I thought Bernard was right to be gloomy. But in fact it's not so bad: I think that Dudley's accusation may do me more good than harm. The people like to feel they have a strong leader. I explained this to Bernard.

He saw the point at once. 'Oh yes indeed. Moreover, strong leadership'll be a new pleasure for them.'

'No it won't,' I replied shortly.

'No it won't,' he agreed without hesitation.

Humphrey arrived at that moment. I did not mince words with him. I reminded him that I had sought to avoid this resignation, and I now realise – too late – that it was his three-point plan which provoked it.

Humphrey had other, surprising news for me. He agreed that the three-point plan had been the last straw. 'But', he added, 'I understand that in any case the Employment Secretary was planning to resign in a couple of months.'

'Was he?' I was astounded. 'Why? When?'

'On the day of the Autumn Budget,' Humphrey revealed. 'On the grounds that the budget is expected to give him insufficient money to deal with unemployment.'

I was shaken. A resignation over the Autumn Budget would have been *really* damaging. And it could have made Dudley extremely popular. In fact, the more I think of it, I've handled this whole crisis pretty well. Brilliantly, in fact. I have forced Dudley to resign on an obscure administrative issue of my choosing instead of an important policy issue of his choosing. No one, either among the voters or the backbenchers, will support him, because no one really understands why he's gone.

I explained all this to Humphrey, who readily agreed that I'd handled the whole affair in a masterly fashion.

[*It is interesting that Jim Hacker never questioned Sir Humphrey Appleby's revelation that the Employment Secretary was planning to resign a few weeks later. Presumably this was because it enabled him to think of his defeat as a victory.*

Bernard Woolley did notice that there was something altogether too convenient about the information and wondered from whence it came.

Later that day he had a private word with Sir Humphrey about it, the gist of which was noted in Appleby's private diary – Ed.]

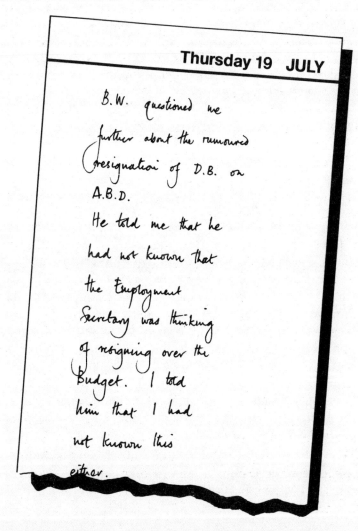

Thursday 19 JULY

B.W. questioned me further about the rumoured resignation of D.B. on A.B.D.

He told me that he had not known that the Employment Secretary was thinking of resigning over the Budget. I told him that I had not known this either.

B.W.[1] questioned me further about the rumoured resignation of D.B.[2] on A.B.D.[3]

He told me that he had not known that the Employment Secretary was thinking of resigning over the Budget. I told him that I had not known this either.

He seemed surprised, and asked me if it was not true.

I attempted to clarify the matter for him. I explained that I had not said it was true. I had said that I *understood* it to be true. The possibility always exists that I could have misunderstood.

BW tried to pin me down. 'So you don't know it's true?'

I explained that, equally, I do not know that it is *not* true. It might be true.

Bernard said that anything might be true. I congratulated him on seeing the point at last. But I was premature: Bernard still didn't understand why I had told the PM that Dudley Belling would have resigned anyway. I should have thought the answer was obvious: to make the PM feel better.

[*And also, Sir Humphrey might have added in the privacy of his personal diary, because the Prime Minister would no longer criticise him over the resignation of a minister he wanted to keep – Ed.*]

Bernard remarked that it was a pity that Dudley Belling had to go. How true! But there was simply no other way to stop his dreadful plan.

[*Hacker's diary continues – Ed.*]

July 20th

Today I had a wonderful idea!

I was sitting in my study going over my conciliatory press release, designed to counter Dudley's angry resignation speech in a way that would make me appear strong, caring, wise and statesmanlike.

I had redrafted Malcolm's[4] wording, so that it read: 'His plan was being studied but there was a danger of much greater cost than was first thought without *necessarily* achieving the employment objectives. So I am puzzled and saddened by his sudden resignation.'

Humphrey and I were having a morning coffee, and a couple of chocolate digestives, looking out over Horseguards Parade sparkling in the morning sun, feeling cosy and safe and warm inside Number Ten. I was still sad that I'd lost a good man, and a terrific plan, a plan that would actually have helped unemployment. And then I had my inspiration!

[1] Bernard Woolley.
[2] Dudley Belling.
[3] Autumn Budget Day.
[4] Malcolm Warren, the Press Secretary.

'Humphrey,' I said quietly, 'now that the Employment Secretary's gone we can recreate his plan.'

At first he didn't seem to see the beauty of it. Nor did Bernard. They looked almost horrified, though clearly they must have been as delighted too – I think they just found it galling that I had had the brilliant insight and not them.

'Don't you see?' I explained. 'I can go ahead with it now. It won't look like weakness any more, it'll look like strength.'

'But the whole point was . . .' began Humphrey, and then stopped. He gets confused, poor chap.

'Was what?' I asked. 'It wasn't to stop the relocation plan, was it?'

'No! No, indeed no, it was to, er, was to . . . establish your authority.'

'Exactly!' I said.

He'd figured it out at last. Sometimes he's a bit slow, but he gets there in the end.

So it's all ended perfectly. By reinstating the plan I can *prove* that I wasn't against it. And it will demonstrate to the world that Dudley's resignation was pointless. And having got rid of that bastard who was plotting against me, I've given a warning to others and shown that I can repel boarders with ease. 'Put defence relocation on the agenda for the next Cabinet,' I told Humphrey with quiet confidence.

'Yes Prime Minister,' he replied, staring at me thoughtfully.

2
Official Secrets

July 27th

It's only a week since I was forced to fire Dudley, a man I had always thought of as an old friend and a trusted ally. Imagine my bitterness and pain when Sir Humphrey revealed that he'd been plotting against me.

And now, only one week later, I'm facing another challenge to my authority – and this time it's from an even more unexpected quarter. My predecessor, the former Prime Minister, has submitted the latest chapter of his memoirs for security clearance – and publication *must* be stopped.

First thing this morning, at Cabinet Committee, we were joined by the Solicitor-General,[1] a couple of junior officials from his department, plus Humphrey and Bernard.

[*The Solicitor-General was one of the two senior law officers of the Government, the Attorney-General being the other. Sir Robin was famous, some would say notorious, for adopting a legalistic holier-than-thou attitude towards his political colleagues, and in so doing he acquired the nickname Good 'Evans – Ed.*]

Robin was at his most proper and pious this morning. 'As you know, we have already approved Chapters One to Seven, and I see no grounds for withholding approval of Chapter Eight.'

'Hold on a minute,' I said hastily. 'It seems to me that it contains some highly questionable material.'

Robin looked surprised. 'Such as?'

I'd been up half the night with it. I had all the page references at my fingertips. 'Page 211 for a start.'

I handed the offending page across the Cabinet table to Robin. He stared at the section I'd marked through his half-moon gold-rimmed reading glasses, then stared at me coldly over the top of them. 'It only says that the Minister for Administrative Affairs supported the pro-

---

[1] Sir Robin Evans.

posal to expand the Sellafield nuclear fuel plant in Cabinet, but spoke out against it in public.'

I was amazed that he couldn't see the problem. 'But that was me! I was the Minister.'

'The point is, Prime Minister, it's not a security leak.'

'The point is,' I responded indignantly, 'it's not true!'

'The documentation is fairly impressive,' he replied dispassionately. [*'Fairly impressive' is Whitehall code for 'irrefutable' – Ed.*]

His cold blue eyes seemed to twinkle with amusement. But I couldn't see anything funny. 'With respect, Prime Minister,' he continued insultingly, 'if he has libelled you, that's a matter for the courts after publication, not for security clearance before it.'

I disagreed flatly. 'It's not as if the only problem is on page 211. Page 224 has a scurrilous accusation about my stopping that chemical plant project because of a baseless press scare. Then there's an indefensible passage about me on page 231.'

Humphrey took the opportunity to read that bit aloud – needlessly, I now feel. '"Hacker was more interested in votes than principles. He ran for cover at the first whiff of unpopularity. He raised the average age of the Cabinet but lowered the average IQ."'

'Thank you, Humphrey, we've all read it,' I said tartly. I couldn't help feeling that around this table there was more than a little pleasure at my discomfiture.

Robin hesitated, then spoke again. He expressed himself carefully. 'Well, as I say, Prime Minister, I'm not in any way supporting or defending him, but it's not an actual security breach. After all, Chapter Five got leaked to the press and we took no action.'

He'd missed the point. 'Chapter Five was very nice about my getting the Qumran contract,' I explained. 'And about my computer security guidelines.'

'But', Robin persisted, 'it had just as much confidential material. And you never even had a leak enquiry about it.'

They all stared at me. Did they know? 'Anyone could have leaked that chapter to the press,' I remarked, with as much innocence as I could muster.

'Anyone!' agreed Humphrey emphatically.

Chapter Five had been in no way comparable. I turned back to the beginning of the manuscript. 'Look at the *title* of this chapter,' I exclaimed in anguish.

Humphrey read it aloud again. '"The Two Faces of Jim Hacker"?'

'That's not a secret, surely?' Bernard was trying to make me feel

47

better – I think! He caught my eye and fell silent.

I returned to the attack. 'I'm sorry, I think that there *are* security implications. Sellafield is nuclear.'

The Solicitor-General shook his head. 'But the Energy Secretary is responsible for Sellafield, he has seen the chapter, and he says that he has no problems.'

Of course he has no problems. It describes him as the ablest minister in the Cabinet. Which in itself is another slur on me. I pointed this out to Robin, who replied legalistically that he didn't think that it was actionable.

I was tired of all this obstructionism. 'Let's be clear about this. We have the right to refuse publication, don't we?'

Robin nodded. 'We do. But if they ignore us and publish anyway, my legal opinion is that we shall have no hope of stopping it through the courts.'

This was a blow. I suggested that, in that case, we lean on the publishers. The Solicitor-General wanted to know on what grounds. I told him the national interest.

Again he defied me! 'But I've said that there's no grounds . . .'

I cut him off. 'Listen,' I said sharply. 'This is obscene, scurrilous filth. It cannot be in the national interest to publish it and undermine confidence in the leader of the nation. This chapter must not be published. Right?'

They all gazed at me bleakly. The meeting broke up. They hadn't said yes and they hadn't said no. But they know what they have to do.

[*Events moved fast. Only a week later a report appeared in the* Daily Post, *London's newest morning newspaper, that Hacker was trying to suppress a chapter of his predecessor's memoirs. And the story quoted freely from the chapter, printing verbatim the sections that Hacker had found most objectionable.*]

25p

DAILY  POST

FRIDAY 3 AUGUST

HACKER ATTEMPTS TO SUPPRESS MEMOIRS

FOILED BY SOLICITOR-GENERAL

BY OUR POLITICAL STAFF

Prime Minister Jim Hacker, in a secret meeting at Number Ten Downing Street last week, tried to suppress the eighth chapter of the as yet untitled memoirs of former Prime Minister Herbert Attwell. The manuscript was sent to the Cabinet Office for security clearance in the usual way.

[*An anxious meeting took place in Bernard Woolley's office at 9 a.m. on the morning the story hit the streets. Present were Bernard Woolley, Sir Humphrey Appleby and Malcolm Warren, the Press Secretary at Number Ten Downing Street. A note of the meeting appears in Sir Humphrey Appleby's diary – Ed.*]

Friday 3 AUGUST

B.W., M.W. and I conferred about the story in the Daily Post. We knew that even if the P.M. had not yet read his daily press digest, he would have heard it quoted on the Today show, to which he always listens while he has his breakfast.

B.W. remarked that he had listened too.

B.W., M.W. and I conferred about the story in the *Daily Post*. We knew that
even if the P.M. had not yet read his daily press digest, he would have heard
it quoted on the *Today* show, to which he always listens while he has his
breakfast. B.W. remarked that he had listened too. The presenters had
chewed up Hacker for breakfast!

We all regarded it as a somewhat amusing and trivial embarrassment of no
particular consequence. The only problem, other than the PM's discomfiture (which was not a problem), was that the leak not only quoted from
Chapter Eight but revealed that Hacker tried to suppress it, which means
that the leak must have come from someone who was at the meeting.

Malcolm had an immediate problem: half of Britain's press corps were in
the press office waiting for Hacker's response, and the other half were on the
phone. The foreign press have also picked it up, and there have been
interview requests from *Le Monde*, the *Washington Post*, and the *Women's
Wear Daily* – which, Malcolm tells me, is an important newspaper across the
pond. Thank God *we* do not live in a matriarchy.
[*Appleby Papers 1540/BA/90077*]

[*Hacker's diary continues – Ed.*]

August 3rd
Humphrey, Bernard and Malcolm trooped in as if they were in
mourning. Grave faces. Eyes lowered. I stared at them angrily.

'Well?' I asked.

There was a silence.

'Well?' I asked again.

They stared intently at their shoes. 'Say something,' I snarled.

There was a pause. Finally Bernard spoke up. 'Good morning,
Prime Minister,' he mumbled.

'Good morning,' the others echoed, apparently grateful to
Bernard for having thought of something safe to say.

I banged the *Daily Post*. 'You've read this?'

They all produced copies of it from under their arms or behind their
backs.

'You realise what this is?' I asked. I pointed at the story.

'It's the *Daily Post*,' said Bernard unnecessarily.

'It's a catastrophe! *That's* what it is!'

Humphrey cleared his throat. 'With respect, Prime Minister . . .'

I let him get no further. 'With no respect at all, Humphrey.' I was
very curt. 'No respect for privacy. No respect for security. No respect
for the national interest. No respect for the elected leader of the
nation. This is unforgiveable! Who leaked it?'

More silence. I waited. 'Who can say?' was Humphrey's eventual and feeble response.

'*You* can say,' I said. 'And you'd *better* say – or else! I want it traced. At once. It must have been somebody at the meeting – I want to know who.'

Humphrey nodded. 'I'll set up a leak enquiry straight away.'

I lost my temper. 'I don't want a bloody leak enquiry!' I shouted. 'Didn't you hear me? I want to know who did it?'

[*Hacker's anger at Humphrey's suggestion was caused by his knowledge that leak enquiries are merely for setting up, not for actually conducting. The purpose of a leak enquiry is to find no evidence. If you really want to find the cause of a leak you call in the Special Branch. Those appointed to a leak enquiry seldom meet, and only report if it is absolutely unavoidable – Ed.*]

'Prime Minister,' said Humphrey gently, apparently in an effort to calm me down, 'when there is a leak, normally one doesn't really want to find out who is responsible, just in case it turns out to have been one of your Cabinet colleagues.'

For once I wasn't worried about that. The Solicitor-General and I were the only ministers left there by then. It can't have been him, he had nothing to gain, and anyway law officers never leak. And I know it wasn't me. Therefore it *must* have been one of the officials. I told Humphrey, then and there, that we would take this right through to the Courts.

Malcolm interrupted. 'I'm sorry, Prime Minister, but I really have to have a statement for the press. They're all waiting. And there are four requests for TV interviews and eleven for radio.'

'Bloody marvellous!' I was decidedly bitter. 'All last week I wanted to go on the air and talk about my successes in achieving détente with the Soviets, and they didn't want to know. Now this happens and they charge in like a herd of vultures.'

'Not heard, Prime Minister,' said Bernard inexplicably.

I told him I'd speak louder. Then I realised I'd misunderstood. 'Herd,' he said, 'not heard. Vultures, I mean, they don't herd, they flock. And they don't charge, they . . .'

'*Yes*? They *what*?' I turned to him, absolutely furious, and waited. More silence. 'Well, what *do* they do, Bernard?'

He could see that he was dicing with death. 'They . . .' he faltered. And he flapped his arms a bit. 'Nothing,' he said, and returned to staring at his shoes again. I have had enough of Bernard's pedantry!

I turned back to Malcolm. 'Don't the press believe in Britain?' I asked rhetorically. 'Why must they always go trouble-seeking and muck-raking? Why can't they write about our successes?'

Malcolm chewed his lower lip. 'Like . . .?'

I stopped to think. 'Like . . . like . . . like my détente with the Russians,' I suggested with relief, thinking of it in the nick of time.

Malcolm considered this idea. 'Well, there are more friendly voices coming from the Kremlin but it hasn't actually led to anything concrete though, has it?'

'It's going to,' I explained. People are *so* picky!

Malcolm glanced at his watch. 'I'm sorry, Prime Minister, but I do have to tell them something about this allegation.'

He was right. We had to say something. I told him to talk to them off the record, attribute his remarks to sources close to the Prime Minister, and be sure to say *nothing* attributable.

He waited, pencil poised.

I began: 'Say that what he says about me is a complete pack of lies.'

Bernard interrupted, worried. 'Um, do you mean, um Prime Minister, about, well, about running for cover and all that sort of thing?' He went pink.

'Yes,' I said. What was his problem?

'Um . . .' Bernard persisted, 'the only problem is, it is the author's opinion. We can't call him a liar for expressing his opinion.'

I didn't see why not, but generously I modified my instructions to Malcolm. 'Well, say it's a pack of lies that I spoke in favour of Sellafield in Cabinet but against it in public.'

'Um . . .!' Bernard appeared to have *another* problem. I narrowed my eyes at him. 'Well, the only thing is, it is sort of true, isn't it?'

'Shut up, Bernard!' I explained.

He wouldn't. 'How do we *say* it's a pack of lies?' he asked with determination.

Malcolm knew. He was already writing it down in the appropriate language. 'The Prime Minister's recollection of events is significantly at variance with his predecessor's.'

Bernard relaxed. 'Oh, I see,' he said, crossed his legs, and sat back in his Chippendale armchair.

'Then say', I told Malcolm, 'that the Cabinet minutes vindicate me completely, but unfortunately under the terms of the Thirty Year Rule they can't be disclosed for another twenty-eight years. Which makes his book deeply unfair as well as totally inaccurate.'

Malcolm got all that. His shorthand is excellent. It's always a good idea to have an ex-journalist as Press Secretary – poacher turned gamekeeper.

'And what about the smears against you personally?' he wanted to know.

'Smear him,' I replied promptly. 'Say the old fool is trying to rewrite history to try to make his premiership look less of a disaster. Imply he's gone ga-ga.'

Malcolm chewed his pencil for a moment. 'Passage of time and separation from official records have perhaps clouded his memory?'

'Fine, as far as it goes. How about the ga-ga bit?'

Malcolm smiled. 'Though no more than one would expect for a man of his age?' he offered.

It seemed all right to me. 'Will that do?' I asked them all.

Malcolm seemed to think so. 'It's okay for refuting what's in the chapter. But what about the story that you tried to prevent publication?'

I could see no problem with that. 'Say that's a pack of lies too.'

Malcolm was perfectly happy. '"A garbled account of a routine meeting. There was never any question of suppression."'

I looked round the table. Humphrey and Bernard were raising no objections. I told Malcolm that I would give no interviews on the subject, and I allowed him to make it a direct quote: 'An insignificant matter of no national importance, typical of the media's trivialisation of politics.'

'Do I attribute that quote to you, Prime Minister?'

'Of course not!' Sometimes I wonder if Malcolm's all there. 'A close Cabinet colleague.'

After Malcolm left we discussed the crisis, and I found that they viewed it far too lightly. My view is that it's a disaster, but Humphrey thinks it's not all that serious.

'Not serious?' I was incredulous. 'Telling the British people they can't trust the word of their own Prime Minister?'

Humphrey was calm and confident. 'They won't believe that,' he asserted. I was tempted to believe him when Bernard piped up.

'They might, you know.' He is *so* discouraging. 'Otherwise, logically, it would mean that they couldn't trust the word of their own *ex*-Prime Minister.'

Humphrey thanked Bernard. [*In other words, Sir Humphrey indicated to Bernard Woolley that he had said enough – Ed.*]

It seemed to me that there was a good chance that, given the choice between my word and my predecessor's, the British public would believe me. They never trusted *him*, that's for sure. Thank goodness I've been able to bring back a little bit of honesty into British political life. [*Hacker's capacity for self-deception was, as with most politicians, one of the essential ingredients of his success. Unless one takes the phrase 'a little bit of honesty' at face value – Ed.*]

We had discussed our rebuttal of the *Daily Post* story for long enough. 'Now,' I said, moving right along, 'about nailing that leak.' [*We have preserved Hacker's mixed metaphors whenever possible, for the insight that they give us into the unusual mind of this great political leader. Bernard Woolley, however, was unable to ignore them – Ed.*]

'I'm sorry to be pedantic, Prime Minister, but if you nail a leak you make another leak.'

I glared at him. He shut up again. 'I want the culprit.' I was implacable.

'Yes, Prime Minister,' replied Humphrey, without argument.

'And I want a conviction.'

Humphrey seemed puzzled. 'Prime Minister, we can try to find the culprit. We can prosecute. But under our current political system there are problems, as I'm sure you must be aware, about the government actually guaranteeing a conviction.'

Of course I knew that. But it's been done often enough, God knows! I suggested a quiet drinkie with the judge.

'Unthinkable!' Sir Humphrey was playing Goody Two-Shoes. It was one of his least convincing performances. 'There is no way, Prime Minister, of putting any pressure on a British judge.'

Who does he think he's kidding? 'So what *do* you do to ensure a conviction?' I enquired.

'Simple,' replied Sir Humphrey promptly. 'You pick a judge who won't need any pressure put upon him.'

I hadn't thought of that. It's always easy when you know how.

'A quiet word with the Lord Chancellor,' continued Humphrey. 'Find a judge who's on the government's side.'

'And who dislikes the *Daily Post*?' I asked.

'They all dislike the *Daily Post*. We need a judge who's hoping to be made a Lord of Appeal. Then we leave justice free to take her own impartial and majestic course.'

I asked if that always does the trick. Humphrey explained that it wasn't foolproof. 'Sometimes they're obviously trying so hard for a conviction that the jury acquits out of sheer bloody-mindedness.'

'So,' I summed up judicially, 'the judge has to have some common sense as well.'

He nodded. I can see that it's not so simple as he makes out.

August 6th

Lunch today with Derek Burnham, the editor of the *Daily Post*. It's no pleasure to have lunch with such a person, but he is a representative of the fourth estate and I kept a metaphorical clothes-peg on my nose.

We lunched in the small dining-room at Number Ten. It's a panelled room, a sort of ante-room to the big state dining-room, adjoining the yellow pillared room. It's an impressive place, yet small enough for intimate luncheons. Sometimes I lunch there with Bernard and other officials if Annie's[1] out and I can't be bothered to go upstairs and make lunch for myself.

Burnham is a nondescript, sandy-haired Scotsman of indeterminate middle age, with dandruff liberally scattered across his collar and lapels.

'So what are you asking me to tell my readers?' he asked me over the tomato soup.

'I'm not asking you to tell your readers anything,' I replied carefully, not neglecting to turn on the charm. 'I'm just giving you my side of the story.'

Derek pretended to be puzzled. 'But it's not that important, is it?'

He wouldn't like to have lies written about him in the newspapers! [*Hacker appears to have forgotten that it was* truth *that was written about him in the papers. Or perhaps he did not really forget, for the truth can be even more painful to read than lies – Ed.*]

'Why the big fuss?' persisted Derek.

'Because', I was indignant, 'I do not have two faces, and I didn't try to suppress the chapter.'

'May I quote you?' he asked mischievously.

I was very specific in my reply. I told him that he may not quote me denying that I have two faces.

He grinned. 'It was worth a try.' He slurped his soup. 'But Jim, I really don't know why you're so upset. I agree the chapter doesn't flatter you, but it's just part of the normal rough and tumble of political life, isn't it?'

I told him that I really didn't think that a responsible paper should print that kind of smear. He gave a non-committal nod. So I asked him why he did.

'Because it sold us over a hundred thousand extra copies.'

[1] Mrs Hacker.

'But didn't you see how damaging these accusations are?'

I'd created a trap for myself. 'That's my point exactly,' he grinned. 'Here's this damaging accusation and it's up to you to clear it for publication, and you are asking me to believe that you didn't try to stop it?'

'Of course I didn't.'

'Why not?'

'This is a free country, Derek,' I said grandly. 'Freedom of speech will always be protected while I'm in Number Ten.'

He wouldn't let go. 'But if it's seriously damaging to you . . .'

'It's not all *that* damaging,' I replied irritably.

He sat back and smiled. 'Fine,' he said. 'So what's all this fuss about?'

I could see that it was difficult for me to have it both ways. I tried a new tack. I explained that I didn't care about the damage to me *personally*, it's the damage to Britain that worries me.

He couldn't see, at first, how Britain could be damaged. Patiently I explained that undermining the leadership seriously damages the nation with foreigners. The pound, that sort of thing.

He didn't buy it. Because when I followed up by asking him to retract the story that I'd tried to suppress chapter eight of that damn book, he said that he couldn't.

'*Wouldn't*' I'd understand, but couldn't? I challenged him. 'You're the Editor, aren't you?'

He took a bread roll. Bernard immediately passed him the butter. 'Prime Minister, an Editor isn't like a General commanding an army. He's just the ringmaster of a circus. I can book the acts, but I can't tell the acrobats which way to jump. Nor can I prevent the bareback rider from falling off her horse.'

Cajoling had clearly failed. It was time to try Pressure. 'Derek,' I said carefully as I filled up his glass of Aloxe-Corton (his favourite, according to Malcolm), 'I don't think it would be helpful if you forced us to the conclusion that we couldn't trust you. Obviously we like to co-operate with the press, but you really are making it hard for us.'

Derek was made of sterner stuff. He sniffed the bouquet, swirled the Burgundy around in the glass to let it breathe, and then looked me squarely in the eye. 'I don't think that it would be helpful if you made us think you were hostile to our paper. Obviously we like to co-operate with Number Ten, but if it's war, then . . .'

I let him go no further. I assured him that war was the last thing we wanted, it wouldn't be helpful to either of us. 'I was merely suggesting

. . . merely thinking . . . there could be exclusive interviews and photo opportunities . . .'

'If I retract?' he enquired sharply.

'If you print the truth,' I corrected him.

He sighed. 'Jim, I have to stand by my story until I get hard evidence that it's not true.'

I couldn't think what evidence there could be to disprove the story. [*Perhaps because the story was true – Ed.*]

'Such as?' I asked.

'The minutes of the meeting.'

'I don't see why not, if my integrity is at stake.' I turned to Bernard. 'Bernard, the minutes bear out my account of the meeting, don't they?'

Bernard stammered incoherently. The eyes of all three of us – Derek, Malcolm and myself – were upon him. He said something like 'Well I er um but well er yes but . . .'

'Good,' I said. 'Derek, you may see them.'

Bernard was looking apoplectic. I thought he was about to have a brain seizure. 'But Prime Minister . . .' he spluttered.

I put him at his ease. 'Yes, yes, I know they're usually confidential, but this is a special case.'

Derek was not content with seeing the minutes. 'May I publish them?'

I told him we could talk about that – I haven't seen them myself. I told Bernard to show them to me this afternoon.

[*Bernard's discomfiture had two origins. It is anybody's guess which fear was causing him the greater panic. First, there was the breach of the Official Secrets Act: the idea of showing minutes of a Cabinet Committee to the press was absolutely without precedent. And even if the breach of the Official Secrets Act was made legal by the instructions of the Prime Minister (by no means a certainty), there was the additional problem that Hacker had sworn to prosecute the official who had leaked the discussion about the offending chapter eight – which was undoubtedly less secret than Cabinet minutes.*

But Bernard Woolley had a greater problem still, which he revealed to Sir Humphrey Appleby immediately he was able to get away from the Prime Minister's lunch with Derek Burnham. Sir Humphrey's personal papers contain a detailed report of the ensuing conversation, followed by a rare and valuable insight into his views on political memoirs and the need for secrecy in government – Ed.]

B.W. arrived in my office in a state of advanced dither. His problem appeared to be that the Prime Minister has told the press that the minutes of Cabinet Committee confirm his story that he did not try to suppress chapter eight of the book.

But, Bernard told me, the minutes are not yet written. I felt that this simplified the problem – all he has to do is write them.

Bernard did not feel that this was the answer. He was concerned that, according to his recollection, the Prime Minister *did* try to suppress the book. And he expressed surprise when I expressed surprise at his recollection.

So I explained to him that what I remember is irrelevant. If the minutes do not say that he tried to suppress the book, then he did not.

B.W. went into a greater dither, and said that he didn't see how he could falsify the minutes. He wanted, he said, a clear conscience. I found myself wondering when he acquired this taste for luxuries and how he got into government with it.

Consciences are for politicians. We are humble functionaries whose duty is to implement the commands of our democratically elected representatives. How could we be doing anything wrong if it has been commanded by those who represent the people?

B.W. does not accept that view. 'No man is an island,' he said. I agreed wholeheartedly. 'And therefore never send to know for whom the bell tolls; it tolls for thee, Bernard.'

Apprehensively, he asked for my suggestions, and their rationale. I gave him these thoughts to ponder:

1. Minutes do not record everything that was said at a meeting.
2. People frequently change their minds during a meeting.
3. Minutes, by virtue of the selection process, can never be a true and complete record.
4. Therefore, what is said at a meeting merely constitutes the choice of ingredients for the minutes.
5. The secretary's task is to choose, from a jumble of ill-digested ideas, a version that presents the Prime Minister's views as he would, on reflection, have liked them to emerge.

Later today Bernard returned to my office, still confused. He had considered all I had said and likened the question of ingredients to cooking. A dangerous analogy. It is better not to use the verb 'cook' in connection with either books or minutes.

Once again this raised the question of truth (whatever that may be) and Bernard's erroneous belief that minutes must in some way constitute a true record.

Patiently, I approached the matter from an alternative point of view. I explained the following points as clearly as I could:

1. The purpose of minutes is not to record events.

2. The purpose is to protect people.
3. You do not take notes if the Prime Minister says something he did not mean to say, especially if this contradicts what he has said publicly on an issue.
4. In short, minutes are *constructive*. They are to *improve* what is said, to be tactful, to put in a better order.
5. There is no moral problem. The secretary is the Prime Minister's servant.

In short, the minute is simply a note for the records and a statement of action (if any) that was agreed upon.

So, we turned to the meeting in question. What happened? The Solicitor-General had advised that there were no legal grounds for suppressing chapter eight. The Prime Minister accepted that there were no *legal* grounds for suppression. [*Our italics – Ed.*] That is all that need be minuted.

It is not a lie. It can go in the minutes with a clear conscience. B.W. departed with his conscience feeling less bruised.

These two conversations with Bernard about this storm in a teacup have prompted in me some fundamental thoughts about its origin:

There is no doubt that the real cause of all this trouble is this business of publishing ministerial and Prime Ministerial memoirs.

When I entered the Civil Service in the 1950s it was still possible for a man of intelligence and ingenuity to defend the thesis that politics was an honest and honourable profession. Ministers did not divulge Cabinet proceedings. Leaking to the press was regarded as a breach of confidence, not an instrument of government. And if a Department fell down badly on a job, the minister resigned.

Equally, members of the Civil Service preserved a cloak of anonymity and a tradition of discreet silence which concealed from the rest of the country the fact that they were running it.

Thus Prime Ministerial memoirs and diaries are, I believe, deeply reprehensible. The uninstructed may gain pleasure, and believe that they are being vouchsafed privileged insights, by reading distressingly frank accounts of how politicians reach their main political decisions (or, more frequently, indecisions). Most politicians have a certain lively style, often achieved by those without the reflective profundity to appreciate, or the intellectual apparatus to communicate, those qualifications and modifications which may make their accounts less readable but which could render them reliable.

Leaving aside the poor quality of literature of most ministerial memoirs, the more important *caveat* remains: revelations of this sort should never be published at all.

In such books the old tradition of the responsible minister and his obedient servant is generally misrepresented as a totally misleading portrait of scheming officials manipulating innocent politicians. Although those at the heart of government are aware that this is an absurd travesty, there is a danger that ordinary simple-minded souls may be deceived into believing there may be some truth in it.

The rot began with the Crossman diaries. And once one Minister reveals the secrets of the Cabinet, the others rush in to 'set the record straight', which means, of course, to show themselves in a favourable light.

After reading a succession of descriptions of the same period from opposed ministers of the same government, all of whom were by their own account uniformly honourable in their dealings and right in their judgements, it is hard to see where to lay the responsibility for decades of unprecedented and unrelieved political squalor.

The only scapegoat available must therefore logically be the Civil Servant. This has culminated in a distressing and regrettable change in public opinion, so that the necessary role of the Civil Service in advising caution, taking soundings, consulting colleagues, examining precedents, preparing options and advising ministers on the likely consequences of their proposals if they reached the statute books is perceived as ingrained bureaucratic obstructiveness rather than an attempt to translate narrow political expediency into broad national benefit.

Of course, there is an argument that by maintaining secrecy we would be simply defending the narrow interests of the Civil Service against the greater benefits of more openness about government. Paradoxically, this has not proved to be the case.

When I first attended Cabinet as a Private Secretary in the 1960s, members were irritated at the stultifying boredom of the proceedings and would interrupt with diverting outbursts of truth which would cause much conflict and dissent. Now that I have returned to the Cabinet as Cabinet Secretary over twenty years later, all members of the Cabinet are peacefully occupied making notes for their memoirs and will only make the statements that they want others to record in theirs.

This has been enormously beneficial to the Civil Service, for an interesting reason: the fact is that the movement to 'open up' government, if successful, always achieves a gratifying increase in the level of secrecy. Once a meeting – in Parliament, local council, Cabinet – is opened up to the public, it is used by those attending as a propaganda platform and not as a genuine debating forum. True discussions will then take place privately in smaller informal groups.

In government these smaller groups often contain one or more senior civil servants, so that some element of intelligence and practicability can be built into proposals before they become public and have to be defended with arguments which represent a victory of personal pride over common sense. So the move to greater openness in public affairs has greatly strengthened the level of secrecy and therefore the quality of decision-making in the higher echelons of government.

This is now jeopardised by Hacker's extraordinary, foolish and unprecedented decision to show Cabinet Committee minutes to a newspaper editor, with the consequent risk – nay, certainty – of publication. It is because Bernard and I were present at the meeting that the damage can be contained, and it is for these reasons that Bernard's minutes should take the form that I instructed him to take. [*Appleby Papers PU/12/3/86/NCH*]

[*Bernard Woolley's fears as to the unprecedented release of minutes that he had written were soon to be fully realised. The minutes were indeed published in the* Daily Post *– Ed.*]

MONDAY 13 AUGUST

25p

DAILY POST

CABINET COMMITTEE MINUTES PUBLISHED – EXCLUSIVE

The Solicitor-General advised that there were no legal grounds for suppressing chapter eight. The Prime Minister accepted that there were no legal grounds.

BRIEF REFERENCE CONFIRMS HACKER'S CLAIM

BY OUR POLITICAL STAFF

For the first time ever, and with the permission of The Prime Minister, the *Daily Post* publishes an extract from the minutes of a secret cabinet committee. They reveal

SIR BERNARD WOOLLEY RECALLS:[1]

I had lost my cloak of anonymity. For the first time in my life I became a public figure – almost the worst fate that can befall a civil servant, in my view. Other than being sent on gardening leave, of course.

It meant that I myself had to answer questions from the press, questions that I was not free to answer, nor able to – questions that required a degree of prevarication and economy with the truth that I, as a non-politician, was ill-equipped to evade.

The morning those minutes appeared in the *Daily Post* I was accosted in Downing Street on my way to work. Questions were fired at me. My answers were not good enough. No doubt you can find it all by looking up the archives.

No 62,839

THE TIMES

TUESDAY 14 AUGUST

Woolley says Prime Minister is above the law

Official Secrets Act not applicable to Hacker.

By our Chief Political Correspondent.

Bernard Woolley, the Prime Minister's Principal Private Secretary, today admitted that the Official Secrets Act does not apply to the Prime Minister.

His replies turn an interesting light on the unwritten British Constitution.

[*All the newspapers carried essentially the same story. The full verbatim conversation is to be found on the BBC Nine O'Clock News filmed report, and we reprint the transcript overleaf – Ed.*]

---

[1] In conversation with the Editors.

BRITISH BROADCASTING CORPORATION

THE ATTACHED TRANSCRIPT WAS TYPED FROM A RECORDING AND
NOT COPIED FROM AN ORIGINAL SCRIPT. BECAUSE OF THE RISK
OF MISHEARING THE BBC CANNOT VOUCH FOR ITS COMPLETE
ACCURACY.

"NINE O'CLOCK NEWS" "NEWSNIGHT"

TRANSMISSION: AUGUST 14th

ACTUALITY:

SHOT OF BERNARD WOOLLEY APPROACHING THE CAMERA IN
DOWNING STREET

KATE ADAM: Can we have a word with you, Mr Woolley,
about the minutes of Jim Hacker's meeting with the
Solicitor-General which were published in the Daily
Post today?

BERNARD·WOOLLEY: Look, I've got to go to work.

ADAM: Just a few questions.

WOOLLEY: I'm sorry, I can't comment.

ADAM: But you'd agree it all looks very suspicious?

WOOLLEY: What?

ADAM: The Prime Minister offered to publish them last
Thursday. Why did it take so long?

WOOLLEY: Well, because they weren't...

     HE HESITATES, AND LOOKS AROUND ANXIOUSLY

ADAM: Weren't cleared? Weren't cleared for publication?
Didn't the Prime Minister clear them last Thursday?

WOOLLEY: Yes, but, well, there's the Official Secrets
Act.

ADAM: That's what we'd like to understand, Mr Woolley.
How <u>can</u> they be cleared for publication if they're
subject to the Official Secrets Act?

- 1 -

WOOLLEY: Well, the Prime Minister can clear anything.

ADAM: So are you saying that the Prime Minister is not subject to the Official Secrets Act?

WOOLLEY: Um, no.

ADAM: No he is or no he isn't?

WOOLLEY: Yes.

ADAM: So when it comes to the Official Secrets Act, the Prime Minister is above the law?

WOOLLEY: Not in theory.

ADAM: But in practice?

WOOLLEY: No comment.

CUT TO:

KATE ADAM TALKING TO CAMERA

ADAM: What Bernard Woolley seems to be saying is that the Prime Minister makes the rules. He would not be drawn further about the content of the minutes, though he denied the rumour that the minutes took four days to appear because Mr Hacker can only type with two fingers.

- 2 -

[*That final comment by Kate Adam resulted in a complaint from Number Ten Downing Street to the Chairman of the Governors of the BBC. The BBC hotly denied that the comment showed any sign of bias against the government.*]

[*Hacker's diary continues – Ed.*]

August 14th
This morning Bernard told me that he had been interviewed by the press. I was not pleased. It is not his job to give interviews.

He explained that he had not meant to do so, but had been trapped into speaking to them.

I asked him what he had said.

'Um . . . Nothing really.'

This answer did not have the ring of truth. If he'd said nothing, he would not have come to confess it. And his eyes were decidedly shifty.

'So what's the problem?' I asked.

'Well . . .' he hesitated, 'they were asking me about you.'

Not very surprising. '*What* about me?'

'About you and the Official Secrets Act, Prime Minister.' [*When Hacker wrote this entry in his diary he had not yet seen the TV news or the morning papers. This conversation with Bernard Woolley took place immediately after he spoke to the press – Ed.*] 'They asked me whether you were bound by the Act.'

'Of course I am,' I confirmed.

'Yes, of course you are,' he agreed.

I waited. Nothing. He stared at the wall unhappily. 'So?' I pressed him.

'Well, it, er, may not come out like that.'

'What do you mean?' I asked with menace in my voice.

'Well, um, thinking back on what I said, and what you said, and what I said you said, or what they may say I said you said, or what they may have thought I said I thought you thought, or they may say I said I thought you said I thought . . .'

He petered out. Grimly, I told him to go on.

He took a deep breath. 'I think I said you thought you were above the law.'

I was aghast! 'You said *that*??'

'Not intentionally. But that's how it seemed to come out. I'm terribly sorry. But they were asking all those questions.'

I couldn't believe it. 'Bernard,' I asked with real curiosity, 'what made you think that, just because someone was asking you questions, you had to answer them?'

He said he didn't know. Nor did I. It was hard to believe. He's never answered *my* questions just because I asked them. I was furious. 'After a lifetime in the Civil Service, an entire career devoted to evading questions, you suddenly decide to answer questions *today*? And from *the Press*?? *You must have flipped your lid, Bernard*!'

He begged me not to shout at him. He was near to tears. He assured me that he wouldn't ever answer any more questions, ever again, ever!

I calmed down. I told him to get Humphrey in at once. And while we waited for Humphrey to arrive, I gave Bernard my eight ways to deal with difficult questions:

1. *Attack The Question.* 'That's a very silly question, how can you justify the use of the words, "above the law"?'

2. *Attack The Questioner.* 'How many years have *you* spent in government?'

3. *Compliment The Question.* 'That's a very good question. I'd like to thank you for asking it. Let me reply by asking you one.'

4. *Unloading The Question.* Most questions are loaded. They are full of assumptions such as 'A lot of people have said that you consider yourself above the law'. There are two possible replies to such loaded questions:
   a) 'Name ten.'
   b) 'Surely in a nation of 56 million people you can find a few people who will say anything, no matter how irrelevant, misguided, or ill-informed.'

5. *Make It All Appear An Act.* This approach only works for live TV interviews: 'You know, I've come to the conclusion that I don't agree with what you suggested I should answer when you asked me that question downstairs before the programme began. The *real* answer is . . .'

6. *Use The Time Factor.* Most interviews are short of time, especially live 'on air' interviews. Reply: 'That's a very interesting question, and there are nine points that I should like to make in answer to it.' The Interviewer will say: 'Perhaps you could make just two of them, briefly.' You say: 'No, it's far too important a question to answer superficially, and if I can't answer it properly I'd rather not trivialise it.'

7. *Invoke Secrecy*. 'There's a very full answer to that question, but it involves matters that are being discussed in confidence. I'm sure you wouldn't want me to break a confidence. So I'm afraid I can't answer for another week or two.'

8. *Take Refuge In a Long Pointless Narrative*. If you can ramble on for long enough, no one will remember the question and therefore no one can tell if you answered it or not.

Bernard listened attentively to this lesson in handling the nosey-parkers from the media. As Humphrey arrived I summed it up for him: if you have nothing to say, say nothing. But better, have something to say and say it, *no matter what they ask*. Pay no attention to the question, make your own statement. If they ask you the same question again, you just say, 'That's not the question' or 'I think the more *important* question is this:' Then you make another statement of your own. Easy-peasy.

When Humphrey arrived I questioned him about the leak enquiry. He was evasive.

'Ah well,' he said, 'the wheels will be turning very soon.'

'I asked for it a week ago,' I said. I reiterated that I wanted it pursued rigorously. And immediately.

Humphrey appeared perplexed. 'Rigorously?'

'And immediately.'

He was still perplexed. 'Immediately.'

'Immediately,' I repeated.

The penny dropped. 'Oh. You mean . . . you *really* want it pursued.'

I told him to watch my lips. 'I-want-you-to-pursue-it-*now*!'

Humphrey remained puzzled, but did not say anything to oppose me. 'If you are serious about it I'll arrange for a genuine arm's-length enquiry – if that's what you *really* want. I'll get Inspector Plod from the Special Branch.' [*Sir Humphrey was speaking figuratively when he spoke of Inspector Plod – Ed.*]

That question settled, I pointed out that we now have to improve our relations with the press. 'These will have worsened today since my esteemed Private Secretary told them that I put myself above the law when it comes to official secrets.'

Humphrey stared at Bernard, deeply shocked. Bernard hung his head.

'Yes, you may well look ashamed, Bernard.' I was not letting him off lightly. I asked Humphrey to let me know the actual constitutional position. He promised to let me have it in writing later in the day.

[Sir Humphrey kept his word. A memo arrived in Hacker's study later that day. We have retrieved a copy of it from the Cabinet Office archives – Ed.]

70 WHITEHALL, LONDON SW1A 2AS

Memorandum

To: The Prime Minister   August 14th

From: The Secretary of the Cabinet

In one sense, Bernard was quite correct. The question you posed, in a nutshell, is what is the difference between a breach of the Official Secrets Act, on the one hand, and, on the other hand, an unattributable off-the-record briefing by a senior official?

The former – the breach – is a criminal offence. The latter – the briefing – is essential to keep the wheels turning.

Is there a real objective difference? Or is it merely a matter of convenience and interpretation? And is it a breach of the Act if there is an unofficial non-attributable off-the-record briefing by an official who is <u>un</u>officially authorised by the Prime Minister?

- 2 -

You could argue that this is not a breach, if it has been authorised by the Prime Minister. Which is Bernard Woolley's position.

You, Prime Minister, will inevitably argue that it is up to you to decide whether it is in the public interest for something to be revealed or not. This would be your justification for claiming that the leak from your meeting with the Solicitor-General, which must have come from an official, is a breach of the Act.

However, this raises some interesting constitutional conundrums.

1. What if the official was officially authorised?

2. What if he was unofficially authorised?

3. What if you, Prime Minister, officially disapprove of a breach of the Act but unofficially approve? This would make the breach unofficially official but officially unofficial.

I hope this is of help to you.

H.A.

[Hacker's diary continues – Ed.]

August 15th

We reconvened again. [*Tautology is part of Hacker's personal literary style, so we have retained it where possible – Ed.*] We'd all seen Bernard's press and the television interview last night. Bernard was the new hot celebrity. He arrived at the office this morning wearing sunglasses and a big hat, in a typically ineffectual effort to avoid recognition.

The press, strange to say, were immediately drawn to enquire about the strange person who would wear sunglasses and a beaver hat on one of the hottest days of the year.

I thanked Humphrey for his helpful memo – a white lie, I felt – and we discussed how to minimise the week's damage. I suggested having another lunch with a Fleet Street editor – a friendly one this time.

Malcolm Warren had joined us. His comment was that none of them would be awfully friendly at the moment.

'Can't we offer one of them a knighthood in the New Year honours?' I asked.

He was doubtful of the ultimate value. 'Giving them knighthoods is a double-edged sword. It can work for *or* against you. The question is, do you have any control over them once you've given it?'

'I should have thought,' I said, 'that any editor would be rather grateful.'

Malcolm shook his head. 'You see, having got an honour, he may feel free to do and say exactly what he likes. Nothing further to lose.'

I could see his point. You don't get gratitude afterwards. In politics, gratitude is merely a lively expectation of favours to come.

Malcolm thought that, instead of trying to butter up the press, we should distract them. 'Let's give them a story.'

'Such as?' I asked.

'Start a war,' he suggested airily, 'that sort of thing.'

'*Start a war?*' I wasn't sure I'd heard him correctly.

'I was just giving an example of a major distraction.'

'Only a small war,' added Bernard.

They were kidding. They must have been. Humphrey joined in. 'If I may intervene, even a small war would be overkill. But, seriously, why don't you expel seventy-six Soviet diplomats. This has been the practice in the past, when we wished to ensure that the press lose interest in some other matter.'

I was shocked. I rejected the suggestion out of hand.

Malcolm persisted. 'It'd be a great headline for you, Prime Minister. "GOVERNMENT CRACKS DOWN ON RED SPY RING." Very patriotic. Goes down excellently with the electorate.'

Humphrey nodded. 'Yes, you see, it must be a story that no one can disprove . . .'

'And which will be believed,' concluded Malcolm, 'even when it's denied.'

'"SOVIET AMBASSADOR'S CHAUFFEUR IS MAJOR-GENERAL IN KGB",' declared Humphrey imaginatively. He was getting quite carried away.

I told them that the whole preposterous notion was completely out of the question. I have been working towards détente for months. It's the only thing that's working for me at the moment.

They all seemed somewhat disappointed. I turned to my Private Secretary. 'What do you think, Bernard?' I enquired ironically. 'You seem to be good at getting things into the papers.'

He blushed. 'Well . . . what about a royal event?' he offered.

I couldn't think what he meant. 'Such as?'

'Well, an engagement . . . pregnancy . . . divorce?'

'You can arrange that?' I asked.

He hadn't thought of that little snag. 'Oh. Well, no, I . . .'

Humphrey had had enough. 'I know,' he said. 'What about "PM'S PRIVATE SECRETARY IN DOLE QUEUE"?'

[*Five days elapsed, and the Leak Enquiry actually reported. The culprit was named. A press officer in the Department of Energy who had been present at the meeting with the Solicitor-General. The Enquiry had no difficulty in finding that he was the source of the leak because (a) there were so few suspects, (b) he owned up immediately. Bernard Woolley and Sir Humphrey Appleby received copies of the Leak Enquiry on the same day. Bernard must have telephoned Sir Humphrey for instructions or advice, because this letter was received from Sir Humphrey dated the day of the report – Ed.*]

70 WHITEHALL, LONDON SW1A 2AS

From the Secretary of the Cabinet and Head of the Home Civil Service

August 20th

Dear Bernard,

Yes, I have read it. This is a potentially difficult situation, as there is no precedent for handling a leak enquiry that actually finds the culprit.

Although the victim is a mere press officer he will undoubtedly be labelled a Senior Civil Servant by the press, simply because he works in Whitehall.

I think we can save him, however.

HA.

A reply from Bernard Woolley:

10 DOWNING STREET

From the Principal Private Secretary

August 20th

Dear Humphrey,
    How can we save him? There's
no doubt he did it.
        Bernard

And a reply from Sir Humphrey:

70 WHITEHALL, LONDON SW1A 2AS

From the Secretary of the Cabinet and Head of the Home Civil Service

August 21st

Dear Bernard,

There will be !

H.

[We print the full texts below – Ed.]

August 20th

Dear Bernard,
Yes, I have read it. This is a potentially difficult situation, as there is no precedent for handling a leak enquiry that actually finds the culprit.

Although the victim is a mere press officer he will undoubtedly be labelled a Senior Civil Servant by the press, simply because he works in Whitehall.

I think we can save him, however.
H.A.

A reply from Bernard Woolley:

August 20th

Dear Humphrey,
How can we save him? There's no doubt he did it.
Bernard.

And a reply from Sir Humphrey:

August 21st

Dear Bernard,
There will be!
H.A.

[Hacker's diary continues – Ed.]

August 21st
A difficult meeting this morning – but with the help of my able and loyal staff I was able to snatch victory from the jaws of defeat.

The Leak Enquiry reported yesterday. I read it last night. The Press Officer from the Department of Energy did it. The evidence is irrefutable. And nobody denied it either.

So when we met this morning I asked for the immediate dismissal of the man, and for a prosecution under Section 2 of the Official Secrets Act.

Humphrey was cautious. 'I think not, Prime Minister.'

I mocked him – foolishly, it turned out. 'You think not? Because he's a Civil Servant, I suppose.'

He was not amused. 'Certainly not, Prime Minister. Because it is not in your interest.'

'Not in my interest to punish people for undermining the whole fabric of government?' I enquired icily.

Bernard said: 'Um, you can't undermine a fabric, Prime Minister, because fabric hangs down so if you go underneath you . . .' He tailed off abruptly as I stared him down.

Humphrey, anticipating my every whim, had already consulted the Attorney-General. 'The Attorney-General's advice is that a prosecution will not succeed, because there are no real security implications.'

I said that I didn't care if it succeeded or not. 'At least it will make an example of him,' I added.

Humphrey continued, as if I had not spoken. 'He also advises that if we prosecute we must first undertake a similar Special Branch enquiry into the earlier leak of Chapter Five.'

I didn't like the sound of that at all. Furthermore, I couldn't see why! The leak of Chapter Five was completely different! It was absolutely harmless!

Humphrey took a different view. 'The Attorney-General says that either both leaks were harmless, or neither.' He gazed at me, wide-eyed, innocent. 'So shall I ask the Special Branch to work on the Chapter Five leak?'

He knew perfectly well that only one person who'd read Chapter Five stood to gain anything from leaking it – and I was not about to have myself prosecuted under Section 2.

'On second thoughts, Humphrey,' I told him, 'I think the Attorney-General is right. Forget that prosecution. Just sack the Press Officer concerned.'

Humphrey shook his head sadly. 'That could be difficult. There is some evidence that the Press Officer was not acting on his own initiative.'

I hadn't noticed that bit. 'Meaning?'

'He was carrying out the wishes of his Secretary of State.'

Appalled, I asked for a full explanation. According to Humphrey, the Press Officer had not leaked Chapter Eight out of hostility to me. The truth is that the Secretary of State for Energy was delighted at being described by the former Prime Minister as the ablest man in the Cabinet. He had mentioned to his Press Officer that, so far from suppressing the chapter, he would not mind seeing it in the press at once. Otherwise the public might never get a chance to read it, because of the attempt by Number Ten to censor it.

I asked Humphrey if he were sure of this.

He nodded. 'I'm sure that this will be the Press Officer's explanation when his case comes up for wrongful dismissal before the Industrial Tribunal. He will argue that he was following an implicit instruction, doing what his Secretary of State wanted done.'

I was bitterly disappointed. The upshot is that we have found the leaker, and I can neither prosecute him nor sack him!

Humphrey obligingly offered an alternative. But not a very practical one. 'I'm afraid, Prime Minister, that if you must sack somebody, the only candidate is the Energy Secretary. He is responsible for his Department.'

'But I can't,' I wailed. 'I lost one Cabinet Minister last month. I can't sack another this month.'

'Quite.' He agreed wholeheartedly. 'To lose one minister may be regarded as a misfortune. To lose both looks like carelessness. Furthermore, as the Energy Secretary didn't do the leaking and denies that he asked for it to be done, he might sue for wrongful dismissal as well!'

I couldn't see how to save my neck. The press were clamouring for the result of the enquiry. Humphrey offered up a press release that Malcolm had drafted, but it was hopeless. Phrases like 'Communication breakdown . . . misunderstanding . . . acted in good faith . . . will be dealt with by internal procedures . . .'

'It's a whitewash,' I complained. 'And not even a very effective whitewash.'

'More of a greywash, really,' agreed Bernard.

Humphrey was not of the same opinion. 'It's no whitewash. It shares out the blame equally.'

That's the *last* thing I wanted. It would have made it seem as if I really *did* try to suppress Chapter Eight! [*Which was true – Ed.*]

Humphrey thought for a moment. 'Perhaps . . .' he volunteered cautiously, 'perhaps we should let the story go out – but smother it.'

I saw instantly what he meant.

'You mean . . .?' I asked.

He nodded.

Silence filled the Cabinet Room. We could all see that there was no alternative. After some moments Humphrey put the plan into action.

'I've been meaning to tell you, Prime Minister – there's some very worrying information on the Foreign Office files. About espionage in the Soviet Embassy and Trade Delegation.'

'No!' I said in a horrified voice.

'I'm afraid so. Evidence against a lot of diplomats.'

'How many?' I asked.

'Seventy-six,' he replied.

I wasn't surprised. 'You know, Humphrey, I think the time has come for firm action. After all, the security of the realm is at stake.'

'Precisely.'

So it was done. 'Expel them,' I ordered. 'And we don't want to keep this secret. Tell the press today, at the same time as we tell them the result of the leak enquiry.'

'Yes, Prime Minister,' said Sir Humphrey. 'Good idea,' he added deferentially. We're quite a team!

3
A Diplomatic Incident

September 3rd
Today, the anniversary of the day World War II broke out, was a day with a couple of extraordinarily appropriate developments, a day full of surprises but a day that will one day be seen as a great day, a day on which a new day may dawn for Britain.

[*Hacker occasionally lurched into passages of purple prose. Generally they are meaningless. At best they are insignificant. But they reveal a Churchillian yearning for a meaningful and significant place in the history books which has sadly been denied him by posterity – Ed.*]

The main topic at the first early morning meeting with Humphrey and Bernard after my brief summer hols was the great delay that we are experiencing on the Channel Tunnel.[1] My concern is the big public ceremony to celebrate the start of the work. [*Naturally – Ed.*] For reasons that were unclear to me, the Foreign Office have been stalling again.

Humphrey didn't see the hurry. Nor did Bernard. 'They say the heads of agreement haven't been signed.'

Typical Foreign Office lethargy. 'It's about time they were,' I complained. It should be a terrific ceremony – big gates inaugurated, a foundation stone laid by the Rt Hon. James Hacker, the Prime Minister. I'll do a speech about this historic link, uniting two great sovereign powers. The coverage will be great. The fact that the FO hasn't agreed everything with the French does not, on the face of it, seem a sufficient reason to hold everything up at a time when my opinion-poll ratings have slipped a bit.

So I told Humphrey my decision: to have a summit meeting with the French President and sort it all out myself.

Humphrey was shocked. 'I had no idea that you were considering such a radical approach,' he said, using one of the most vicious adjectives in his vocabulary.

---

[1] A 1980s project for a tunnel under the English Channel, connecting Dover with Calais.

'Well, I am.'

Immediately he tried to undermine my self-confidence. 'Prime Minister, do you really believe that you personally are capable of concluding this negotiation with the French?'

I couldn't see why it should be so difficult. 'Yes I do. What are the outstanding points of issue?'

He replied, 'They are mainly concerned with sovereignty. Where do you believe the frontier should be?'

The frontier? I'd never considered it. He meant the frontier between Britain and France, presumably.

[*This entry in the diary tells us all that we need to know about Hacker's thought processes. It is as well to remember the adage: if God had intended politicians to think, he would have given them brains – Ed.*]

I couldn't see a problem. 'What's wrong with it wherever it is now?'

'You mean', enquired Humphrey, 'the three-mile limit? Who would own the middle of the tunnel?'

I had meant the three-mile limit. I'd never considered the middle of the tunnel at all.

[*Undoubtedly so. Hacker had only considered the favourable publicity to be obtained from the opening ceremony – Ed.*]

'You see,' Humphrey explained, 'the British position is that we should own half each. But of course, we could follow your idea, in which case most of the tunnel would be an international zone, administered by the United Nations perhaps? Or the EEC?'

I felt that the Foreign Office had got it right for once – dividing the tunnel in the middle is perfectly fair.

But Humphrey explained that the French *don't* think it is fair. They want an Anglo-French frontier at Dover. A ridiculous notion! 'Perhaps,' Humphrey suggested with a little smile, 'perhaps you would be happy to concede fifty per cent of the French case?'

In the interests of fairness, I told Humphrey, I'm always happy to concede fifty per cent.

'Oh dear,' replied Humphrey with evident satisfaction. 'Since the French have demanded one hundred per cent to start with, they'll end up with seventy-five per cent.'

A trick question. Which explained Humphrey's little smile. He was now looking triumphant, the silly man, because he'd caught me out. Anybody could do that. [*A little unintentional honesty there – Ed.*]

'*Obviously*,' I told him, keeping my temper with difficulty, 'we have to divide the tunnel in the middle. That way we can have sovereignty over half the tunnel, and so can they.'

'And who has sovereignty over the trains?'

I'd never thought of that. Humphrey, who after all has had the benefit of doing some homework on this, threw a barrage of irritating, niggling, pettifogging questions at me.

'If a crime is committed on a French train in the British sector, who should have jurisdiction? The British or the French?'

'The British,' I replied. He stared at me, that irritating little smirk playing around his lips. 'No, the French,' I said. 'No, the British.'

He didn't give me his opinion. He just went on with the questions. 'If a body is pushed out of a British train within the French sector, who has jurisdiction?'

'The French?' I tried. No response. 'No, the British,' I said. No, um . . .'

'If,' said Humphrey relentlessly, 'if a British lorry is loaded on to a French train in the British sector, who has jurisdiction?'

I was pretty confused by now. [*And, indeed, previously – Ed.*]

So was Bernard. 'Could criminal jurisdiction be divided into two legs?' he asked. 'Home and away?'

Humphrey ignored Bernard. 'Should we have a frontier post in the middle of the tunnel, half-way across?'

'Yes,' I said. He stared at me and I lost confidence again. 'No,' I added.

'Or should we have customs and immigration clearance at either end?'

I was beginning to see how complex the whole issue was. 'No,' I decided initially. 'Yes,' I concluded a moment later, having reconsidered.

'Or both ends?' There were limitless possibilities, it seemed.

'Yes,' I agreed.

Sir Humphrey hinted that I was being less than decisive. Very true. But after all, as I pointed out, these were questions for the lawyers in the negotiation.

'Precisely, Prime Minister. But I thought you said you wanted to handle it yourself.'

I was getting irritated. 'I don't want to handle abstruse points of international law, Humphrey, I want to sort out the basic political points at issue.'

'So,' said Humphrey, in a tone of extravagant mock surprise, 'Sovereignty is not political? How interesting.' He's got an endless supply of these cheap shots. He knew what I meant.

[*Hacker was being somewhat optimistic. It is improbable that Sir Humphrey knew what Hacker meant. After years of studying this manuscript we do not know what he meant. At times we are forced to wonder whether Hacker knew what he meant – Ed.*]

'I take it', asked Sir Humphrey, continuing this rather insolent cross-examination, 'that you will agree to the Tunnel being built with the most modern technology?'

'Of course.'

'Then,' replied Humphrey, 'you have just conceded that ninety per cent of the contracts will be placed with French companies. And do you want the signs to be in French first and English second?'

'No!' I was adamant.

'The French do.'

'We don't agree.'

'You can't have your ceremony until we do.'

I suggested a compromise. 'We could have the English first on the signs at the British end. And French first at the French end.'

'What about the trains?'

I was becoming furious. 'For God's *sake*, Humphrey, what does it matter?'

He remained calm. 'It matters to the French,' he explained. 'What about the menus? French or English?'

I looked for a compromise. 'Can't they change the menus half-way?'

He shook his head sadly. 'The French will be adamant. That's why both the British and the French Concorde are spelt the French way – with an E on the end. Of course, if you want to concede all of these points with the French we could have immediate agreement with them. Alternatively – ' he plunged in the knife ' – you can leave it to the Foreign Office to do their best.'

Do their best? It seemed that he did not expect the FO to get a good deal either.

He confirmed that this was his view. 'I'm afraid they won't. But it will be better than you could get, Prime Minister.'

I'm afraid he's right. And yet, it made no sense. 'Humphrey,' I asked, 'do we never get our own way with the French?'

'Sometimes,' he allowed.

'When was the last time?'

'Battle of Waterloo, 1815.' Could he be right? While I pondered this question, delving into my encyclopaedic memory and knowledge of history, Sir Humphrey raised the vexed question of hijacking.

'What if terrorists were to hijack a train? And threaten to blow up the train and the tunnel.'

What a horrific thought that was! 'My God,' I exclaimed. 'Let's give France jurisdiction over the whole thing. Then they'd have to handle it.'

Sir Humphrey smiled a complacant smile. 'You see, Prime Minister?' He was patronising me now. 'If you were handling the negotiations you would have just conceded *everything* to the French. In fact, I believe that the French will come up with some totally underhand ploy to regain the advantage. But no doubt you have anticipated that, Prime Minister.'

The sarcasm was unmistakable. I had to concede that I could not possibly handle the negotiations. With some nations, yes. With the French, never. Also, I could see another, bigger advantage in staying out of it. 'If humiliating concessions are going to be made, I'd like the Foreign Secretary to be in charge.'

'Very wise, Prime Minister.' At last we were in agreement. And we moved on to another matter that has been causing me the most profound ongoing irritation. 'May we now discuss the equally vexed question of your predecessor's memoirs?'

As if we hadn't had enough trouble with Chapter Eight, it seems that he'd now started work on his final chapter, the one that concerns his resignation and my accession to the Premiership. And, to that end, he wanted access to certain government papers.

I asked if we couldn't find *any* way to stop these bloody memoirs before they ruin my career. Little did I know that my wish was about to be granted.

Humphrey shook his head sadly. 'Memoirs, alas, are an occupational hazard.' And he sighed deeply, like Eeyore.

I can't think why he was sighing. I'm the one who's being skewered. And it's not even what he's written that upsets me – it's the betrayal! Until I read the first eight chapters of his book I thought he was a friend of mine!

For instance, in the draft that arrived this morning he'd called me two-faced. I'd shown it to Bernard.

'Very wrong' was Bernard's gratifying comment.

I was grateful for the vote of confidence.

'And unforgiveably indiscreet,' Bernard went on.

'Indiscreet?' I looked at him, surprised.

'And wrong!' Bernard added emphatically.

'How can he tell such lies about me?' I asked rhetorically.

'What lies?' asked Bernard. 'Oh I see,' he said.

Really, Bernard is sometimes remarkably slow on the uptake. How could he have thought I'd changed the subject? But apparently he did.

Why has the former Prime Minister written this garbage? Simply so that he'll increase the sales of the book by inventing stories? I think not. Some people lie not because it is in their interest but because it is in their nature. 'He is a vile, treacherous, malevolent bastard,' I told Bernard, 'and if he's hoping to get any more honours or quangos or Royal Commissions he's got another think coming. He will not get one ounce of official recognition as long as I'm here.'

I regretted this outburst, because at that moment the phone rang. Bernard took the call.

'Yes? . . . look, is this important, because? . . . Oh! . . . Ah! . . . Oh! Dead on arrival? . . . I see.'

Solemnly he replaced the receiver.

'Bad news, Bernard?' I asked.

'Yes and no,' he replied cautiously. 'Your predecessor, the previous Prime Minister of Great Britain and Northern Ireland, has just died of a heart attack.'

'What a tragedy,' I said immediately. I know how to say the right things on such occasions.

'Indeed,' replied Bernard and Humphrey in chorus.

'A great man,' I said, for the record.

'A great man,' they repeated in unison.

'He will be sorely missed,' I said. After all, *someone's* bound to miss him.

'Sorely missed,' echoed the double act on the other side of the Cabinet table.

'And so will his memoirs,' I added.

'Which will never be finished,' said Bernard.

'Alas!' sighed Humphrey.

'Alas!' I said.

'Apparently, Prime Minister,' said Bernard, 'he expressed a hope that he might have a state funeral, just before . . . the end. But in view of your wish to give him no further honours . . .'

Bernard was quite wrong. A funeral was an honour that I was happy to arrange. I told Bernard that he had completely misunderstood me. 'I am sure, Bernard, that a tremendous number of people will want to attend his funeral.'

'To pay him tribute, you mean?'

'Of course,' I said. That was certainly one reason. And to make sure he's dead is another.

[*Working funerals are the best sort of summit meeting. Ostensibly arranged for another purpose, statesmen and diplomats can mingle informally at receptions, churches and gravesides, and achieve more than at ten official 'summits' for which expectations have been aroused. This is presumably why Hacker immediately agreed to a state funeral for his late and unlamented predecessor – Ed.*]

September 4th

A splendid list of acceptances for the funeral already. They're all RSVPing like mad. So far we have seven Commonwealth Prime Ministers, the American Vice-President, the Russian Foreign Minister, and six European Prime Ministers – excellent. And I am the host! I shall be there, among all these great statesmen, at the centre of the world stage. Bearing my grief with dignity and fortitude. Dignified grief goes down terribly well with the voters. Especially when shared with other world leaders. Marvellous thing, death. So uncontroversial.

However, there was one interesting query on the list. The French Prime Minister. I asked Bernard and Humphrey about this when we met to discuss the pleasurable matter of the funeral arrangements.

'I imagine that's what the French Ambassador is coming to see you about tomorrow,' said Humphrey.

I was more immediately concerned with the placing of the TV cameras. 'There will be plenty of room, won't there?' I wanted definite assurances. 'We want them outside Number Ten, along the route, outside the Abbey,[1] inside the Abbey, and one looking straight at my pew.'

Humphrey looked doubtful. 'That would mean putting the camera in the pulpit.'

'Will that be all right?' I checked.

'It won't leave a lot of room for the Archbishop,' said Humphrey.

I understood the problem. 'So where will he preach from?' I asked.

'I think he will need the pulpit.'

This was a bigger problem than I'd thought. 'So where will my camera be?'

Humphrey thought for a few moments. 'Well, there's always the High Altar. But the Archbishop may need that too.'

---

[1] Westminster Abbey.

He'll just have to do without it. [*Apparently the Archbishop was under the impression that the funeral was a religious ceremony. Nobody had told him that it was a Party Political Broadcast – Ed.*]

September 5th

Today I saw the French Ambassador. It's all worse than I thought.

But first I saw Bernard. 'The French Ambassador is on his way. But I know what his news will be: the French Prime Minister isn't coming, the President's coming instead.'

'The President?' I was overjoyed. 'That's wonderful.'

'No, no, Prime Minister. It's terrible!'

Humphrey had heard the news too and, flustered, he hurried in to join us.

I couldn't see the problem – at first. I've not had all that much experience with the French. Bernard could see it all too clearly.

'When the Queen visited France three years ago, Prime Minister, she presented him with a labrador puppy. And now he's bringing one of its puppies to present her with in return.'

Humphrey sank into his chair, aghast. 'No!' he gasped. 'That's what I'd heard! So it's true!'

'I'm afraid so, Sir Humphrey.' Bernard was using his funereal voice.

'I knew it,' said Sir Humphrey, fatally. 'I *knew* they'd do something like this.'

I still couldn't see the problem. 'It seems rather a nice gesture to me.'

'It's a gesture all right.' Humphrey smiled a sour smile. 'But hardly a nice one.'

'Why not?'

'Because Her Majesty will have to refuse it. And there will be . . . repercussions!'

The problem, it seemed, was quarantine! Dogs can't just be imported. This puppy will have to spend six months in quarantine at Heathrow.

It still didn't seem particularly tragic to me. 'The French will understand that, won't they?'

'*Of course* they'll understand it. Privately. That's why they're doing it. But they'll refuse to understand it officially.'

I suddenly saw the problem. The French were creating a diplomatic incident to get their own way over the sovereignty of the Channel Tunnel. I explained this to Humphrey and Bernard, who seemed grateful for the insight. Then, decisively, I sent for Peter Gascoigne, the Foreign Affairs Private Secretary. 'What do we do?' I asked.

'I don't know.' He'd already heard the news and had apparently been struck down by depressive illness as a consequence. He had the look of a desperate man about him.

I hardly expected such a hopeless response. The Civil Service can usually think of *something* to do. 'But you're my Foreign Affairs Secretary,' I informed him. 'I expect some positive suggestions.'

'I'm sorry, Prime Minister, but the Home Office is responsible for quarantine.'

I think he was passing the buck. Or the puppy. I sent for Graham French, the Home Affairs Private Secretary. While we waited for him I explored with Peter the possibility of getting the French to withdraw the gift.

'We've tried everything,' Peter told me desperately. 'We've suggested an oil painting of the puppy. A bronze. A porcelain model. Not a hope.'

'Can't you get them to stuff it?' I asked.

Humphrey intervened. 'There's nothing we'd sooner . . . oh, taxidermy? No chance.'

Graham hurried in. 'Graham,' I said, 'tell your chums at the Home Office that they've got to find a way round these quarantine regulations.'

He reacted rather stiffly. 'I'm afraid that's out of the question, Prime Minister.'

I wasn't expecting to be contradicted. I asked him to explain himself.

'In the first place,' he said, blinking at me nervously, 'we enforce the regulations rigorously with all British citizens and all foreign nationals. Without exception. And in the second place, the Quarantine Act is signed by the Sovereign. She can't be the only one to break her own laws. It would be quite wrong ethically and for health reasons, and is completely out of the question.'

At that moment the intercom buzzed. The French Ambassador had arrived. Things were all happening too fast. Yet nothing can be posponed because the funeral is only three days from now.

So while the Ambassador waited a moment in the little waiting room next to the Cabinet Room[1] I told my staff that we *have* to find a way out of this. I told Peter to get back to the Foreign Office at once and tell them to talk to the Home Office. Graham was to do the same

[1] See *Yes Prime Minister*, Volume I, Chapter 4, pp. 114ff.

at the Home Office. Both were to keep in touch with Bernard, who would liaise with the Palace. Humphrey was to talk to the law officers in the hope of finding legal loopholes (they all shook their heads firmly at this suggestion), and I told Humphrey he'd be responsible for co-ordinating the whole thing.

'What whole thing?' He seemed confused.

'Whatever whole thing we think up to deal with this French plot,' I explained.

'Oh, that whole thing.' Sometimes Humphrey's a bit slow. 'Certainly, Prime Minister. I'll set up an operations room in the Cabinet Office.'

I seemed to be the only one with any ideas. I asked Humphrey if *he* had any suggestions. He suggested that I didn't keep the French Ambassador waiting any longer. So I sent for him and I asked Humphrey to stay and give me support.

'Do I need any papers?' asked Humphrey, flapping a bit at the thought of the impending confrontation.

'Just a sponge and a towel,' I told him grimly.

The French Ambassador spoke almost perfect English as he slipped elegantly into the room. 'Prime Minister. You are most kind to give me your time.' He is small, slim, and utterly charming.

I told him it was a pleasure.

'I understand you are anxious to finalise the agreement for the Channel Tunnel?'

'Yes, very much so . . .' I began, but out of the corner of my eye I saw Humphrey shaking his head slowly, almost imperceptibly, an unmistakable cautionary signal. I backtracked rapidly. 'But, on the other hand, no *real* hurry,' I said. I'm sure the Ambassador didn't notice.

In fact, he seemed eager to help. 'But it would be nice if we could reach some conclusions, wouldn't it?'

'Nice?' I glanced at Humphrey. He shrugged. 'Nice,' I agreed. 'No question.'

'And', continued the Ambassador, 'my Government feels that if we were to take advantage of the funeral – my condolences, by the way, a tragic loss – '

'Tragic, tragic!' I echoed tragically.

'. . . take advantage of the funeral for you and our President to 'ave a few words . . .'

'Of course, of course,' I interrupted. 'The only thing is, I shall be host to a large number of distinguished guests, and I'm not sure . . .'

His Excellency took umbrage. 'You do not wish to speak to our President?'

'Of course I do.' I smiled reassuringly. 'Yes. No question.' Since my conversation with Humphrey a couple of days ago, I'm well aware of the dangers of my becoming directly involved in negotiating with the French. So I tried to explain that I'd rather simply *speak* than negotiate. I tried to imply that actual negotiations were slightly beneath me.

He understood that kind of arrogance. But he wouldn't let go. 'Don't you think that these little quarrels between friends are best resolved by just talking to each other, face to face?'

'Between *friends*, yes,' I replied. Humphrey blanched.

But the Ambassador was unperturbed. 'I think otherwise our President would be very hurt. Not personally, but as a snurb to France.' I *think* he meant snub. It sounded like 'snurb', but I don't know what a snurb is.

Anyway, I reassured the excellent Excellency that we had no intention of snurbing France, and that I regard the French as *great* friends.

He was pleased. I hoped he'd leave, but no. He had quite a considerable agenda of his own, and we moved on to item two.

He claimed that he was concerned about his Embassy's security during the President's visit. This was rather surprising. I looked at Humphrey. Was there any reason for concern? But no, I could tell from Humphrey's expression that this was just another French ploy. Together, we assured the Ambassador that the Commissioner of the Metropolitan Police has everything absolutely under control.

The Ambassador was not satisfied. 'My Government requests that the French police be permitted to guard our Embassy.'

Humphrey was flashing me the clearest possible warning signals. His look said 'Say no at all costs.' So I told the French Ambassador that it was impossible to grant such a request.

He pretended indignation. 'It is surely not *impossible*.'

I decided to go on to the attack. 'Are you saying that you don't trust the British police?'

'My Government makes no comment on the British police,' he replied carefully. 'But the President would be happier if the French police were in charge.'

I could see that Humphrey was itching to get at him. So I let Humphrey off his leash and sat back in my swivel chair.

'The problem, Excellency,' said Humphrey smoothly, somehow

continuing to make the word Excellency sound like an insult, 'is that there are seventy-three Embassies in London. No doubt they would all want their own police. Most would carry machine-guns, given the opportunity. Her Majesty's Government is not convinced that this would make London a safer place.'

The irony went *right* over his head. But he seemed to accept the refusal with diplomatic good grace. 'My Government will be most disappointed. But now I can move on to a happier matter. Our President will be bringing a little present which he will be presenting to Her Majesty.'

I forced a smile. 'How charming.'

'A little puppee,' he explained unnecessarily. Why did he bother, he must have known that we knew? 'She comes from the litter of the very same labrador that Her Majesty graciously presented to Monsieur le Président on her State visit to France.'

I waited. I expressed no pleasure, no thanks. So he continued to the bitter end. 'Perhaps you will let us know the arrangements for the presentation?'

I sighed. 'Your Excellency,' I said patiently. 'It is of course most kind. A charming thought. But as you know it cannot be presented for six months. Our quarantine laws.'

Of course he refused to understand. He told me it was absurd. He reminded me that the Queen presented the dog during her State visit.

I explained that we would be delighted for his President to do the same thing. But the law's the law.

'Surely', enquired the Ambassador, his manner visibly cooling, 'your laws are only to exclude infected animals?'

I concurred.

'But you are not suggesting that the President of France would present the Queen of England with a diseased puppy?'

'No, of course not.'

'Then it's settled.'

'No it is not settled.' I was firm. 'I must ask you to suggest to the President that he find a different gift.'

His Excellency informed me that this would be completely out of the question. 'Were it the President alone, perhaps . . .' He shrugged. 'But the President's wife, our First Lady, has set her heart on it. She is determined.'

A neat move. It now appears that if I now say no, I will be insulting a lady. The first lady.

I told him that we would make every endeavour. But it may not be possible. [*This is the firmest form of refusal known to the language of diplomacy – Ed.*]

The Ambassador rose to his feet. 'Prime Minister, I do not have to tell you the gravity of the affront my Government would feel if Her Majesty were to refuse a request to present a gift in exchange for the one the President accepted from her. I fear it would be interpreted as both a national and a personal insult. To the President *and* his wife.'

I'd had enough of this bullshit. I stood up too. 'Excellency, please ask the President not to bring that bitch with him.'

Humphrey gasped. The Ambassador looked utterly stunned. And I suddenly realised the ambiguity of what I'd said.

'The puppy,' I said hastily. 'I meant the puppy.'

Tonight Annie and I had a quiet evening at home together, in the flat above the shop. [*The top-floor flat in Number Ten Downing Street – Ed.*] We had to go over all *her* arrangements for the funeral. She wanted to know why we had to lay on so many visits for the wives. I explained that the Foreign Office likes it – it keeps them out of the way. They can't be with their husbands, their husbands are busy.

'Only at the funeral itself,' said Annie.

I explained that she'd missed the point of the whole funeral: they're coming for the politics. This is a *working* funeral. As a matter of fact, when we were all at that funeral in Norway a few months ago, the French, the Germans and I were all so busy negotiating EEC farm quotas in the hotel that we forgot to go to the Cathedral.

Annie thought that was very funny. 'Didn't they notice?'

'We got there before it finished. We blamed security. You can blame security for almost anything nowadays.'

In fact, this funeral will be a heaven-sent opportunity. Literally! Much better than a summit, because there are no prior expectations. The public don't expect their leaders to return from a funeral with test ban agreements or farm quota reductions. So we can actually have serious negotiations, whereas a 'summit' is just a public relations circus in which the press never give the politicians a real chance. Journalism wants to find problems. Diplomacy wants to find solutions.

Annie wanted to know if anyone at all would be coming to the funeral to pay tribute to a friend. I laughed. If only his friends came we wouldn't even fill the vestry, let alone the Abbey. No, my illustrious predecessor has undoubtedly done more for the world by dying than he ever did in the whole of his life.

She asked if the service was agreed. Funny old Annie, she's a churchgoer, she cares about these things. I told her that there'd be lots of music, which was all I knew about it.

'That's nice,' she said.

'Yes,' I said. 'That way, we can have useful discussions when the organ's playing. Unfortunately, we have to shut up for the lesson and the prayers.'

Annie smiled. She was getting the point. 'What about the sermon?'

'That's when our guests catch up on jet-lag,' I explained.

Altogether, this funeral has come at exactly the right moment. Apart from the little local problem of squelching those damn memoirs, it will improve my standing in the polls to be seen with all the world leaders and there's lots of things to sort out between NATO and the Warsaw Pact. Also it's a good opportunity to make more friends in the Third World.

'Jim,' asked Annie, 'there's something I've never understood. If we're the First World and the poor are the Third World, then who's the Second?'

'Good question,' I said. 'I've never heard anyone admit to being Second World. We think it's the Soviet bloc, maybe they think it's us – but because no one ever raises the question it's not a problem. Diplomacy, Annie!'

Above all, the Middle East is looking ominous again. I'm sure that, if I could only find the time, I could bring the various warring parties together in peace and harmony. But if we don't sort out some of these problems in the next three days, we'll have to hope that somebody else important dies within the next three months.

September 6th

A variety of suggestions for dealing with the dog crisis poured in from the Foreign Office and the Home Office today, each more foolish than the last.

[*The first came from Sir Ernest Roach, Permanent Secretary at the Home Office, and is reproduced overleaf – Ed.*]

HOME OFFICE
QUEEN ANNE'S GATE
LONDON SW1H 9AT

Memorandum

From: The Permanent Secretary   September 6th

To: Bernard Woolley

Dear Bernard,

    We have two possible approaches to this problem under
discussion:

    1. We could pass an enabling Act of Parliament, enabling
        this particular dog to remain in the UK. An enabling
        Act can enable anything.

    2. We could turn the whole of Buckingham Palace into a
        dog quarantine zone, thus fulfilling the letter if not
        the spirit of the law.

    Please let me have the Prime Minister's reactions.

[Hacker's diary continues – Ed.]

The Home Office's first two proposals are completely cracked. An enabling Act *can* enable anything – in this case it would enable me to lose the next election.

The dog quarantine zone idea leaves one fairly important question unanswered – what would happen to the Queen's other dogs?

The Foreign Office outdid the Home Office. Moments after I'd sent Graham away with a flea in his ear, a memo arrived from King Charles Street.[1]

Foreign and Commonwealth Office

London SW1A 2AH

Memorandum

From: The Permanent Secretary September 6th

To: Peter Gascoigne

Dear Peter,

We can only think of one technical way around this problem: make Buckingham Palace notionally an extension of the French Embassy. Then the dog could still be on foreign territory.

Reactions please.

Dick

---

[1] The Foreign Office is situated on the corner of Whitehall and King Charles Street.

[*Hacker's diary continues – Ed.*]

I gave them my bloody reactions! I told them that, as always, they had revealed themselves to be weak, indecisive and stupid in the face of a genuine emergency. I reminded them that I am currently engaged in a fight for the sovereignty of the Channel Tunnel. What did they suppose I felt about the sovereignty of the Palace?

The Civil Service is usually so frightfully smart and condescending – *especially* the Foreign Office. Life is simple when you have so many precedents to follow; but they're like computers: put them into a *new* crisis, for which they've not been programmed, and their brains short-circuit.

[*It must have been very painful for senior Foreign Office officials to be told that they were weak, indecisive and stupid. What would have made it more painful was being told by someone as weak, indecisive and stupid as Hacker. What would have made it most painful was that Hacker was correct – Ed.*]

Meanwhile, Number Ten was in a frenzy all day. All the phones were ringing in the Private Office *all* the time.

Bernard was on excellent form. He remembered to phone the Palace and check that Her Majesty was never told *officially* that this gift has been proposed – that way, she cannot be implicated in refusing it.

But even Bernard was at a loss on the matter of this damn dog. All he could suggest was that our Ambassador in Paris tried to 'nobble' it . . . slip it some poison, borrow some umbrella tips from the Bulgarians. [*A reference to the murder in 1978 of Georgi Markov, a Bulgarian dissident working for the BBC's[1] External Services, who was stabbed with a poisoned umbrella tip at a London bus stop – Ed.*]

This sounded like an extremely tricky covert operation, with profoundly embarrassing consequences if discovered. The British voter can stomach rising unemployment, rising inflation, rising taxes, a falling pound, a falling stock exchange – but it would *never* re-elect me if I were thought to be implicated in the demise of a labrador puppy, dispatched to meet its Maker in the Great Kennel in the sky under mysterious circumstances. The British know their priorities!

Meanwhile, in the absence of a solution to the problem with the French, other arrangements continued apace today. We have laid on interpreters for numerous meetings. There were even interpreters

---

[1] British Broadcasting Corporation.

listed for my meeting with the American Vice-President, but I assume that was just a typing error. [*Almost certainly correct. After all, the English-speaking nations can, with a certain generosity of spirit, be said to include the Americans. In fact, it may be thought that the 'special relationship' between us is purely due to the fact that the Americans are no more noticeably multilingual than we are – Ed.*]

The Prime Ministers are flying in tomorrow and Bernard tells me that the Band of the Royal Marines is going crazy – it has to learn to play all the national anthems. There was great relief when we learned the Argentinians weren't coming – not because we defeated them in the Falklands but because the Argentinian national anthem is in three movements and lasts six minutes.[1]

Seating in the Abbey was the big question today. I had to approve it. Incredibly, they had done it alphabetically, which would have resulted in Iran and Iraq sitting next to each other, plus Israel and Jordan in the same pew. We could have started World War III.

Bernard rang through to the Abbey, and was told that it had been noticed that they were all sitting together but that the feeling at the Abbey was that as they were all from the same part of the world they might feel more at home. Bernard was forced to explain that proximity does not equal affinity.

Somebody else pointed out that as Ireland was in the same pew it might make things better. I pointed out that Ireland doesn't make *anything* better. Not for us. Ever!

Peter, my Foreign Affairs Private Secretary, came up to the study to brief me on the various issues we could expect to encounter. Bernard was there too, of course.

'The Spanish Ambassador says his Foreign Secretary will want a word about the unity of nations. And the Italians want a word about the European ideal.'

These were clearly coded messages. I asked what they meant.

Peter translated. 'The Spanish want Gibraltar back and the Italians want to enlarge the EEC wine lakes.' [*When EEC Foreign Ministers returned home after top-level meetings, it would come as a surprise to their governments if they claimed that their time had been spent trying to promote the European ideal. The EEC was just a customs union – politicians won brownie points only by heroically defending their national interest – Ed.*]

---

[1] In fact, the long version lasts for about four minutes (depending on the speed at which it is played) and the shortened form one minute forty-eight seconds. It is interesting to note that Hacker was given this incorrect information by the anti-Argie lobby in the FO.

'The New Zealanders', continued Peter, 'want an *ad hoc* meeting of Commonwealth leaders to discuss alleged British racist support of South Africa.'

I asked why they were raising this again. It was explained to me that there were two possibilities: it was either because of their anger about EEC butter quotas which exclude New Zealand dairy products – or maybe it was a manifestation of the guilt they feel over their about-turn on nuclear policy.

Peter proposed a royal visit for New Zealand. Send the Queen herself if possible. An excellent idea, though rather a long-term solution and no help to the immediate embarrassment unless the offer of the royal visit shuts them up. And Peter warned me that we could expect serious trouble from the South Africans anyway.

'Problems with human rights?' I asked.

'No. They're trying to unload more grapefruit.'

I was briefed about correct modes of address. Apparently the correct mode of address when speaking to a Cypriot Archbishop is not Your Ecstasy, it's Your Beatitude. And if the Papal Envoy says 'We desire to wash our hands' it means he's been caught short.

In the middle of all this Bernard received an urgent call from the Palace. We all held our breath. Had she heard about the puppy and, if so, did she have a view?

But no: the Palace had heard that there was a problem with the red carpets at Heathrow. (Which there was, but had been solved, I know not how.) And Her Majesty was worried that the President of the Ivory Coast wishes – apparently – to award her the Order of the Elephant.

I boiled over. 'Bernard, Peter, for God's sake!' I shouted. 'We can't have another animal. Especially an elephant! The whole of Whitehall, the Foreign Office, the Home Office, the Cabinet Office and the DHSS[1] have been tied up with one puppy for nearly a week. Government has been paralysed. No elephants!!'

But I was mistaken. Apparently it's not a real elephant that the Ivory Coast wants to send – it's a medal. The problem is that the honour is conveyed by a wet kiss.

I'm leaving that one to the FO.

September 7th
Tomorrow is the funeral of my illustrious predecessor. And today we

---

[1] Department of Health and Social Security.

licked the French. I don't know which of these events gives me a greater feeling of satisfaction.

But things did not start auspiciously.

First thing this morning Bernard entered the Cabinet Room with two files – one of them one inch thick, the other six inches thick.

'What on earth is that, Bernard?' I asked.

He indicated the slim file. 'The Channel Tunnel file, Prime Minister.'

'No,' I said. 'The thick one.'

'Oh.' He looked hopeless. 'That's the puppy file.'

'How far have we reached with it?'

'It weighed in at three and a half pounds this morning.'

'The puppy?'

'The file,' he replied seriously.

We had told the French that airport security would regretfully have to impound the puppy and quarantine it at Heathrow. The French had not replied. But in order to make it sound a little better the FO had let the French know that, as Heathrow Airport is en route from Buckingham Palace to Windor Castle, the Queen will be able to visit it on the way.

I was suprised. 'Can you visit quarantined dogs?'

Bernard didn't know either. 'If she can't,' he replied, tired of the whole business, 'she can sort of wave as she drives down the M4.'

The real question was what measures the French would feel free to take against us, after this alleged and manufactured rebuff. The likelihood was that they would go public over the story if we don't give in to them over the Channel Tunnel.

We were certainly completely unprepared for what happened next. Sir Humphrey burst into the room unceremoniously.

'Prime Minister!' He was quite breathless. 'I have urgent news.'

'Good news?' Hope springs eternal.

'Yes . . . and no.' He was cautious. 'The police have just found a bomb in the grounds of the French Embassy.'

I was horrified. 'Who put it there?'

'We don't know yet. Lots of people could have a motive.'

'Us, for a start!' said Bernard.

'Still,' I said, trying to look on the bright side, 'it's a good job we found it. I suppose.' That must have been the good part of Humphrey's news.

Humphrey had more to say. 'The other news is even worse. The French President isn't flying in for the funeral.'

I couldn't see why that mattered. In fact, it sounded like good news to me. It *still* sounded like goods news (not quite as good, but nearly) when Humphrey said that the President was still coming, but by car – secretly. The plane is a security decoy, a blind.

'That sounds like a good idea,' I said. But I didn't see why it mattered.

'It's a brilliant idea!' said Humphrey, tight-lipped with anger. 'He can bring the bloody puppy in the car!'

Humphrey was right. Was there nothing we could do? 'Are you prepared, Prime Minister, to give instructions for the French President's car to be stopped and searched as he comes here as your invited guest to the funeral?' I had been completely outmanoeuvred. 'Are you prepared to violate their diplomatic immunity and search the diplomatic bag?'

I was confused. 'You can't put a puppy in a bag.'

'It would be a doggy bag,' said Bernard.

'Suppose we did search, and found it?' I was considering my options. 'That would really set the cat among the pigeons.'

'And let the dog out of the bag,' said Bernard.

'But . . . what would be even worse . . . suppose we were wrong?' explained Humphrey. 'Just suppose it wasn't there.'

He was right. I couldn't take the risk. Violating their diplomatic immunity wrongfully? It would be a catastrophe.

'*But,*' said Humphrey, ever the Devil's Advocate, 'if it *is* in the car they will drive it into the French Embassy, and the puppy will be on French territory. Here in the middle of London.'

'Hanging over our heads,' I observed gloomily.

'We'd better pray it's house-trained,' said Bernard.

SIR BERNARD WOOLLEY RECALLS:[1]
That evening we held a diplomatic reception at Number Ten. The evening was full of humour, mostly unintentional.

My role was, of course, to make the Prime Minister's guests welcome. Especially the French. I remember introducing Mrs Hacker to a Monsieur Berenger from UNESCO.[2] He was having a frightfully good time, and informed us both that he thought it was an excellent funeral. The last one he'd been to was Andropov's,[3] which had been awfully gloomy.

I also had the pleasure of introducing him to the Commissioner of the

[1] In conversation with the Editors.
[2] United Nations Economic, Social and Cultural Organisation.
[3] Former head of the KGB, then General Secretary of the Communist Party and President of the USSR, then dead.

Metropolitan Police. I explained that Monsieur Berenger was in London as the diplomatic representative of UNESCO. 'Ah yes,' said the bobby, pulling knowledgeably at his little white toothbrush moustache, 'gallant little country.'

[*Hacker's diary continues – Ed.*]

Star-studded reception at Number Ten – and yours truly wiped the floor with the French. Although in all honesty I must admit that it was a sensational French own goal which brought about my victory.

Everyone was very jolly. No one was at all sad about tomorrow's funeral. The American Vice-President came armed with a new Polish joke which he'd got from Gromyko.[1] 'You've heard the new Polish joke? Jaruzelski!'[2] And he laughed loud and long.

The Vice-President wanted an urgent word about the NATO bases in Germany. It wasn't possible at the party, so we made a deal to discuss them in the Abbey tomorrow. Then he disappeared into the crowd, hopefully searching for some non-aligned countries who would speak to him. [*The definition of a non-aligned country is that it is non-aligned with the United States – Ed.*]

And the Russians were in great form. The Soviet Ambassador sat down next to Sir Humphrey on a Sheraton sofa in the White Drawing-room and reminisced with a gang of us about my predecessor. 'You know, the death of a past Prime Minister is a very sad occasion.'

'Very sad, very sad,' murmured Humphrey dutifully and sipped his white wine.

'But he is no loss to Britain,' continued the Russian. 'You know what his trouble was?'

A leading question. I could think of plenty of answers but I waited for the Soviet viewpoint. 'He had plenty here . . .' the Ambassador pointed to his forehead' . . . and plenty here . . .' he put his hand on his heart. 'But nothing *here*!!' he growled, and made a grab for Sir Humphrey's private parts.

Humphrey squeaked, leapt to his feet and dropped his glass of Macon Villages, while the Russian Ambassador yelled with laughter. I laughed so much that I choked and had to leave the room. And the Russian Ambassador was right, by the way.

I didn't see Humphrey after that for quite a while. He was conspicuous by his absence. I thought he was either recovering his dignity or

---

[1] The Soviet former Foreign Minister, at the time President of the USSR.
[2] The puppet Prime Minister of Poland.

trying to sponge the red wine off his trousers. I'd been looking for him because I wanted the security of his knowledge and advice when I talked to the French President, a conversation that I did not relish and couldn't postpone much longer.

Then Bernard and the Police Commissioner, an unlikely pair, unobtrusively ushered me out of the party in the State rooms, across the panelled lobby and into my study for a private word. Humphrey was waiting there.

'What's all this?' I asked.

'The bomb in the French Embassy garden was planted by the French police,' said the Commissioner.

At first I thought he was joking. But no!

'It was to see if they could catch us out. To prove our security inefficient.'

This was the best news I'd heard for months. They showed me a file of evidence. A matching detonator was found in their hotel. They had confessed.

I was ecstatic. The French cops smuggling explosives into the UK gave me just the opportunity I needed. I told Humphrey to give me a couple of minutes alone with the President, and to interrupt as soon as I pressed the secret buzzer that I have in my desk for that very purpose. [*To contrive apparently chance interruptions – Ed.*]

Well, they showed Monsieur le Président into my study. I apologised to him for dragging him out of the party for a few moments, and indicated that I wished to discuss the Tunnel. But he didn't want to discuss the Tunnel yet. 'First of all, may we clear up a silly misunderstanding? About this little puppy I shall be presenting as a return gift to Her Majesty tomorrow?'

So they *did* smuggle it in! 'Monsieur le Président,' I said, putting my foot down firmly, 'I'm extremely sorry but there is no misunderstanding. I cannot ask the Queen to break the law.'

He smiled. 'I do not want the Queen to break the law, I merely ask the Prime Minister to bend it.'

Again I apologised, formally, and said no. He was haughty, magnificent and deeply hurt. He remarked that if the French people ever learn of this 'rejection' they would take it as a national slap in the face. As if there was any doubt that they would learn of it. Personally I believe that the French people (unlike the British) have infinitely more common sense than their leaders, and would do no such thing.

So we returned to the Tunnel. And now the President pressed home the advantage that he thought he had created. 'As for the

Tunnel, you make it very difficult for me. The French people will not accept a second slap in the face. And you are rejecting our very reasonable proposal for French sovereignty up to but not including Dover. But setting that aside, there is also another question: which shall be the *langue de préférence*?'[1]

I went to my desk, ostensibly to pick up a piece of paper and a pen. I slid my left hand beneath the desktop and pressed the buzzer. He didn't notice. 'Surely,' I said reasonably, 'if half the signs put French first and half English, that would be fair.'

'Fair, yes, but not logical.'

'Does logic matter?' I asked.

'Does the law matter?' he responded.

'Of course it does,' I said. 'Britain is the only European country without rabies.'

Humphrey burst in without knocking. He was carrying the file. 'Monsieur le Président, please forgive me. Prime Minister, I think you should see this urgently.'

I sat at my desk. I opened it. I read it. 'No!' I gasped, and stared penetratingly at M. le Président. He didn't know what it was, of course. I read on, keeping him in suspense. Then I rose accusingly.

'Monsieur le Président, I'm afraid I have to ask you for an explanation.' And I handed him the file full of evidence of the French bomb plot. He read it. His face gave away nothing.

'I hope I do not have to explain the gravity of this,' I said, very much hoping that I *did* have to.

No such luck. He looked up from the file. 'Prime Minister, I am deeply sorry. I must ask you to believe I had no knowledge of this.'

Probably he didn't. But I wasn't letting him off the hook. Nor would he have done, in my position. 'This is an attempt, by guests, to deceive Her Majesty's Government. And there is the serious crime of illegally smuggling explosives into the UK.'

'You must know', he replied reasonably, 'that the French Government never know what French Security are doing.'

'You mean you are not responsible for their actions?'

This was not what he meant. He couldn't deny responsibility. 'No, but . . . if this report is true I must ask you to accept my profound regrets.'

The truth of it was easily confirmed. And then Humphrey went in for the kill. 'You see, it makes it very difficult for the Prime Minister over the Channel Tunnel.'

[1] First language.

I agreed. 'When news of this bomb is published the British people will want to concede very little.'

'They'll wonder if it's safe to go through it!' murmured Humphrey.

'It might be full of official French bombs,' I added.

M. le Président and I stared at each other. He remained silent. The ball was in my court. 'Of course,' I suggested, 'in the interest of Anglo-French friendship we could overlook the crimes of your security men.'

He offered to meet me half-way. Literally! 'I suppose . . . we could agree to sovereignty only half-way across the Channel.'

Humphrey made a note, very ostentatiously.

I said: 'We would like half the signs to place the English language first. And, above all, we want the opening ceremony in two months. In Dover first, and Calais second.'

'I think that is an excellent idea,' he said with a big smile. 'As an expression of the warmth and trust between our two countries.'

We all shook hands.

'Show us a draft communiqué at the funeral tomorrow, would you, Humphrey? And make sure that none of the press find out about the bomb plant. Or the labrador puppy. After all,' I said, looking pointedly at the President, 'if one of the stories gets out, the other is bound to as well, isn't it?'

'Yes, Prime Minister,' he said, permitting himself the slightest trace of a smile. The communiqué would make a wholly successful and utterly joyful day out of what was already a very happy occasion!

4

A Conflict of Interest

October 1st

The newspapers this morning made pretty depressing reading. I remarked upon this to Bernard when I met him in my study after breakfast. 'They're all saying that since I've been in office nothing has changed.'

'You must be very proud,' said Bernard.

I explained to him that it was a not a compliment, even though it might appear so from a Civil Service perspective. 'I've read ten of London's morning newspapers,' I admitted, which is surely above and beyond the call of duty, 'and there's not a good word about me in nine of them.'

'But the tenth is better?' queried Bernard, mistaking my implication.

'The tenth is worse!' I explained. 'It doesn't mention me at all.' [*Notoriety is generally preferable to obscurity in the minds of politicians – Ed.*]

All the papers are basically saying the same thing – that I'm a windbag. [*And some of the cartoonists. See overleaf – Ed.*] I showed Bernard. He was as astonished as I. [*Honesty, though doubtless an essential requirement for a successful Private Secretary, must at times be tempered with discretion – Ed.*]

'It is quite extraordinary. The newspapers say that my administration is all rhetoric, that I talk and talk but nothing ever gets done. But it's not true – as I *keep* saying, there are numerous reforms in the pipeline, a great new change of direction is promised, there are great schemes in development, a whole new philosophy of government, and a profound movement in the whole social fabric and geo-political climate of this country.'

Bernard nodded sympathetically. He was in full agreement. 'So what is actually happening, then?' he asked.

'Nothing, obviously! Not yet!' I was impatient. Rightfully so. After all, these things take time. Rome wasn't built in a day.

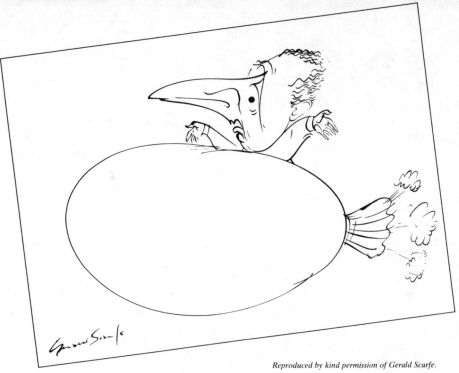

Reproduced by kind permission of Gerald Scarfe.

The truth is that the origin of this latest absurd burst of criticism is that bloody rumour about another big scandal in the City.

So when Humphrey joined us I told him that I had decided to respond to all this press criticism. 'The press are demanding action about the scandals in the City. They shall have it!'

Humphrey looked interested. 'What kind of action?'

'I shall appoint someone,' I said firmly. I was glad he didn't ask me who, or for what, because I haven't yet worked that out. As a matter of fact, I shall eventually need him to help me work that out.

Instead, he asked a question that I didn't expect. 'Prime Minister, when did you make this momentous decision?'

'This morning,' I replied with pride. 'When I read the papers.'

'And when did you first think of it?' He was courteously cross-examining me.

'This morning,' I said, suddenly aware that the suddenness of my decision made me look slightly foolish. 'When I read the papers.'

'For how long, may I ask, did you consider the pros and cons of this decision?' He is sometimes so obvious! He was trying too hard to make me feel that the decision was hasty.

'Not long.' I was defiant now. 'I decided to be decisive.'

He could see that my decision, though hasty, was right, for he dropped the subject. [*A fascinating example of the power of the experienced politician to believe what he wanted or needed to believe – Ed.*]

Bernard tried to comfort me. 'Prime Minister, I must say that I think you worry too much about what the papers say.'

I smiled at him. How little he knows. 'Bernard,' I said with a weary smile, 'only a Civil Servant could make that remark. I *have* to worry about them, especially with the Party Conference looming. These rumours of a City scandal won't go away.'

But Humphrey was unflappable. 'Let's not worry about it until there's something more than a rumour. May I show you the Cabinet agenda?'

I wasn't interested. 'Please, Humphrey,' I said. 'The papers are far more important.'

'With respect, Prime Minister,' replied Humphrey impertinently, riled by my refusal to look at his silly agenda, 'they are not. The only way to understand newspapers is to remember that they pander to their readers' prejudices.'

Humphrey knows nothing about newspapers. He's a Civil Servant. I'm a politician, I know all about them. I have to. They can make or break me. I know exactly who reads them. *The Times* is read by the people who run the country. The *Daily Mirror* is read by the people who think they run the country. *The Guardian* is read by the people who think they ought to run the country. The *Morning Star* is read by the people who think the country ought to be run by another country. *The Independent* is read by people who don't know who runs the country but are sure they're doing it wrong. The *Daily Mail* is read by the wives of the people who run the country. The *Financial Times* is read by the people who own the country. The *Daily Express* is read by the people who think the country ought to be run as it used to be run. The *Daily Telegraph* is read by the people who still think it *is* their country. And the *Sun*'s readers don't care who runs the country providing she has big tits.

[*This critique of London's newspapers was found in Number Ten Downing Street shortly after Hacker's eventual departure. Xeroxed copies were found all over the building: the Cabinet Room, the Private Office and, of course, the Press Office.*]

[*Shortly after the conversation about the City reported above, Sir*

Humphrey Appleby met Sir Desmond Glazebrook for lunch at Wheeler's Restaurant in Foster Lane, a well-placed restaurant in the shadow of St Paul's Cathedral, known for the wide spaces between tables, most of which are placed in their own wood-panelled booths. Discreet conversation is therefore possible in this restaurant, which has become a favourite City watering hole.

Sir Desmond Glazebrook was an old acquaintance of Sir Humphrey's. He was at this time still the Chairman of Bartlett's Bank, one of the 'High Street' banks. Sir Humphrey's diary records the menu – Ed.]

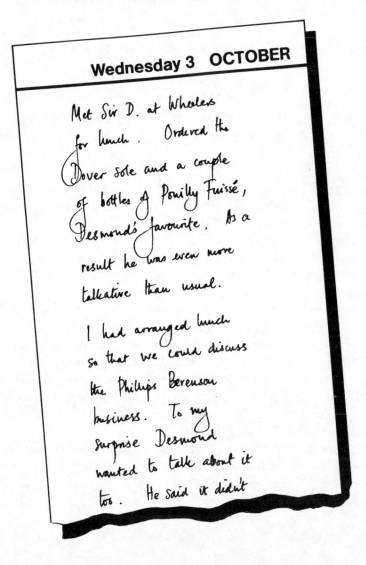

Wednesday 3 OCTOBER

Met Sir D. at Wheelers for lunch. Ordered the Dover sole and a couple of bottles of Pouilly Fuissé, Desmond's favourite. As a result he was even more talkative than usual.

I had arranged lunch so that we could discuss the Phillips Berenson business. To my surprise Desmond wanted to talk about it too. He said it didn't

Met Sir D. at Wheelers for lunch. Ordered the Dover sole and a couple of bottles of Pouilly Fuissé, Desmond's favourite. As a result he was even more talkative than usual.

I had arranged lunch so that we could discuss the Phillips Berenson business. To my surprise Desmond wanted to talk about it too. He said it didn't look too good, which is the closest I've ever heard him come to admitting to rampaging fraud and theft among his City friends.

All that the press have said, so far, is that it's a case of another investment bank that's made bad investments. But he implied that it's the tip of the iceberg. Not only have they broken the insider trading regulations, which everyone knows by now though no one can say so yet, they have broken the basic rule of the City. [*The basic rule of the City was that if you are incompetent you have to be honest, and if you are crooked you have to be clever. The reasoning is that, if you are honest, the chaps will rally round and help you if you make a pig's breakfast out of your business dealings. Conversely, if you are crooked, no one will ask questions so long as you are making substantial profits. The ideal City firm was both honest and clever, although these were in short supply – Ed.*]

I tried to find out if Phillips Berenson had been breaking the law. Glazebrook was evasive. He said he wouldn't put it like that. This struck me as virtually conclusive.

I asked specific questions:
(1) Were the Directors of Phillips Berenson siphoning off shareholders' money into their own companies?
(2) Were they operating tax fiddles?
(3) Were there capital transfers to Lichtenstein companies?
(4) Was there bribery?

Desmond's answers were even more evasive, yet crystal clear in their implications. In answer to (1) he acknowledged that this had occurred, although the money might have been intended to be repaid later; nevertheless, this repayment has not yet occurred.

In answer to (2) he agreed that Phillips Berenson had placed their own interpretation on Treasury regulations. It was felt that *someone* had to interpret them, especially as the Treasury's own interpretation didn't seem quite appropriate.

As to (3), capital transfers had occurred 'a bit'. And (4) he did know of undisclosed advance commissions to foreign government officials [*City code for bribery – Ed.*].

And what has brought it all to a head? Phillips Berenson are going to go bust. This is when it matters that they broke the rules – now that the whole story is likely to come out.

Desmond feels passionately that it must be hushed up. This surprised me. He has a big vested interest. I had not realised until today that a huge high street bank like this could be affected by the failure of a small investment bank. But it transpires that Bartletts has been supporting Phillips Berenson in a big way. Glazebrook revealed that they are 'in' for £400 million.

He was rather defensive. It appears that the problem lay with all that Arab money which they had at 11%. They would have looked rather silly if they didn't lend it to somebody at 14%. Trouble was, there weren't all that many people whom you could trust to pay 14%.

Having lent the money at 14% to people who – it turned out – couldn't pay, Bartletts kept putting in more and more money to keep its creditors afloat. And yet they still sank.

Why didn't Bartletts (or Desmond) know that these people were crooks? Why didn't they make enquiries? With hindsight, it's easy to understand: you simply don't make those sort of enquiries in the City. They had seemed like decent chaps, so the *Decent Chap Rule* applied: decent chaps don't check up on decent chaps to see if they're behaving decently. Furthermore, there's no point: if they're honest it's a waste of time – and if they're not honest you don't find out until it's too late anyway.

Then you have two options:
(a) either you blow the whistle on them and you lose all your money, or
(b) you keep quiet and become an accomplice in the crime.

Therefore – and I can quite see why – Desmond Glazebrook chose the third option: namely, to stay ignorant so that the Board of Bartletts Bank could emerge as honourable men who were shamefully deceived by a lot of rotters. Ultimately, the chaps in the City don't mind that. Nor do they really mind people being crooks. What they do mind is people *finding out* that people are crooks. Worse still, people finding out that people *knew* that people were crooks.

But the question remains: the whole mistake has cost Bartletts £400 million. Is ignorance worth paying £400 million for?

Glazebrook felt that it was. Ignorance is safety – at least safety from the law. And, of course, it's not the Bank directors' own money.

So we moved on, over the trifle, to discuss solutions to this thorny problem. Glazebrook felt that there is only one answer: the Bank of England must rescue Phillips Berenson – quietly, with absolutely no publicity. That way we keep it all in the family, and Bartletts Bank would get its money back.

There is one tiny drawback in this scenario: Bartletts gets its money back not from its creditors but from the taxpayer. However, this is not an insuperable problem. Its feasibility will all depend on the new Chairman of the Bank of England – who has not yet been appointed. Unfortunately, the likelihood is that the PM will appoint one Alexander Jameson.

Virtually everyone in the City is against Jameson. It's not simply that he behaves honestly. That, apparently, doesn't matter in itself. It is not seen as a fatal flaw, because smart people can be honest and still succeed. But Jameson goes one step further – he commits the one unforgiveable crime in the City – he moralises [*i.e. he actually tried to stop dishonesty in others – Ed.*]. He conducts search-and-destroy operations. And, as Desmond Glazebrook rightly points out, the world doesn't work like that.

We in Whitehall have also experienced his interference and his moralising. He did a frankly awful report on waste and inefficiency in the Civil Service, containing 209 practical recommendations for reform. It took eighteen months of laborious committee work to whittle them down to three.

Desmond wants Jameson stopped. I agree. But it could be difficult. The appointment of the Chairman of the Bank of England is really a Treasury recommendation. But we cannot let that stand in our way because it's not just the Phillips Berenson case that will be affected if Jameson gets the job and starts all his confounded amateur Sherlock Holmesing. All sorts of other little matters could emerge. He could uncover a major scandal. Followed by collapse of confidence. Sterling crises. The pound could fall through the floor.

It would, of course, be best for all of us if all these City fiddles could be cleared up. But that's just naive optimism, I fully realise. Pie in the sky. The bottom line (as our American cousins like to say) is that the City earns this country £6 billion a year. We can't hazard all that just because a few chaps do a few favours for a few other chaps, who happen to be their friends, without telling the shareholders.

It might be *right* to put a stop to it. But it simply wouldn't be reasonable. The repercussions would be too great. The time is not ripe. [*Appleby Papers RR/2056/LFD*]

[*Hacker's diary continues – Ed.*]

October 5th
Party Conference coming up. I've been working with Dorothy[1] on my speech today, but I'm not happy with it.

She claimed that it's only a first draft, but that isn't the problem. The problem is that it contains no good news. I pointed this out to her and she shrugged. 'We couldn't think of any.'

Feeble! There's always a way. And if there isn't any good news you just have to make the bad news look good.

For instance, I told her, you have to say *something* about the Health Service. Care for old people, mothers and children, that sort of thing. Growing up into a healthy nation.

'Value for money? suggested Dorothy.

'We can't say that,' I pointed out. 'Everyone knows that costs are completely out of control.'

---

[1] Dorothy Wainwright, Hacker's Chief Political Adviser.

Dorothy suggested an alternative: 'We're spending more than ever before to make our Health Service the best in the world.' Excellent!

We turned to Defence. I had meant to talk to Party Conference about defence cuts, but I haven't been able to get the MOD to make any yet. Dorothy had got the idea already. She's very quick on the uptake. 'This government will not put the security of the nation in jeopardy by penny-pinching and false economies.' [*Not that Hacker would have put the nation in jeopardy by, for instance, merging all three music schools of the three armed services. It was a doubtful necessity to have separate music colleges for the Army, Navy and Air Force respectively. There could hardly have been, for instance, a specifically Royal Naval method of playing the bassoon – Ed.*]

We turned to the EEC. A knotty problem. I don't want to attack it because I desperately need the agreement on quota reductions. I can't afford to have all those bloody Europeans ganging up on me again. 'Wholehearted commitment to our friends in Europe' was Dorothy's excellent wording, 'but still vigilant and vigorous in our determination to see that Britain gets a fair deal.'

She's very good. Finally, we turned to the economy, the biggest problem of all. No good news there at all, really. I was plunged into melancholy at the mere thought of having to put a good face on it in public.

Dorothy tried to comfort me. 'We'll find something.'

I asked her if any further bad news was likely to break during the party conference.

'Don't ask me. You're the one who sees the secret Treasury papers.'

'I wasn't really thinking of that, Dorothy.' I sighed heavily. 'I was thinking of the Phillips Berenson business.'

'Ah.' She was non-committal. And looking as lovely as ever – slim, blonde, blue-eyed, cool – a vision of wisdom, beauty and unflappability. She always makes me regret that I'd never had a nanny.

I pressed her. [*Not literally, we think – Ed.*] 'What do you make of it all?'

'I'm suspicious.'

'Why?'

'Because . . .' she replied thoughtfully, 'because of the statements from the Chairman of the Stock Exchange, the Chairman of the Clearing Banks Association, and the Governor of the Bank of England.'

I was puzzled. 'But none of them really said anything.'

She smiled. 'That's why I'm suspicious. If there'd been nothing in these rumours they'd all be falling over themselves to say so.'

Very shrewd. Very wise. She was right, of course – there *must* be more to it than meets the eye. 'Can you find out a bit more about it?'

'I'll try,' she promised.

The whole thing is so *unfair*! City scandals always look bad for the government and it's absolutely nothing to do with me at all! Yet, if the story breaks during Party Conference it could really hurt me.

Dorothy suggested that, to counteract the damage if damage there is, I could announce a wide-ranging review of malpractice. Not a bad idea exactly, but it did sound rather inadequate.

Then I realised that there is one thing I *can* do. I can announce the new Governor of the Bank of England. 'If I choose the right man I can make it look as if no further City scandals will be tolerated.'

Dorothy seemed slightly confused. 'You mean . . . appoint some-one really good?' She was having difficulty in grasping this concept.

I nodded vigorously, stood up, and paced about the study, greatly enthused with the idea. 'Yes!' I was excited. 'Someone vigilant and vigorous.'

She was even more puzzled. 'That'd be a break with tradition,' she observed, and asked me if it were Alexander Jameson I had in mind.

She's no fool. However, I haven't yet made my final decision, and I don't need to yet. I know they'd hate it in the City if I appointed Jameson, and if it turns out there is nothing in this Phillips Berenson affair it may not be necessary.

'If!' said Dorothy.

We continued to work on my speech. We'd reached the economy before we digressed. I couldn't see *what* I could say about that! I mean, if I'd inherited a mess like that from the other party I could blame all the problems on them for the next three years at least. But how do I tell my party that my late, unlamented Right Honourable predecessor had navigated us all up shit creek and then departed with the paddle?

Dorothy tried manfully. 'You could say: "We have come through some difficult times together."'

I didn't dignify such a pathetic offer with a reply. I eyed her balefully. She tried again. '"All the industrial world is facing severe problems."'

I shook my head. 'America and Japan are doing all right.'

'Okay,' she said, not giving up. 'How about "All the European nations are facing severe problems"?'

113

It was the best we could think of, but not great stuff to lift the party's spirits and send them out happy.

Dorothy needed more information. 'What about output?'

'Down!'

'As far down as last year?'

'No,' I said.

'Great! "We are halting the rate of decline in the nation's output."' Very good. She thought for a few moments. 'Is unemployment coming down at all?'

'Not much,' I replied, but I could see she had a way of dealing with it.

I was right. '"We shall make the attack on unemployment our top priority!",' she offered. Not bad!

'Pay?' she asked.

'It's rising too fast,' I admitted.

'"We cannot afford to pay ourselves more than we earn. The world does not owe us a living."'

True, but not awfully inspiring. Just a bit of Jimmy Carter moralising really. Nobody likes being preached at, especially not by politicians. I wondered if we could turn this section into an attack on greedy unions and spineless managers, thus directing the heat from me and putting the blame fairly and squarely where it belongs.

Dorothy suggested a more diplomatic formulation. '"Both sides of industry must strive to work together in peace and harmony for the sake of Britain."'

One final reference was necessary: to interest rates, which are undoubtedly too high. If *only* they'd come down before Conference it might save my bacon. But I just don't seem to get that kind of luck. We thought about it for hours, but we just couldn't find anything good or positive to say about interest rates.

So we discussed how to finish up. As the whole picture is really a total disaster, the only viable option is to wave the Union Jack. So I'll finish with some rubbish about Britain's unique role on the world stage, and the nation's great destiny.

Dorothy wanted me to say that I'd 'devote every effort to building a peaceful and prosperous world for our children and our children's children'. At least that bit would be honest. It's probably about how long it will take.

SIR BERNARD WOOLLEY RECALLS:[1]

The Prime Minister was indeed exercised about his speech to Party Confer-

[1] In conversation with the Editors.

ence. And he had a considerable problem on his hands. You do need *some* good news if you want to rally the morale of the party faithful.

He made it known to me that he was planning to appoint Alexander Jameson as Governor of the Bank of England. Naturally I reported this to Sir Humphrey Appleby. I must admit to a certain *naïveté*, for I saw this as good news.

Sir Humphrey quickly disabused me. 'It's *appalling* news!' He was so agitated that he rose from his desk and strode angrily about his office, pausing occasionally at the bullet-proof net curtains to stare out over Horse Guards Parade.

At first I couldn't quite see the danger of appointing Jameson, but I readily accepted that Sir Humphrey had greater wisdom or fuller information than I. So I asked him if he were going to try to change the Prime Minister's mind.

He turned and smiled at me, then replied with characteristic precision. 'No, Bernard, I am *going* to change the Prime Minister's mind.'

I couldn't help smiling back, though. I couldn't see how this goal was to be achieved. Jameson was a genuinely good choice, so far as I was aware, and the PM was extremely keen on him – it appeared to be the only hopeful piece of news that he could present to the massed groundlings at Blackpool.

Sir Humphrey found it no deterrent that the PM was keen on Jameson. In fact, he seemed to regard it as a positive bonus. 'That will be my starting point. If you want to suggest that someone is perhaps not the ideal choice [*i.e. rubbish them – Ed.*], the first stage is to express absolute support.'

The reason, as I now understood, is that you must never be on the record saying that somebody is no good. You must be seen as their friend. After all, as Humphrey explained so cogently that morning, it is necessary to get behind someone before you can stab them in the back.

The interesting thing about expressing support for Jameson is that it was indeed the right thing to do. Jameson *was* good. He was extremely honest and efficient. And Sir Humphrey planned to say so. And this is why Sir Humphrey's tactics were so confusing to me at first.

But I should have been patient. He spelled it out.

'*Stage One*: Express absolute support.

'*Stage Two*: List all his praiseworthy qualities, especially those that would make him unsuitable for the job.

'*Stage Three*: Continue to praise those qualities to the point where they become positive vices.

'*Stage Four*: Mention his bad points by defending and excusing them.'

Stage Three is simply done, I learned that day, by oversimplificaton. You *label* someone. If, for instance, someone is a good man he can seriously be damaged by calling him 'Mr Clean'. Strange, but true.

Humphrey had heard that Jameson was a churchgoer, information which I was able to confirm. Indeed, I added, he had once been a lay preacher.

Humphrey's face lit up. His joy was beautiful to behold. 'Splendid news! We can certainly use that against him.'

I asked for an illustration. Sir Humphrey turned to me and spoke as if speaking to the Prime Minister. 'What a charming man. Hasn't an enemy in the world. But is he *really* up to dealing with some of the rogues in the City?'

Ingenious. But I wasn't sure it would wash. For, as I explained to Sir Humphrey, Jameson was in reality a pretty tough customer.

Humphrey remained blissfully unconcerned. 'In that case, we'll go on to Stage Four and say he's *too* tough. For instance, "it probably doesn't matter that he was a conscientious objector, no one has ever *really* questioned his patriotism". Or "I thought the criticisms of him for bankrupting his last company were not entirely fair". That sort of thing.'

It was clear to me that Humphrey would be coming to praise Jameson, not to bury him. Never before had I grasped the lethal possibilities of praise. Humphrey explained that the same principle can be applied to the personal lives of those who cannot be smeared by praise in their professional lives. All you need do is hint at something that cannot be easily disproved. And if it *is* disproved, you never *said* it anyway, you merely hinted.

The best approach is to hint at a hidden scandal. For instance:

1. If not married – Homosexuality.
2. If married – Adultery, preferably with a lady who is beyond reproach, such as one of the royals or a television newsreader.
3. If happily married – Puritanism or Alcoholism. Or undisclosed Psychiatric Treatment.

The possibilities are most infinite. Careers can be brought to a juddering halt by generously referring to a chap as a great stimulator, a wonderful catalyst, a superb cook, an innovative chess player. As for oversimplification the stages are frightfully easy:

1. Take someone's idea – say, a chap who believes that education subsidies should be funnelled through the parents rather than through the Local Education Authority.
2. Simplify it to the point of absurdity – 'He believes in a complete free for all'.
3. Admit there was some truth in it *once*. 'But we've all realised that there is a less extreme way of solving the problem.'
4. Label him with the idea every time his name is mentioned. 'Ah yes, the educational vouchers man.'

I learned a lot that day that I was able to apply fruitfully as I rose high in the Civil Service. Indeed, I would go so far as to admit that my eventual rise to Head of the Home Civil Service was not wholly unconnected with the techniques that I acquired that morning in Sir Humphrey Appleby's office.

[Hacker's diary continues – Ed.]

October 8th

Dorothy brought me in a new draft of my Party Conference speech. It's marginally better but still pretty uninspiring. And I remain deeply concerned about this Phillips Berenson scandal and its implications for us all.

However, at my morning meeting with Humphrey (and Bernard) my Cabinet Secretary seemed to disagree with me. 'I'm sure it's not that serious' is how he casually dismissed it.

This was like a red rag to a bull to Dorothy. In fact, that's how she always responds to him. I can never make up my mind whether their endless disagreements are highly creative or just a bloody nuisance. But certainly her intention was to defend my position. 'It certainly is serious, Humphrey,' she retorted sharply.

He was patronising. 'No, no, dear lady, I think that the bank over-lent to one big borrower, that's all.'

'There's more to it than that. Some of the Phillips Berenson directors have a slightly shady past, you know.'

He stared at her coldly. 'Can you prove it?'

'No,' she acknowledged honestly. 'It's just my antennae.'

Sir Humphrey chuckled and turned to me. 'I think, Prime Minister, we're in the realms of female intuition.'

Dorothy went white with anger. Tight-lipped, she stood up and smoothed down her tight-fitting black linen skirt. 'We shall see,' she snapped, and headed straight for the door.

'We shall indeed,' murmured Humphrey with a confident smirk.

I wondered why he had such confidence. He gave me no hint. So I told him the good news: that I intended to appoint Alexander Jameson as the new Govenor of the Bank of England.

I wasn't sure what his reaction would be. I was certainly quite unprepared for the great enthusiasm with which he received the news.

'Oh, the Lay Preacher! What a nice chap!'

The Lay Preacher, I thought, must be a nickname. I asked how he got it and was, I must admit, mildly surprised by Humphrey's answer. 'Well, he is one, isn't he?'

I couldn't see how it was particularly relevant, though I'm always a little put off by fanatics of any kind, especially religious ones. But even in these secular days one can hardly hold it against a chap that he believes fervently in God, irrational though that seems to many of us. So I stuck to the point. 'But Humphrey, do you think he's good?'

'Good is *exactly* the word,' replied Humphrey. 'A really *good* man. Did a terribly good job at the White Fish Authority, too.'

The White Fish Authority doesn't sound a totally essential job. Perhaps he spends rather too much time on preaching. '*Where* does he preach?' I wanted to know.

'In church, I suppose. Frightfully religious. Extremely honest. Honest with absolutely everyone.'

Humphrey obviously likes him a lot. And yet . . . there's something about his enthusiasm that worries me. 'It's good, isn't it, to be honest with everyone?' I asked. After all, I was appointing a man to help clean things up.

He was unequivocal. 'Of course it's good. If he finds a scandal anywhere, even here in Number Ten, he'll tell everybody. No doubt about that.'

'You mean . . . he's indiscreet?'

Humphrey looked uneasy. 'Oh dear,' he replied with a sigh, 'that's such a pejorative word. I prefer merely to say that he's obsessively honest.'

I was becoming concerned. I'm all for honesty, God knows, but there's a time and a place for everything. And we are discussing politics. Handling people, that sort of thing. 'Do you think, quite candidly, that he's the right man to bring the City into line?'

'Absolutely,' said Humphrey without hesitation. 'If you want a Saint. Of course, there are those who say he doesn't live in the real world. He *is* extremely puritanical, even for a bible-basher.'

Jameson was beginning to sound like more trouble than he's worth. Or as much trouble, anyway. I indicated to Humphrey that I wanted to hear absolutely all the *cons* as well as the *pros*. Reluctantly he continued. 'Well, I must admit that he is *so* honest that he might not understand their little games. But it probably doesn't matter that the City would run rings round him. And *I* don't think it's true that OPEC[1] would eat him for breakfast.'

He must be a friend of Humphrey's. *Of course* it matters if the City runs rings around him. But would it? I find it very hard to believe. And *who says* OPEC would eat him for breakfast?

I told Humphrey I was confident that he is neither so weak nor so stupid. 'I've heard that he's highly intelligent and very tough.'

Humphrey readily agreed. In fact, I began to see that this may be the root of the problem. 'Very tough, Prime Minister, yes indeed. A bit of an Ayatollah, in fact. The only question is, do you want to risk a Samson who might bring the whole edifice crashing down?'

---

[1] Organisation of Petroleum-Producing Countries.

I couldn't deny that that's a bit of a worry. I fell silent. Humphrey continued to enthuse about him till it began to get on my nerves. 'He certainly is no respecter of persons. He's very stimulating, and a great catalyst. The only thing is that, although treading on toes is sometimes a necessity, he tends to make it a hobby. And of course, he does like everything in the open, he talks very freely to the press – he's not awfully realistic about that.'

I asked Humphrey if he knew anything else at all about Jameson.

'Well . . . one wonders if *anyone* can be *that* moral – I've heard . . .' and then he hesitated.

I was all agog. 'Yes?'

His invariable discretion took over. 'Nothing. Anyway, I'm sure it won't come out.'

'What?' I asked, desperate to know.

'Nothing.' He was trying to reassure me now, but completely without success. 'I'm sure it's nothing, Prime Minister.'

I'm not sure that I can use this man, in spite of Humphrey's enthusiastic recommendation. How little he understands me!

[*News travels fast in Whitehall, and in a matter of hours the rumour reached Sir Frank Gordon, Permanent Secretary of the Treasury, that Sir Humphrey was 'rubbishing' Alexander Jameson. In this situation the Cabinet Secretary and the Permanent Secretary of the Treasury had conflicting needs, opposed ambitions, and different fears.*

The following day Sir Humphrey duly received a particularly friendly note from Sir Frank, which has been fortunately released to us under the Thirty Year Rule and is reproduced overleaf – Ed.]

H M Treasury

Permanent Secretary

October 8

My Dear Humphrey,

You may well have heard that the Treasury would like Alexander Jameson to be the new Governor of the Bank of England.

We believe that it is about time that the Bank had a Governor who is known to be both intelligent and competent. Although an innovation, it should certainly be tried.

The Treasury has endured these City scandals for long enough. The Chancellor of the Exchequer is quite fed up with having to defend the indefensible, and so is the Treasury.

Furthermore, we believe that an honest financial sector cannot damage the national interest. The City is a dunghill and I propose that we clean it up now. Jameson is our man.

Yours ever,

Frank

[*Sir Humphrey did not hasten to reply. But some days later Sir Frank received the letter reprinted below – Ed.*]

70 WHITEHALL, LONDON SW1A 2AS

From the Secretary of the Cabinet and Head of the Home Civil Service

12 October

Dear Frank,

Thank you so much for your letter. It is always a
pleasure to hear from you.

I was most amused by your droll remarks about the
Governor-to-be of the Bank of England. I am fully
seized of the need, from the Chancellor's point of
view, for a clean-up in the City. It would indeed
be in the Chancellor's own interest.

But I am sure you will agree that we must all
ensure that the nation's interest is paramount. And
although an honest financial sector cannot damage the
nation in the long term, there would be significant
short-term problems.

An inquiry into the City would undoubtedly
cause a loss of confidence, the pound would plunge,
the share index would plunge - and the Government
would plunge with them.

This would not be in the Chancellor's interest,
nor the Prime Minister's. If I might borrow your
analogy of the City as a dunghill, may I ask what is
left when you clean up a dunghill? Nothing! Except
that the person who cleans it up usually finds themselves covered in dung.

Yours ever,

[signature]

[*Sir Frank's hostility to the Bank of England embodied a traditional Treasury attitude. Bank of England officials are paid more than Civil Servants, and envy is a factor in the relationship. Further, the Bank is a luxurious institution, serving superb meals in the canteen to its abundantly large quota of staff. The Treasury, on the other hand, is intellectually rigorous and slightly contemptuous of the calibre of those who work at the Bank. The Treasury élite, unlike the Foreign Office élite, are a meritocracy traditionally disdainful of intellectual inadequacy, and even junior officials may express well-reasoned dissent in front of politicians.*

Sir Frank did not apparently let the matter drop. His reply to Sir Humphrey is missing, but it provoked a strong reply from Sir Humphrey which we were fortunate enough to find and which we reprint opposite – Ed.]

70 WHITEHALL, LONDON SW1A 2AS

From the Secretary of the Cabinet and Head of the Home Civil Service

16 October

Dear Frank,

I do not regard this situation as my problem. As you know, sixty per cent of Phillips Berenson's outstanding loans are with a mere three foreigners of dubious repute. The Bank of England was charged with the responsibility of supervising Phillips Berenson, but the supervision was a farce. That is why the Bank of England wants a cover-up - to disguise the undoubted truth that their investigators are a bunch of amateurs.

I understand that you want a clean-up. But I beg you to consider the full implications. The Bank of England may have been responsible for supervising Phillips Berenson, but the Treasury is responsible, in turn, for supervising the Bank of England.

If we have a clean-up, therefore, which would inevitably be a very public affair, the Chancellor might ultimately find that he were held responsible. Then he would be defending the really indefensible this time.

In order to survive the stirring up of this hornets' nest the Chancellor would need considerable support from the P.M. But, strangely, the P.M. isn't all that keen on defending the indefensible.

In fact, the only way that the Chancellor could persuade the P.M. to rescue him would be to convince the P.M. that he (the Chancellor) had been let down by his senior permanent officials.

Think it over, Frank.

Yours ever,

[*Sir Humphrey's deadly threat won the day. The Treasury stopped pushing for a clean-up and Jameson's chances of becoming Governor of the Bank of England were significantly reduced to almost nil. Sir Humphrey, acting for once in what he believed were Hacker's best interests, had ensured that Sir Frank would now also oppose Jameson if and when it were necessary.*

This development was not, however, known to Hacker. His diary continues – Ed.]

October 17th

I discussed, with Dorothy Wainright and Bernard Woolley, the report I received yesterday on Phillips Berenson.

Dorothy had been absolutely right. It's deeply shocking. Full of irregularities and malpractices. I'm not sure exactly what the difference is by the way, but Phillips Berenson appears to have had an awful lot of malpractices even for a merchant bank. [*'Irregularity' means there's been a crime but you can't prove it. 'Malpractice' means there's been a crime and you can prove it – Ed.*]

It seems that we have got hold of a confidential auditor's report. Actually, it's more than confidential – nobody has seen it. [*In Whitehall, 'confidential' usually means that everyone has seen it – Ed.*]

I asked Dorothy how we got hold of it.

'The Senior Partner at their accountants is a friend of mine.'

'Just friendship?' I wanted to be quite clear about this.

She smiled. 'Apparently he's looking forward to reading the New Year's Honours List.'

That seemed a fair deal. I asked her how we'd do that. In which section?

Bernard leaned forward confidentially. 'How about through the Welsh Office? For services to leaks?' He is irrepressible.

What really suprised me about the whole business is that a High Street clearing bank like Bartletts should be so deeply involved.

But it didn't surprise Dorothy. 'Look at their Chairman – Sir Desmond Glazebrook!'

'You mean, he's a crook too?' I was amazed.

'No,' she explained. 'But he's a bumbling buffoon.'

She's right, of course. I've had dealings with him before.[1]

Dorothy said, 'It's easy to see how he became Chairman. He never has any original ideas, he speaks slowly, and because he doesn't

[1] See *The Complete Yes Minister*, Chapters 7 and 13, pp. 152ff. and 297ff.

understand anything he always agrees with whoever he's talking to. So obviously people think he's sound.'

She's dead right. And the trouble is, I've been invited to consult him about appointing the new Governor of the Bank of England. Not that it's necessary to consult anyone – I still intend to get Jameson, even if he is a lay preacher. He's the only chap who could do the thorough clean-up of the City that we need.

'I think you may find', said Dorothy, 'that Sir Desmond doesn't want you to appoint Jameson to do a clean-up.'

'Do I have any alternative?' I asked rhetorically, tapping the Phillips Berenson audited accounts. 'After this!'

She could see the point. 'No . . . not if it gets out.'

'Some of it is bound to get out!'

Dorothy wasn't so sure. 'If it gets to court, all of it will come out. But if the Bank of England does a rescue they can probably keep the worst of it quiet. The bribery and embezzlement, anyway. And the directors investing all the insurance premiums in their private Lichtenstein companies just before the insurance business crashed.'

I wasn't quite clear at first what she was recommending. 'Prime Minister, appoint Jameson right away. Then *you* are protected if it all comes out before he starts. And it's *something* good to announce at Party Conference.'

[*Interestingly, on this rare occasion Dorothy Wainright and Sir Humphrey were both doing all that they could to protect Hacker – and yet their recommendations were totally opposed. She wanted Jameson appointed for Hacker's immediate protection, and he wanted to avoid at all cost the loss of confidence in the economy that would inevitably accompany doing the right thing, i.e. cleaning up the City. She believed, on the other hand, that before you can increase confidence you must first reduce it.*

The crisis festered on, undiscovered by the public, and unreported by the Press for fear of libel actions. Two days later Sir Desmond Glazebrook paid his unwelcome visit to Number Ten – Ed.]

[*Hacker's diary continues – Ed.*]

October 19th
Dorothy and I were again discussing the vexed question of the Governorship of the Bank, when the intercom buzzer rang.

'Who', I asked, 'will Desmond Glazebrook want me to appoint?'

'Sir Desmond Glazebrook,' said Bernard from beside the intercom.

'You're absolutely right, Bernard,' said Dorothy.

He looked blank. 'What about?' he said. It wasn't surprising he was confused, he'd merely been announcing Sir D's imminent arrival. But Dorothy, I realised, was not joking – she meant that Glazebrook would be recommending himself for the job.

I asked if she were serious. She nodded. 'After all, who has the most interest in a cover-up?'

A good point. I took a deep breath and told Bernard to send him in. Bernard reported that Sir Humphrey was with Sir Desmond and that they were both on the way up to the study.

While we waited I asked Dorothy if Sir Humphrey and Sir Desmond knew about the auditors' report on Phillips Berenson. 'Yes,' she said with a warning look. 'But they mustn't know you know. Or you'll have to make the senior partner an Earl.'

When Desmond arrived it was easy to see what made him such a success in the City – tall, distinguished-looking, a full head of white hair, droopy Harold Macmillan eyelids with a moustache to match, casually elegant, the epitome of the English gentleman with all that implies – amateurism, lack of commitment and zero intellectual curiosity. He arranged his impeccable self in my chintz floral armchair and stared at me with his air of baffled amusement. Most people believed that the look of amusement was an act – I knew that the bafflement was as well.

'How good of you to come,' I began. 'As you know, I have to appoint a new Governor of the Bank of England. I'd welcome your views.'

Desmond answered with confidence. 'I certainly think you should appoint one. Bank needs a Governor, you know.'

Humphrey was not unaware that Desmond's confidence was misplaced. 'I think the Prime Minister has more or less decided that. It's a question of who.'

'Ah,' said Desmond wisely, as a little light penetrated into his grey matter. 'Ah,' he said again, processing this information. 'That's tricky,' he went on. 'It's a question of who, is it?' he verified. 'Well,' he concluded, 'it needs to be someone the chaps trust.'

'Yes,' I agreed. 'I feel we need someone really intelligent. Upright. Energetic.'

Desmond looked nervous. 'Well, hold on!'

'You don't agree?' I asked.

He weighed up the question with care. 'Well, of course it's a jolly interesting idea, Prime Minister. But I'm not sure the chaps would trust that sort of chap.'

Dorothy intervened. 'I think the Prime Minister is worried about financial scandals. Are you worried about financial scandals, Sir Desmond?'

'Yes, well, of course we don't want any of those. But if you go for the sort of chap the chaps trust, you can trust him to be the sort of chap to see the chaps don't get involved in any scandals.'

'You mean he'll hush them up?' Dorothy could never resist a provocative question.

Desmond was shocked. 'Good Lord, no! Any hint of suspicion and you hold a full inquiry. Have the chap straight up for lunch. Ask him straight out if there's anything in it.'

'And if he says no?' I asked.

'Well, you've got to trust a chap's word. That's how the City works.'

Perhaps that's how it doesn't work. Moving on, I questioned him about Phillips Berenson. 'What do you know about it?' I asked him.

'What do you know about it?' he countered, cautiously.

'Only what I read in the papers,' I replied.

'Oh. Good.' He seemed highly relieved. 'Well, they're in a bit of trouble, that's all. Lent a bit of money to the wrong chaps. Could happen to anyone.'

'Nothing more?'

'Not as far as I know,' he said carefully.

Dorothy was not satisfied. 'You'd give your word on that?'

Desmond hesitated. His word was important to him. City gents as thick-headed as Desmond know that their reputation for honesty is not to be trifled with – what else have they got? 'I'll look into it for you, if you like.'

Dorothy, a real terrier, just wouldn't let go. 'You haven't heard any rumours?'

'Of course there's always rumours,' he replied, relaxing visibly. That was a full toss and thoroughly deserved to be hit straight to the boundary.

'Rumours,' repeated Dorothy. 'Of embezzlement. Bribery. Mis-appropriation of funds. Insider trading.'

Desmond tried to take the heat out of it. He smiled amicably. 'Come, come, dear lady, those are strong words.'

Dorothy was immune to his charm. 'So it's not true?'

'There are different ways of looking at things,' he replied, with a total honesty wholly unconnected to the question he'd been asked.

Dorothy was curious. 'What's a different way of looking at embezzlement?'

'Well, of course, if a chap embezzles you have to do something about it.'

'Have a serious word with him?' I enquired ironically.

Desmond doesn't fully appreciate irony. 'Absolutely,' he replied. 'But usually it's just a chap who gave himself a short-term unauthorised temporary loan from the company's account, and invested it unluckily. You know, horse falls at the first fence. That sort of thing.'

I could see that we were getting nowhere. Obviously Dorothy had been right, Glazebrook did not want me to appoint Jameson. So I asked him who *he* thought should be the Governor.

'Well, Prime Minister, as I say, it's not easy. Not all that many chaps the chaps trust. I mean, it's not for me to say, but if one were to be asked, assuming one were thought to be . . . of course one is committed to one's current job, but if one were to be pressed I dare say one could make oneself available . . . as a duty one owes to, er . . . the nation . . .'

I suddenly realised what he was driving at, and cut through the flannel. 'I was thinking of Alexander Jameson.'

'Ah,' he said, deflated. How could he even *think* that he could be Governor. I'm certainly amazed by the apparently limitless capacity for self-deception that I find in others. [*But never, apparently, in himself – Ed.*]

'What are your views on him?' I asked.

Desmond damned him with faint praise. 'He's a good accountant.'

'Honest?'

'Yes.'

'Energetic?'

'I'm afraid so.'

'So you'd recommend him?'

'No.' Desmond was unequivocal. Not surprising – anybody that interprets the word energetic as a criticism would hardly be on Jameson's side. 'City's a funny place, Prime Minister. You know, if you spill the beans you open up a whole can of worms. I mean, how can you let sleeping dogs lie if you let the cat out of the bag? You bring in a new broom and if you're not very careful you find you've thrown the baby out with the bathwater. Change horses in the middle of the stream, next thing you know you're up the creek without a paddle.'

'And then what happens?' I asked.

'Well! Obviously the balloon goes up. They hit you for six. An own goal, in fact.'

I got the message. Leave things as they are. *Laissez-faire*. Humphrey was nodding in agreement, with feigned admiration, as he sat at the feet of this latter-day Adam Smith.

[*Modern readers may wonder why Sir Desmond Glazebrook wanted to be the Governor of the Bank of England, having already reached the dizzy heights of Chairman of Bartletts Bank. In fact the Governor, though less well paid, was viewed as the top job in the City, with the highest status, influence, trappings and even a little real power. There is something romantic, mysterious and above all* secret *that creates the traditional allure of Threadneedle Street. Furthermore, the Governorship of the Bank can be seen as service to the nation, not merely as enriching oneself further, thus firmly establishing oneself on the list of the Great and the Good to whom further honours, quangos, Royal Commissions and fact-finding missions to sunny climes will be offered upon eventual retirement – Ed.*]

October 24th

This evening I sat in my dressing-room at the Winter Gardens, Blackpool. There was a tatty, grimy old silver star on the door. I didn't feel like a star. I didn't even feel like a sheriff. I felt full of despair.

My walk along the cold and windy sea-front, accompanied by what seemed to be the entire Lancashire constabulary who were clearly out to impress me with their security arrangements, had been wet and bleak. I'd met no one except several dozen cameramen and reporters, all of whom asked me what I was going to say in my speech.

Of course they didn't seriously expect an answer. What worried me was fear that they already knew that I had nothing to say. For, only half an hour before I went on, I was leafing disconsolately through the dog-eared script on my dressing-table and realising – as if I didn't know already – that the speech was *completely* devoid of content.

Of course, that would have made little difference to the reception. I'd have got a standing ovation no matter what! Three and a half minutes. That's if they *didn't* like the speech. Dorothy had made that the minimum; my late unlamented predecessor got three minutes last year so come what may it was to be an extra thirty seconds. All the key people had been issued with stop-watches this morning.

But everyone knew that the ovation was mere window dressing. They would only show a few seconds of that on the news. They'd also show some of my empty phrases, some scattered and half-hearted applause, and then the Political Correspondent would come on and point out that I'd had no good news to offer the party or the country.

Hopelessly I picked up the pencil and stared at the speech once again. 'I need to say something positive,' I said to Dorothy, as make-up was smeared over the bags under my eyes by a pretty girl from our TV consultants.

She leafed through the pages. Nothing came to her mind either, I could tell. 'With the economy in the state it's in, it's the best we can say,' she answered. 'Unless you want to say the tide is turning?'

'There's no evidence,' I complained.

'We don't need evidence – it's a party conference not the Old Bailey. You just need conviction.'

Gloomily I thought that a conviction was what I'd get at the Old Bailey. And my profound melancholy was not lightened when Bernard stuck his head round the door of the dressing-room.

'Prime Minister . . . Sir Humphrey's downstairs with the Burandan High Commissioner. Can they have a word with you?'

I couldn't imagine what about, but I could see no harm in it. While we waited Dorothy said, 'Unemployment is terrible, interest rates are too high, there's not enough investment. What do we do?'

There seemed to be no way out. We couldn't get more investment without cutting interest rates. Yet how could we cut them? There was a case for bringing interest rates down – and a case for keeping them up. Dorothy wanted them brought down in the interests of social justice – but social justice is just another word for inflation.

'Can't you lean on the Chancellor to lean on the Treasury to lean on the Bank of England to lean on the High Street Banks?' she wanted to know.

It seemed rather a tall order to accomplish all that in the remaining twenty minutes before I went on. My option was to announce the appointment of the Lay Preacher, Mr Clean, Alexander Jameson, in the hope of HACKER TAKES NO MORE NONSENSE FROM THE CITY headlines.

[*Hacker's intention to make this announcement even when he was well aware of the risk involved was a result of what is known to the logicians in the Civil Service as the* Politicians' Syllogism:

Step One: *We must do something.*
Step Two: *This is something.*

Step Three: Therefore we must do this.
Logically, this is akin to other equally famous syllogisms, such as:
Step One: All dogs have four legs.
Step Two: My cat has four legs.
Step Three: Therefore my dog is a cat.
The Politicians' Syllogism *has been responsible for many of the disasters that befell the United Kingdom in the twentieth century, including the Munich Agreement and the Suez Adventure – Ed.*]

There was only one thing puzzling me: Humphrey knew I was about to deliver my most important speech since my elevation to Number Ten. Why had he chosen this moment to introduce me to the Burandan High Commissioner?

I was soon to learn. They bustled into the dressing-room and were no sooner seated than Humphrey jumped right in at the deep end.

'The High Commissioner', he began, 'is concerned at the rumour that you intend to appoint Alexander Jameson to the Bank of England, who will inevitably start an investigation into Phillips Berenson.'

I couldn't see how this could affect Buranda, and I said so. 'Phillips Berenson was a shady bank that lent sixty per cent of its money to three foreigners of dubious repute,' I pointed out.

The High Commissioner spoke. 'Two of those three foreigners were the President of Buranda and the Chairman of the Buranda Enterprise Corporation.'

Thank you, Humphrey Appleby, for dropping me in it like that. 'Ah,' I replied thoughtfully.

The High Commissioner did not beat about the bush. 'If you attack these loans the President of Buranda will have no option but to interpret this move as a hostile and racist act.'

'*Racist?*' I couldn't believe my ears.

'Of course,' replied the Burandan High Commissioner. He seemed to have no doubt on the matter.

I tried to explain. 'I . . . I wouldn't dream of attacking your President *per se*, I would merely . . .'

I was lost for words. Bernard made a suggestion. 'You would merely say that he was of dubious repute?' I silenced him with a look.

'May I further point out', continued the implacable Burandan, 'that a racist attack on our President would undoubtedly create solidarity and support from all the other African States.'

'Commonwealth countries, Prime Minister,' Humphrey reminded me unnecessarily.

'We would move to have Britain expelled from the Commonwealth. Our President would be obliged to cancel Her Majesty's State visit next month, and Buranda would immediately sell all the British Government stock that it has brought.'

I turned to Humphrey and whispered, 'Would that cause a run on the pound?'

He nodded gravely. Then he turned invitingly to the High Commissioner. 'Anything else?'

'Isn't that enough?' I snapped at Humphrey. I indicated that the meeting must end because of my imminent appearance on stage. I thanked the High Commissioner, and I promised that I'd give his words the most serious attention.

I kept Humphrey in the room after the African diplomat had gone. I was livid! 'How *dare* you put me in this position?' I shouted.

Stubbornly, he stuck to his guns. 'It's not me, Prime Minister, its Buranda. And the Commonwealth Club is yet another reason for not opening up this can of worms.'

I was furious. 'The President of Buranda is a crook! He doesn't belong to the Commonwealth Club, he should be blackballed.'

'He is already, isn't he?' said a smiling Bernard. 'Sorry,' he added at once, just before I throttled him.

I was angrier with Humphrey than I'd ever been before. 'Humphrey, what are you *playing* at? I don't get it! Why are you so adamant that I should allow another cover-up in the City? What's in it for you?'

Humphrey's reply seemed both desperate and sincere. '*Nothing*, Prime Minister. I assure you. I have no private ulterior motive. I'm trying to save you from yourself. I'm on your side.'

'How can we believe that?' said a sceptical Dorothy, who clearly didn't.

'Because this time it's true,' cried Humphrey revealingly. We stared at him. 'I mean, this time I am *particularly* on your side.'

I had reached the end of my tether. I knew I had to say something good in my speech. I could think of nothing other than announcing that the lay preacher would become Governor of the Bank.

'How about announcing a cut in interest rates?' said Humphrey.

I was about to tell him not to be silly when I realised, from the expression on his face, the he literally had a concrete realistic proposal up his sleeve. [*Not literally, we presume – Ed.*] But I couldn't see how it was to be done. 'Jameson will never agree to a cut in interest rates for political reasons,' I told Humphrey.

'Desmond Glazebrook would,' said Humphrey. 'If you made *him*

Governor of the Bank of England, he'd cut Bartlett's Bank interest rates in the morning. You could announce both in your speech.'

'How do you know?'

'He's just told me. He's here. He'll allow you to be first with the good news.'

I was literally torn. [*Hacker had his own non-literal meaning of the word 'literally' – Ed.*] I was genuinely confused about what was right. [*On the contrary, Hacker knew that it would be right for the country if he appointed Jameson. He was perhaps referring to the fact that it would be right for himself, or his party, to choose Glazebrook. And politicians frequently labour under the misapprehension that what is right for them personally is by definition what is right for their country – Ed.*] My problem was that Sir Desmond was such an improbable choice for Governor. He is such a fool. He only talks in clichés. He can talk in clichés till the cows come home.

Dorothy's disapproval was aimed, fair and square, at Humphrey. 'It's jobs for the boys,' she accused him.

He shrugged. He couldn't deny it. But he pointed out that a cut in interest rates would give me a considerable success in my speech.

Dorothy was thinking ahead. 'Won't a cut in interest rates mean that prices will go up?'

She's right, of course, but frankly at that moment I just didn't care, so long as I got a standing inflation. [*We believe that Hacker meant 'ovation', but after serious consideration we elected to print his slip of the tongue because it is so revealing – Ed.*]

Dorothy seemed bitterly disillusioned. 'So you don't want an honest man in charge of the City?'

This struck me as unfair. Desmond Glazebrook's not exactly dishonest. It's just that he's too thick to understand when he's being honest and when he's not. 'The fact remains', I said, as I prepared to walk on stage, 'that the Government simply cannot work without the good will of the City. Can it?'

'No Prime Minister,' said Humphrey.

'And there's no point in upsetting them needlessly, is there?'

'No Prime Minister.'

'Dorothy,' I said, 'fix my speech to announce the cuts in interest rates. Humphrey, get Sir Desmond up here at once.'

'Yes Prime Minister,' they chorused. Within two minutes Desmond had the job, and I was on TV. I got a six-minute ovation. Proof positive that I had made the right decision.

5
Power to the People

October 29th

This morning I had a TV appearance. I hadn't looked forward to it very much. As usual they wanted to interview me about bad news, that's all they're ever interested in. The particular disaster on the agenda today was the ongoing permanent catastrophe of local government, about which I can do practically nothing!

'Almost everybody in Whitehall *and* in Parliament,' I said to Bernard, 'of *whatever* party, agrees that there are a few councils which are run by a bunch of corrupt morons who are too clever by half.'

Bernard didn't disagree. He merely commented that the most that a moron can be is *less* clever by half. He hates to express an opinion on anything that's remotely controversial. But I demanded that he gave me his opinion.

'They're democratically elected,' he remarked cautiously.

'That depends on how you define democracy,' I pointed out. 'Only about twenty-five per cent of the electorate vote in local elections. And all they do is treat it as a popularity poll on the political leaders in Westminster.'

'Nonetheless, they are still representatives.' He's persistent as well as wrong-headed.

'But who do they represent?' I challenged him. 'Nobody knows who their councillor is. And the councillors know that nobody knows who they are. Or what they do. So they spend four totally unaccountable years on a publicly subsidised ego trip, handing out ratepayers' hard-earned income to subsidise lesbian awareness courses and Borough Pet Watch schemes to combat cat theft! They ruin the schools, they let the inner cities fall to bits, they demoralise the police and undermine law and order, and then they blame us.'

'They blame you,' said Bernard punctiliously.

'That's right!' I agreed. '*Me!*'

'Will you say all that?'

'I just said it!' I snapped. 'Don't you bloody listen?'

Bernard explained that he'd meant would I say it all on television. What does he think? Of course I wouldn't! It would make me look intolerant. [*It is interesting that Hacker believed that he was not intolerant. Some more ideological politicians might have been proud to be intolerant on this score, and might have felt it would be popular as well. Hacker, however, wanted to be liked, and his greatest problem with these local authorities was that they made him less popular – Ed.*] People assume that I'm responsible because I'm Prime Minister. And now the leader of the Houndsworth Council, that bloody Agnes Moorhouse woman, is threatening to withhold funds from the police, and ban them from council property. If she gets away with it, it'll mean the Government has virtually handed over control of the country to the local councils.

Bernard had looked up the relevant statute. 'She can't do that,' he said. 'Section 5 of the Police Act, 1964, says that Councils have to provide an adequate and efficient police force.'

I'd seen the latest *Guardian* interview with Ms Moorhouse, and I allowed myself to be the devil's advocate for a moment. 'She says that until the police are fifty per cent black they will not be either adequate or efficient.'

'She can't prove that, can she?' Bernard asked.

Who knows? Her current all-white police force is actually the least efficient and most inadequate in the country. Everyone round here is terrified that if we took her to court she'd prove her case.

[*Unfortunately the transcript of Hacker's radio interview that day has not survived, and for that reason we believe that it was not significant. However, the following morning Hacker called a special meeting with Sir Humphrey Appleby to discuss the London Borough of Houndsworth – Ed.*]

October 30th
'Humphrey,' I began, 'it's clear to me that we have to do something about Agnes Moorhouse. Her borough is almost a no-go area.'

He nodded sagely. 'Indeed, Prime Minister.'

'Well . . . what?' I asked.

He gazed hopefully up at the moulded plaster ceiling, and thoughtfully scratched the back of his neck. 'How about a strongly worded letter?'

Not much of a suggestion, in my view. She would simply send us an

135

even more strongly worded letter. Copied to all the newspapers.

Bernard wondered if he might draw her attention to the law, but I don't think that would be much help either. She's a lawyer, getting round the law is what she gets paid for.

In truth, Humphrey and Bernard were rather at a loss. They simply don't understand people who don't play by the rules. It's more or less incomprehensible to them that a strongly worded letter might fail to do the trick. It would certainly bring *them* into line.

Humphrey doodled on his notepad, quietly thinking. Finally he suggested, 'Why not just ignore her?'

I stared at him. 'And have everyone say I've handed over control of the country to the militant loonies? No, Humphrey, someone must have a word with her. And point out the security implications.'

I waited, but the penny didn't drop. 'One of the law officers?' he asked puzzled.

'No,' I said. 'It can't be a political confrontation. It must be an official.' I waited again. Still nothing. 'With security responsibilities,' I hinted.

It dropped at last! 'No! No, Prime Minister, no!' He was desperate not to do it, and I couldn't really blame him. 'Surely it's up to Scotland Yard? The Home Office. MI5. The Special Branch. Lord Chancellor. Department of the Environment . . .'

'White Fish Authority?'

'White Fish Authority!' he repeated in deadly earnest, then realised I was being facetious. 'The point is, not me! It's not fair.'

'The point is, Humphrey,' I explained, 'you are the man who co-ordinates the security services.'

'Yes, but . . .'

'Or should we give that responsibility to someone else?'

My threat was unmistakable. He stopped dead in mid-sentence.

I smiled sympathetically. 'So that's agreed. A quiet word. Reach a gentleman's agreement.'

Humphrey scowled. 'But she's not a gentleman. She's not even a lady!'

'Never mind,' I consoled him. 'I want you to handle her.'

His eyebrows shot up into his hairline. 'Handle her?' Clearly he regarded that as a fate worse than death. I couldn't disagree.

[*Sir Humphrey refers to his gruelling and thought-provoking meeting with Agnes Moorhouse in his private diary – Ed.*]

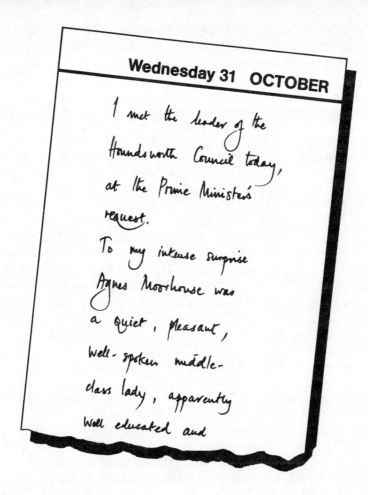

Wednesday 31 OCTOBER

I met the leader of the Houndsworth Council today, at the Prime Minister's request.

To my intense surprise Agnes Moorhouse was a quiet, pleasant, well-spoken middle-class lady, apparently well educated and

I met the leader of the Houndsworth Council today, at the Prime Minister's request.

To my intense surprise Agnes Moorhouse was a quiet, pleasant, well-spoken middle-class lady, apparently well educated and properly brought up. This makes her attitude towards us even more puzzling.

She is extremely hostile, though I must say she has excellent manners. She accepted a cup of tea on her arrival, of course, but she was disdainful of my friendly query as to whether she was Miss or Mrs Moorhouse. I had merely been concerned to address her correctly. But in reply she asked me in a surly fashion if her marital status was any concern of mine.

Of course it's not. Nor have I the faintest interest in it. Meanwhile, she made a clear choice in favour of Orange Pekoe over Typhoo Tea-bags, which demonstrated that she was not wholly uneducated in, or unappreciative of, the better things in life.

137

I enquired with caution if she wished to be called Ms Moorhouse (which is pronounced 'Mis' and seemed wholly appropriate for her). She told me I could call her Agnes. Which, by the way, I had no particular wish to do so. She asked me what she should call me, and I indicated that Sir Humphrey would be quite acceptable.

However, as I was feeling far from first-name terms in this relationship, and being therefore somewhat unwilling to call her Agnes, I opened the conversation by addressing her as 'dear lady'. This mode of address is habitual, and was not intended to carry any resonances of irony. Nor was it intended to be patronising. However, the lovely Agnes told me to 'leave it out' and that she didn't want any 'sexist crap'.

I was now quite confirmed in my first impression of her, namely that this was not awfully likely to be a meeting of minds. But realising that if any progress were to be made we had to get past this interminable problem of how to address each other, I came swiftly to the point. I said that we needed to understand each other and I expressed the hope that we were basically in agreement in that, although she doubtless had her own views as to how Britain should be run, we both agreed that society needs a fundamental base of order and authority.

She claimed that was half true.

'Half true?' I asked.

'You agree, but I don't,' she said. Very droll. An amusing debating point but hardly a serious answer.

In short, she claims that our political system as presently constituted abuses its authority in order to preserve élitist privileges. And that, in so doing, great suffering is caused to the homeless, the unemployed and the aged.

She seemed to feel I was out of touch with ordinary people. I can't imagine where she got such a strange idea. Patiently I explained that I was fully informed about the disadvantaged members of our society, that I'd read all the published papers, seen all the statistics, studied all the official reports. Whereupon she fired a string of irrelevant questions at me: 'What does half a pound of margarine cost? What time do Social Security offices open? How long can you run a one-bar fire for 50 pence in the meter?' and so forth.

Of course I didn't have the foggiest idea of the answers, nor do I see the relevance of the questions. But she seemed to imply that if I had known the answers my attitude to authority would be different.

This is a preposterous notion. We all agree that it would be marvellous if there were no poverty, and we all sympathise with those who are less well off than ourselves. But we simply do not have the resources to achieve an equally high standard of living for everyone. Indeed, the whole notion of 'equality' in an economic sense is a mirage. There will always be somebody who is better off than oneself.

To my astonishment she rose from her chair and started wandering round my office appraising the value of everything she saw, as if she were on a Sunday afternoon outing to Portobello Road. She asked me if my desk was my own. And the portraits. And the porcelain. She knew full well that they were government property, and she estimated that the contents of my office would fetch about 'eighty grand', which I believe is the vernacular for £80,000. 'Enough to keep twenty one-parent families for a year,' she said.

I think that 'eighty grand' is a gross overestimate, but even if she's right she's economically illiterate. I was about to explain to her how depriving the rich does not create any more wealth for the poor in the long term – indeed, the contrary is the case – when she asked me about my salary. I refused to tell her my income but she had looked it up. Is there no privacy any more, no respect? Is nothing sacred?

She had the audacity to propose that I drop my income to £100 per week, leaving £75,000 a year left over for the needy. Once again I tried to explain that my salary is merely part of a complex economic structure. But her mind is closed. She said that when she is in power – God forbid – she will simplify the structure.

All of this I bore in silence. It was my duty. I bit the bullet. But then the damnable woman went too far! She suggested that I was making a profit out of serving my country.

She had done a little research on me, or certainly on my salary. But I too had not been idle in advance of our meeting, and I now asked her a series of questions: for instance, how her policy of banning sexist calendars in council offices helped poverty.

Her answer was most instructive: sexism, she claimed, is 'colonialism against women'. It would have been more correct to describe such calendars as obscene – but the word obscene is now misapplied to describe war, financial fraud or other forms of conduct which may be wrong but are not obscene.

Clearly Agnes thinks colonialism is, by definition, wicked. And by applying the word to sexist calendars the case is proven, without having to be argued further. So I asked her if colonialism against women is reason for Houndsworth's encouragement and approval of the adoption of children by lesbian working single mothers.

'Yes,' she said. 'I am against prejudice in all forms. I do not think that children should be brought up in an atmosphere of irrational prejudice in favour of heterosexuality.' Several more questions begged there, I noted.

Then I asked whether her policy of allowing only free-range eggs to be sold in her borough helped in the fight against heterosexual prejudice, the fight for women's rights, or the fight against poverty.

Her answer: 'Animals have rights too.' Colonialism against chickens, I suppose. But when I laughed she became very emotional. 'A battery chicken's life isn't worth living. Would you want to spend your life unable to breathe fresh air, unable to move, unable to stretch, unable to think, packed in with six hundred other desperate brainless, squawking, smelly creatures?'

Of course I wouldn't. That's why I never stood for Parliament. But the point I was trying to get across to her was that battery hens make eggs more plentiful, and therefore cheaper, and therefore they provide food in her borough for the needy, about whom she professes to care so much.

She refused to concede the point. 'The price of the suffering caused to the chickens is too high.' Funnily enough, I can see her point a little. I prefer to buy free-range eggs – but then, I can afford them. In fact, her concern for the animal kingdom is the reason for her starting a neighbourhood Pet Watch scheme to combat the theft of cats. I indicated that the sum of money might be better spent on the needy – but doubtless she would argue it's being spent on needy cats.

By now I was making Agnes angry. She asked me what I have against our dumb friends. My reply – that I have nothing against them, for I have a great *many* friends in local government – did not amuse her at all.

We bickered for quite a while. Finally, having totally failed to establish any rapport between us, we stopped exchanging slogans and turned to the matter on the agenda: her wish to withhold funds from the police, ban them from council property, sack the Chief Constable, and allow several no-go areas.

I enquired sardonically if she did not even believe in colonialism against criminals, but yet again my little joke fell on stony ground. Agnes believes that people only become criminals because of the unfairness of society. However, this good-natured theory takes no account of heredity, or of the numerous privileged and wealthy criminals whom society has treated extremely well.

She also believes that the police in her borough are insensitive and racist. I'm sure that many of them are the former and some are the latter. But it is still in the interests of all of us, *especially* those ordinary poor people on the high-crime housing estates, to have adequate law enforcement.

This she does not accept either, and this is where I lose all sympathy with her. She acknowledged that she did not mind if those people were in danger of being mugged, raped and bombed by Molotov cocktails.

I tried to explain that it could lead to the overthrow of our whole system of government, our way of life. 'Yours,' she said with a smile, 'not theirs.'

She was, in short, happy to abolish parliament, the courts, the monarchy – everything! I offered her some matches, to burn down my office. But she declined with a smile. I asked her why.

'I might need it,' she said.

[*Hacker's diary continues – Ed.*]

November 3rd
Tonight I sat in my favourite armchair in the flat upstairs, doing my

boxes. I thought I'd be alone all evening, but Annie got back early from Birmingham.[1]

I told her that I had told Humphrey to have a meeting with the dreaded Agnes Moorhouse. Annie was amused: 'That sounds like an interesting social experiment.'

Actually Humphrey said the meeting went very well, but I noticed he didn't want to talk about it too much. And Bernard tells me that he had four whiskies in the ten minutes after she left.

Annie said she had her own troubles with local government too, in our constituency. 'It's the Town Hall. They've just cancelled the Old People's Christmas party.'

I was shocked. 'Why?'

'Something about new staff overtime agreements. They said it was all your fault. If you gave them the money, they'd have the party.'

That's exactly what I complain about! It's so unfair. Every piece of stupidity and incompetence in every Town Hall in Britain is supposedly my fault. And yet I have virtually no control over them. I'm going to ask Dorothy to do a 'think' paper on local government for me. Tomorrow!

November 6th

I had a most instructive meeting with Dorothy today. She had plenty to tell me about local government – apparently she's been thinking about it for months, knowing that I'd get round to it sooner or later.

'In a nutshell,' she began, 'there is a sort of gentleman's agreement that the officials won't tell how incompetent the politicians are so long as the politicians don't tell how idle the officials are.'

Just like here at Number Ten, I thought. I asked Dorothy what, if anything, we could do about it.

'Do you really want to know?'

I was surprised by the question. 'Of course I do.'

'It's a Them and Us situation. The Local Authorities ought to be Us.'

I was confused. Did she mean Us the people or Us the government?

'In a democracy', Dorothy pointed out quite reasonably, 'that ought to be the same thing.'

All very well in theory, but we all know that it never is. It turned out that she meant Us the people. 'Local Authorities ought to be running things for Us, they ought to be part of Us . . . but they're not,

---

[1] Hacker's constituency.

they're running things for Them. For *their* convenience, for *their* benefit.'

I knew that. Everyone knows that. But what was the answer? Fight them?

'No,' said Dorothy, 'turn Them into Us.'

I was confused. I asked for an example.

'Suppose you want to stop a major government project,' she said. 'What do you do?'

'That's easy,' I said. 'Join the Civil Service.'

She laughed. 'No, seriously, if you're an ordinary person?'

'I can't remember what that was like,' I confessed.

She asked me to imagine that I was an ordinary person. That wasn't awfully easy either.

'Imagine that you want to stop a road-widening scheme. Or a new airport being built near your house. What do you do?'

I couldn't think of anything much. 'Write to my MP?' I suggested hopefully.

She wasn't impressed. 'And that does the trick?'

'Of course not,' I admitted. After all, I know *I'd* never take much notice of that. 'But surely that's what ordinary people do, they're stupid.' [*Hacker apparently never considered the personal implications of that remark: the cause and effect relationship of a stupid electorate and his own election – Ed.*]

What Dorothy was driving at was this: what ordinary people do is form a group to fight official plans they don't want. The group represents the local people. The Local Authority, on the other hand, does *not* represent the local people, only the local political *parties*!

'When the local community really cares about an issue it forms a committee,' Dorothy said. 'It makes individual members of that committee responsible for finding the views of a couple of hundred households each. They go round the streets and talk to people, on the doorsteps and in the supermarket; they drum up support and raise money. Now, how is this committee different from the local council?'

'They're decent sensible people,' I said.

'What else?' she asked.

'They *know* the people they represent,' I said.

'That's right,' said Dorothy. 'So they do what the people who voted for them actually *want* done. And the money they raise isn't like rates, because they spend it on what people actually *want* it spent on. Why? Because it's their money. Local councils overspend because they're spending other people's money.'

She's right, of course, for instance, the ordinary people in my neighbourhood at home would love the old folks to have their Christmas party. But the Town Hall would rather spend the money on a new Town Hall, or a fact-finding mission to the Bahamas.

'I see what you mean,' I said. 'Abolish the councils and put everything under the control of Central Government.' [*Hacker had completely missed the point. That would have been Sir Humphrey's solution – Ed.*]

But Dorothy's idea was even more radical. 'The idea is to return power to the ordinary people and take it away from the Town Hall machine. Make local government genuinely accountable.' And she produced this month's edition of *Political Review*. In it there's an article by someone called Professor Marriott. His plan is this:

1. *Create City Villages* – little voting districts with approximately 200 households in each district.
2. *Create Village Councils* – each council elected by the two hundred households.
3. *Give each Village Council money* – a thousand pounds a year, taken out of the rates or local taxes, just to spend on their own little area – a couple of streets, a city village.
4. *The Chairperson of the Village Council becomes the Borough Councillor* – this means that there would be five or six hundred councillors to a borough. Just like Parliament.
5. *Elect an Executive Council for the Borough* – this means that every local authority would have a parliament and a cabinet.

It sounded very appealing, though I wasn't too excited about the idea of a parliament electing a cabinet. That would be carrying participation to a ridiculous extreme and would set a very dangerous precedent. Dorothy insisted that it was the answer to local government. 'The result would be that every councillor would be in door-to-door touch with the people who voted for them.'

She's right. It's brilliant. Who would ever vote for Agnes Moorhouse if they had actually met her? [*More people probably – Ed.*] And the implications are tremendous! This could be like the Great Reform Act of 1832. All of these councils are, in fact, rotten boroughs – with half a dozen people in local parties deciding who shall go to the Town Hall for four years.

If I bring this off I shall be the Great Reformer. I see it now. Hacker's Reform Bill. A place in the history books. I shall present it myself. I immediately had ideas for how to open the debate, which I tried out on Dorothy.

'The strength of Britain does not lie in offices and institutions. It lies in the stout hearts and strong wills of the yeomen . . .'

She interrupted. 'Women have the vote too.'

'And yeowomen . . .' That didn't sound right. 'Yeopeople, yeopersons . . .' I rephrased it. 'The people of our island race. On the broad and wise shoulders . . .'

She interrupted me again. 'Shoulders can't have wisdom.'

I pressed on. 'On their broad shoulders and wise hearts . . . heads, *in* their strong hearts and wise heads lies destiny. We must trust their simple wisdom. We must give back power to the people.' She applauded.

'Dorothy,' I said humbly, 'I'm proud to be the man who will introduce this new system. What shall we call it?'

'Democracy,' she said. And her blue eyes sparkled.

SIR BERNARD WOOLLEY RECALLS:[1]

Whitehall, the most secretive square mile in the world, was paradoxically a sieve. And it was not long before Sir Humphrey Appleby heard that Dorothy Wainwright had recommended Professor Marriott's ideas to the Prime Minister. He asked me in for drinks in his office after work one evening that week.

I too had read Professor Marriott's article but I must confess that, being still slightly green compared with old Humphrey, the wider implications of the theory had not quite sunk in. So when he raised the subject I remarked that in my opinion it was about time that we reformed local government.

The expression on his face told me at once that I should have been slightly more equivocal. So I indicated that I had merely meant that I was not wholly against reforming local government. As his expression remained the same I felt it wise to add that I could see that there might be many convincing, indeed one might say conclusive, arguments *against* reform. I was grateful that he didn't ask me to specify those arguments because, to be quite honest, I didn't see what they could be. More fool me!

Humphrey, of course, had thought it through in his customary meticulous fashion. He explained that if we once create genuinely democratic local communities, it won't stop there. Once they were organised, such communities would insist on more powers, which the politicians will be too frightened to withhold.

The inevitable result would be Regional Government.

This, as every Whitehall chap fully understands, would be very bad news! Let me give you an example: if there is some vacant land in, say, Nottingham, and there are rival proposals for its use – a hospital or an airport, for instance – our *modus operandi* is to set up an interdepartmental committee.

[1] In conversation with the Editors.

That's what we always have done and it's what we always shall do.

This Committee creates months of fruitful work as all the interested Departments liaise: the Department of Health, the Department of Education, the Department of Transport, the Treasury, Environment, and so forth. We all have to see the papers, hold meetings, propose, discuss, revise, report back, and redraft. It's the normal thing.

And why? Because it generally results in a mature and responsible conclusion. But if we had regional government they would decide the whole thing, themselves, in Nottingham. Probably in three or four meetings? How? Because they're amateurs.

You might argue – as I did, that day with Humphrey – that, as it's their city, they should have that right. But I was wrong, and so would you be, for the following reasons:

First: they can't be trusted to know what's right.

Second: there would be so much less work to do in Whitehall that Ministers could almost do it on their own. Therefore we, the Civil Service, would have much less power.

Third: there's nothing wrong with the Civil Service having less power *per se.* Indeed, I personally have always shunned power. [*We remind readers that when Sir Bernard retired he was Head of the Home Civil Service – Ed.*] But the unfortunate corollary of the Civil Service having less power is that the *wrong people* get more power.

Once Sir Humphrey explained this to me, I quickly saw the error of my ways. At the top of his list of wrong people with power were politicians, local and national.

At first I thought I'd found a flaw in his argument: since the politicians are put there by ordinary voters, I couldn't see how they *could* be the wrong people. Surely, in a democracy, power ought to be vested in the voters?

Sir Humphrey put me right. 'This is a *British* democracy, Bernard. It is different. British democracy recognises that you need a system to protect the important things and keep them out of the hands of the barbarians. Things like the arts, the countryside, the law, and the universities – both of them. And *we* are that system.'

He was right, of course. We, the Civil Service, run a civilised meritocracy, a smoothly-running government machine tempered only by occasional general elections. Ever since 1832 we have been gradually excluding the voters from government. Now we have got to the point where they vote just once every four or five years purely on which bunch of buffoons will try to interfere with our policies.

And I had been happy to see all that thrown away. As Sir Humphrey talked I flushed pink with embarrassment, and hung my head in shame.

'Do you want the Lake District turned into a gigantic caravan site?' he asked me. 'You want to make the Royal Opera House a Bingo Hall and the National Theatre into a carpet sale warehouse?'

'It looks like one, actually,' I replied defensively.

Humphrey was pained. 'We gave the architect a knighthood so that no one would ever say that.' I bit my lip. 'Do you want Radio 3 to broadcast pop music for twenty-four hours a day? And how would you feel if they took all the culture programmes off television?'

I tried to defend myself. 'I don't know. I never watch them.'

'Nor do I,' said Humphrey. 'But it's vital to know that they're *there*.'

Our meeting ended. But I was still confused by one thing. To my certain knowledge Jim Hacker, both before he became Prime Minister and ever since, had always said that he wanted to reform the Civil Service.

Since he was the duly elected, democratically appointed Prime Minister [*depending on your definition of democracy*[1] – *Ed.*], I felt that whether or not we had a duty to reform local government, we *certainly* had a duty to reform the Civil Service. And if local government reform inevitably led to regional government, and therefore civil service reform, perhaps it was our duty to help.

I subsequently plucked up courage and wrote this in a letter to Sir Humphrey. He later told me that he had shredded it. I believe he did so out of kindness, in the knowledge that if my letter had remained on file and ever been seen again it would have fatally damaged any chance I had of reaching the dizzy heights of Permanent Secretary. I shall always be grateful to him for his generosity and foresight.

But I did keep Sir Humphrey's handwritten reply to me [*handwritten, so that there would be no copy in the office – Ed.*] which you may reprint if you wish.

[*Naturally we accepted Sir Bernard's kind offer, and we transcribe this rare personal letter from Sir Humphrey below – Ed.*]

My Dear Bernard,

Whether or not the Prime Minister has said that he wants to reform the Civil Service is completely beside the point. No matter what he has said, it is not what he really wants.

So, you may ask, what *does* he really want? A better Britain? Yes. Better weather? That too. But what is the main objective of all politicians, what is it that obsesses them, day and night, for the whole of their lives? Popularity! Popularity, fame, publicity, their pictures on television, their voices on the radio, their photos in the newspapers. And why? Not just because it gives them a warm glow. Champagne gives them a warm glow, but they're not obsessed with it.

No, the answer is that popularity is essential to them because they want to be re-elected. Government is fame and glory and importance and big offices

[1] See *Yes Prime Minister*, Volume I, Chapter 1.

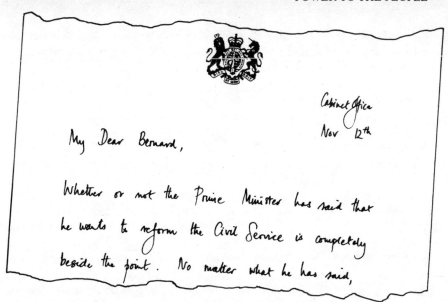

Cabinet Office
Nov 12th

My Dear Bernard,

Whether or not the Prime Minister has said that he wants to reform the Civil Service is completely beside the point. No matter what he has said,

and chauffeurs and being interviewed by Terry Wogan. Opposition is impotence and insignificance and people at parties asking you if you know Sir Robin Day.

Therefore, the only real job of a government is to get re-elected. And since constituencies of 60,000 voters are far too big for people to know their MP, the electors make up their minds on the basis of television and radio and the press. And then they vote for any idiot that a few dozen people in the constituency party chose as their candidate.

In other words, a politician does *not* really represent the electors. His job is public performance and image-building and generally being famous and popular.

So now we must ask: *what do the politicians REALLY want from the Civil Service*?

1. *Publicity*. They want publicity for all the good things they've done (or think they've done). This is why we have over one thousand press officers in Whitehall. And why we spend so many hours helping them with speeches, articles and photo opportunities.

2. *Secrecy*. They want secrecy about anything that could be used against them. This is why we have the Official Secrets Act. And why we classify every document from the Trident missile specification to the tea ladies' rota.

3. *Words*. They want us to help perpetuate the myth that they were elected democratically. This is why we help them write scripts for various charades, such as parliamentary debates. And we also write papers for Cabinet, so that the Prime Minister can update his colleagues on things that they have have missed in the newspapers.

4. *Government*. They need us to govern the country. This is the most important task of all. The politicians have no training for it, no qualifications, no experience. And no interest in it either.

5. *Pretence*. Finally, they need us to keep up the pretence that they are making all the decisions and we are only carrying out orders. This is why they take a lot of work off our shoulders, such as:
   a) ceremonial banquets;
   b) unveilings;
   c) launchings;
   d) official openings;
   e) foreign delegations, etc.

They do all of that work and leave us free for what we do best.

Therefore, politicians have no real wish to reform the Civil Service. Under our present political system we do precisely what the system requires of us. We do everything they need. And we do it, if I may say so, brilliantly.

So therefore it must follow as does night the day that if the Prime Minister wants to reform the Civil Service he would have to start by reforming the political system.

But how can he? It is the system that has got him where he is. You do not kick away the ladder you climbed up. Especially when you're still standing on it.

The fact that he proposed this when he was in Opposition all those years ago is completely understandable. Oppositions always want to change the system that is keeping them out of office. But once they are in office they want to keep it. For instance, no one *in office* has ever wanted to change our electoral system to proportional representation. And although every Opposition pledges itself to repeal the Official Secrets Act, no government has ever done so.

In conclusion, Bernard, it is our duty to ensure that the Prime Minister comes to see things this way. It is not for his own good. And we are not without allies: Professor Marriott himself, and Agnes Moorhouse, as you will see.

Yours ever,
H.A.

[*Bernard Woolley kept the letter safely, and it became one of his articles of faith as he strove in later years to help Ministers, and indeed Prime Ministers, understand their proper role.*

While he puzzled long and hard over Sir Humphrey's final paragraph, not understanding how Professor Marriott and Agnes Moorhouse – of all people – could be allies in this situation, Sir Humphrey had a second meeting with Ms Moorhouse. He made a brief note about it in his private diary – Ed.]

Tuesday 13 NOVEMBER

I met Ms Moorhouse again today. I was determined to be courteous, no matter what. So when, after I thanked her for giving up her time, she replied, "Wasting it, you mean?" I did not rise to the bait. On the contrary,

I met Ms Moorhouse again today. I was determined to be courteous, no matter what. So when, after I thanked her for giving up her time, she replied, 'Wasting it, you mean?' I did not rise to the bait.

On the contrary, I told her the plain truth: that the Prime Minister is so worried about her attitude to the police that he is proposing a wholesale reform of local government. Namely:

i)   street representatives
ii) voting communities of 200 households (average)
iii) selection of local authority candidates by the whole electorate.

I gave her a paper to read which gave the plan in full detail. She was horrified, of course. 'It strikes at the very heart of our democratic social reforms,' she told me.

'By which you mean that the people do not want your policies,' I said.

She denied it. 'Of course they would want our policies if they could understand all the implications. But ordinary voters are simple people, they don't see their needs, they're not trained to analyse problems. How can they know what's good for them? They need proper leadership to guide them the way they ought to go.'

'Do you not think that the people might vote for such leadership?'

She looked doubtful. 'The people don't always understand what's good for them.'

'I do so agree with you,' I told her.

She was surprised. So I explained that the Civil Service has always given such unobtrusive leadership. That is how the Civil Service has survived the centuries. We have made the country what it is today. But no one would ever vote for us.

And so we found that we had much common ground. We are both confident, Agnes and I, that we know what's right for the country. The principal necessity is to have a small group in charge and just let the people have a mass vote every few years. Secondly, it is not advisable for the voters actually to know the people they're voting for, for if they were to talk to them they could fall for all sorts of silly conventional ideas.

At this moment Ms Moorhouse had what she took to be an original insight, although in truth I had been painstakingly leading her towards it.

'Humphrey?'

'Yes, Agnes?' We were quite cosy by now.

'This would be a disaster for you too.'

I explained that I had indeed realised that Community Councils would inevitably lead to regional government. And that was precisely why we had to stop the Prime Minister.

She was surprised. This was the first time that she realised that I too wanted to stop the Prime Minister. And that if I were to meet with success I would need her help.

I requested that she gave me a written assurance that she would stop harassing the Houndsworth police force. She promised to write a letter guaranteeing that the police would not be made more democratically accountable [*same thing – Ed.*].

Our meeting ended most amicably. She told me that I was a great loss to the militant revolution. I, in turn, expressed my true feeling that she was a great loss to the Civil Service. On this note of mutual respect and regret, we parted.

[*Hacker's diary continues – Ed.*]

November 14th

A meeting was scheduled this morning with Professor Marriott. Apparently Humphrey arranged it. I didn't know about it.

Bernard offered an explanation. 'I think he feels, Prime Minister, that if you're adopting his scheme it would help to talk to him.'

Dorothy remarked that Humphrey must have an ulterior motive.

'Why?' I asked.

'All Humphrey's motives are ulterior,' she replied simply.

I looked at Bernard. 'Are they? How *does* Sir Humphrey feel about these reforms?'

Bernard's answer was unclear. 'Well, I think, that is, I'm sure, if, if it's, er, if it's what you want, then Sir Humphrey would, er, er . . .'

'As hostile as that?' I asked. 'Get him in here anyway.'

When Humphrey appeared in the Cabinet Room Professor Marriott was conspicuous by his absence.

'Where's the Professor?' I asked.

'He's just outside,' replied Humphrey obligingly. 'Shall I bring him in now?'

'Just one thing,' I said commandingly. 'What's *your* view of this plan to reform local government?'

'I think it's a brilliant way of bringing real democracy into the government of Britain.'

What was he up to? I couldn't work it out. 'You mean you're in favour?'

'That's not what he said,' Dorothy remarked accurately.

He ignored her, as he always does. 'Prime Minister, if you genuinely want full democratic government, you will have my unquestioning support. Would you like to see Professor Marriott now?'

Marriott was a tall, amiable fellow, nervously adjusting his bow tie, rightly overwhelmed at meeting me. We shook hands, exchanged a few pleasantries, and finally Humphrey came to the point.

'Professor Marriott has a sequel to his original article, due to be published next month. Even more exciting than the first one.'

I asked the Professor to tell me more.

'Yes,' encouraged Humphrey, 'tell the Prime Minister about the benefits to Parliament.'

The Professor was only too delighted. 'Well, you see, under this scheme each borough would have its 500 street representatives and the local MP would be able to talk to them all in one hall.'

'So that they'd really be able to get to know each other,' added Humphrey helpfully.

'Exactly,' said the Professor. 'And they'd be able to tell the people in their street all about him. Personal word-of-mouth recommendation for the MP.'

151

This sounded terrific to me. I glanced at Dorothy, but she was looking decidedly less enthusiastic. She indicated that she wanted to speak.

'Where would the constituency party come in?' she asked pleasantly.

Marriott beamed. 'Well, that's the marvellous thing, you see. The party organisations would be completely bypassed. MPs would become genuinely independent.'

I was aghast.

'You see,' continued Marriott enthusiastically, 'if they were personally known to all their constituents, or to their community representatives, then whether MPs could get re-elected or not would be nothing to do with whether or not the party backed them. It would depend on whether the constituents felt the MP was doing a good job.'

Humphrey smiled at me. 'So if MPs weren't dependent on the party machine they could vote against their own government party and get away with it,' he explained.

'Exactly,' said the Professor again. 'Because there'd be no need for "official" candidates, election would depend on the reputation of each individual MP, not the image of the party leader. It's the end of the party machine. The end of the power of the whips.'

I couldn't begin to grasp how such a system could possibly work. 'So . . . how would the government get its unpopular legislation through if it couldn't twist a few arms? How would it command a majority?'

Marriott's answer was all too clear. 'That's the whole *point*. It couldn't! A government couldn't *command* a majority! It would have to deserve it. Just like in 1832, when an MP's constituency was only about 1200 voters, there could only be legislation if a majority of the MPs were actually in favour of it. And MPs would only favour it if the voters did too. Parliament would be genuinely democratic again.'

I couldn't believe my ears. Who in their right mind could possibly come to the Prime Minister with such a dangerous proposal? Only some damn-fool academic. As far as I was concerned the good professor could return to the ivory tower from whence he came – and pronto!

'That you so much, Professor,' I said with finality. 'Absolutely fascinating.' And I stood up and shook hands.

He was surprised. Beads of sweat broke out on the high dome of his receding forehead. 'Oh, er, thank you, Prime Minister,' he said, and

Bernard whisked him out of the room before his feet could touch the ground.

The heavy panelled door closed with a soft thud. Humphrey smiled at me. 'Isn't that splendid, Prime Minister? Real democracy!' He clapped his hands together and rubbed them with glee.

I ignored him and turned to Dorothy. 'Is he right? Would that happen?'

'I'm afraid it probably would.'

Glassy-eyed, I repeated the dreadful threat aloud. 'MPs free to vote how they like? It's intolerable.'

'Just like the 1832 Reform Act,' Humphrey confirmed.

'But,' I explained to Humphrey, as if he didn't know, 'the whole system depends on our MP's voting the way I tell them. Under this system they could follow the dictates of their constituents.'

'Or their consciences,' agreed Humphrey.

'Exactly!' I said, echoing that bloody Professor. 'Dorothy, this whole scheme's a complete non-starter.'

Dorothy asked what I was going to do, in that case, about Agnes Moorhouse and the police. I was stuck. But to my surprise Humphrey indicated that he had the answer. 'I've had another talk with her, Prime Minister. It's all arranged. I wrote you this memorandum.'

And he handed me a sheet of paper.

[*Fortunately the memorandum in question was found beside the cassette on which this portion of the diary was dictated, and is reproduced overleaf – Ed.*]

70 WHITEHALL, LONDON SW1A 2AS

Memorandum

To: The Prime Minister   14 November

From: The Secretary of the Cabinet

Certain informal discussions have taken place, involving a full
and frank exchange of views, out of which there arose a series
of proposals which on examination proved to indicate certain
promising lines of enquiry which when pursued led to the
realisation that the alternative courses of action might in
fact, in certain circumstances, be susceptible of discreet
modification, in one way or another, leading to a reappraisal
of the original areas of difference and pointing the way to
encouraging possibilities of significant compromise and
co-operation which if bilaterally implemented with appropriate
give and take on both sides could if the climate were right have
a reasonable possibility at the end of the day of leading,
rightly or wrongly, to a mutually satisfactory conclusion.

[Hacker's diary continues – Ed.]

I stared at the sheet of paper, mesmerised. Finally, I looked up at Humphrey. 'Could you summarise this please?' I asked.

He thought hard for a moment. 'We did a deal,' he replied.

He did a deal with Agnes Moorhouse? Splendid! 'How did you fix it?'

He smiled humbly. 'Oh, the old system has its good points, you know. It works things out in its own time.'

I sat back in my chair, relaxed, content to ask no more. 'Yes, it does, doesn't it?' I murmured happily.

'And . . . the Marriott plan?' he asked. He knew what my answer would be.

'I don't think the nation's ready for total democracy, do you?' He shook his head sadly. 'Shall we say next century?'

'You could still be Prime Minister next century,' Dorothy interjected.

'Well, the one after,' I said.

'Yes, Prime Minister,' said Humphrey, quite content. In fact we were all content, Humphrey, Dorothy and me. Friends at last.

6
The Tangled Web

[*The day after Hacker, Dorothy Wainright and Sir Humphrey Appleby agreed to postpone democracy until the twenty-second century, Hacker answered questions in the House of Commons. This was a twice-weekly event: Prime Minister's Question Time. The Prime Minister was likely to be asked about almost anything at all, and was given no notice of the questions. To be more precise, the first question from an MP was likely to be: 'Will the Prime Minister list his official engagements for today?' The supplementary question could be about absolutely anything: e.g. 'Will the Prime Minister find time to consider rising interest rates?' Or 'Will the Prime Minister find time to consider the scandal of Agnes Moorhouse creating no-go areas for the police of the London Borough of Houndsworth?' Or 'Will the Prime Minister find time to consider the scandal whereby 25% of Honours go to less than 1% of the population, most of whom are in government?'*

The Prime Minister can react in a number of ways: honestly, dishonestly, with a mass of figures. He can counter-attack, flatter, or make jokes. The latter is the most dangerous and least recommended response.

Hacker, like all Prime Ministers, would prepare for Prime Minister's Question Time with great care. Bernard Woolley and the Parliamentary Questions Secretary – a Principal from the Private Office – would meet for a briefing from 2.30 to 3.10 p.m. in the Prime Minister's room at the House. They would be armed with a three-volume book which lists what each MP on the Order Paper has asked before, what are that MP's special interests, and – most important – what have been the previous answers.

The Prime Minister is obliged to give an answer to a question about policy. However, if the question demands a purely factual answer, the Prime Minister may be able to give a written reply.

The burden can be lightened by planting some of the questions. Questions come from alternate sides of the House, and a government backbencher hoping for preferment may well inform the Prime

Minister of a potential question – 'I always like to be of service, Prime Minister' – or even offer: 'What would you like me to ask, Prime Minister?'

Furthermore, the job of the Prime Minister's Parliamentary Private Secretary is to 'nobble' an MP: 'The Prime Minister would like you to ask this question.' Nonetheless, the Prime Minister can confidently expect two-thirds to three-quarters of questions to be hostile. And the most awkward questions of all frequently came from the government side – from disappointed, disaffected and sour senior backbenchers who have either been overlooked or sacked from office.

Thus it is that, as a result of Prime Minister's Question Time, a tornado may suddenly appear in what has been a cloudless blue sky – Ed.]

SIR BERNARD WOOLLEY RECALLS:[1]
Jim Hacker had been asked whether he had been tapping MPs' telephones. He had given this excellent answer: 'Much as I respect and value the opinion of this House, I must confess to having no desire to listen to the words of honourable members for any longer than I actually have to,' and he got a big laugh. [*The MPs who laughed would have been largely from his own party, those hoping to be promoted or those afraid of being sacked. This amounts to virtually all of them – Ed.*]

But on our return to Number Ten later that afternoon Sir Humphrey buttonholed me in the narrow twisting corridor that led to the Cabinet Office. He asked me how our great statesman was that afternoon.

'Very cheerful,' I replied. 'He did very well at Question Time this afternoon.'

'Indeed? In whose opinion?'

'His,' I said. In fact I was joking. Everyone had been really impressed with his answer on tapping MPs' phones.

Everyone except Humphrey. Indeed, he seemed so very concerned that I began to fear that there was more to this than met the eye. He ticked me off for not warning him of the question – as Cabinet Secretary, Humphrey co-ordinated all government security. I explained that it was an unforeseen supplementary, but he remarked disagreeably that it was a foreseeable unforeseen supplementary.

It was more than clear from Sir Humphrey's demeanour and agitation that, although the Prime Minister denied that he ever authorised bugging an MP's telephone, this answer was not the truth!

The idea of a British Prime Minister deliberately lying to the House of Commons was deeply shocking to me. It was hard to believe. But Humphrey

---

[1] In conversation with the Editors.

held a fat file under his arm, and informed me that it contained a mass of incriminating information – including the transcripts.

Humphrey asked to see Hacker immediately. I wondered if we might not leave it a little longer, as the Prime Minister was basking in his success and didn't get many moments of unalloyed pleasure. But Humphrey took the view that Hacker got more pleasures than he deserved, and adamantly insisted upon an immediate meeting.

[*Hacker's diary continues – Ed.*]

November 15th

I gave some brilliant answers in Question Time today. I was on absolutely top form. So I wasn't a bit surprised when Humphrey unexpectedly appeared in the Cabinet Room later that afternoon.

'Prime Minister, I want to talk to you about Prime Minister's Question Time this afternoon.'

'Thank you,' I said, with suitable and becoming modesty. 'I accept your congratulations. Wasn't I brilliant, Bernard?'

Bernard replied without hesitation. 'I believe, Prime Minister, that your replies this afternoon will not be quickly forgotten.'

Humphrey tried to speak but I wouldn't let him. From his manner I might have detected storm clouds on the horizon, but I didn't. Foolishly I insisted on recounting my triumphs. 'Let me tell you what happened, Humphrey,' I crowed. 'The first question was about that Home Office cock-up over the shortage of prison officers. My reply was masterly. "I refer the Honourable Member to the speech I made in this House on April the 26th."'

'Did he remember what you'd said?' Humphrey asked.

''Course he didn't. Nor did I, come to that. But it was the perfect evasive blocking answer, and as he couldn't remember what I'd said any more than I could we went straight on to a question about unemployment and whether the Department of Employment fiddle the figures.'

Bernard corrected me. 'You mean "periodically re-structure the base from which the statistics are derived without drawing public attention to the fact"?'

'Exactly,' I repeated, 'fiddle the figures.'

Humphrey, in spite of himself, was interested. 'Of *course* they do,' he said.

'I know that,' I said. 'But I gave a great answer. I said that I'd found no significant evidence of it.'

Bernard said, 'That's because you haven't been looking.'

'And because we haven't shown you,' Humphrey added.

'I know, Humphrey. Thank you. Well done. So then we went straight on to a googlie about the Department of Energy's looming plans for the disposal of nuclear waste. The question was trying to get me to admit that the Cabinet's divided.'

'It is!' remarked Humphrey.

'I know it is,' I said. 'So I said, "My Cabinet took a unanimous decision."'

Humphrey smiled. 'Only because you threatened to dismiss anyone who wouldn't agree.'

He was right, of course. But it certainly made them agree unanimously. Anyway, by this time my backbenchers were cheering my every word. 'Then there was a question about why, despite all that money we've spent on the new anti-missile missile, it was scrapped as obsolete the day before the first one came off the production line.'

Humphrey was curious as to how I wriggled out of that one.

'This was my master-stroke. I didn't! My reply was sheer genius. I simply said, "Our policy has not been as effective as we'd hoped, and clearly we'd got it wrong."'

Humphrey's mouth fell open. He was profoundly shocked that I'd made such an admission. But it was a brilliant answer. It took the wind right out of their sails. A completely honest answer always gives you the advantage of surprise in the House of Commons.

Bernard was enjoying it in retrospect too. 'There was actually a supplementary, Sir Humphrey. The Prime Minister was asked when he would request the resignation of the responsible Minister.'

That one was too easy. A full toss. I hit it straight to the boundary. '"I will ask for his resignation when he makes a mistake that could have been seen at the time, not with the benefit of hindsight."' My side of the house were on their feet, cheering, stamping, waving their order papers. It was a day to remember!

But unfortunately, it turned out to be a day to remember for other reasons too. Of course I should have detected that something was up from the way in which Sir Humphrey had slunk into the Cabinet Room. I had mistaken his funereal air of impending disaster for simple envy at my brilliance in handling the House so well without any assistance from him. But there was more to it than that.

'I understand', he remarked casually, 'that there was a question about bugging an MP?'

'Stupid question,' I said. 'Why should we bug Hugh Halifax? A

159

Friend the Secretary of State for Education and Science about the nature of the curriculum.

PRIME MINISTER

Engagements

Q1. **Mr. Tyler** asked the Prime Minister if he will list his official engagements for Thursday 15 November.

The Prime Minister (Mr. James Hacker): This morning I had meetings with ministerial colleagues and others. In addition to my duties in this House, I shall be having further meetings today.

Mr. Tyler: Is the Prime Minister aware of the disgraceful shortage of prison officers caused by the Home Office's present policy?

The Prime Minister: I refer the hon. Gentleman to the speech I made in this House on 26 April last.

Q2. **Sir Fred Broadhurst** asked the Prime Minister if he will list his official engagements for Thursday 15 November.

The Prime Minister: I refer the hon. Gentleman to the reply that I gave some moments ago.

Sir Fred Broadhurst: Will the Prime Minister assure me that the Department of Employment does not periodically re-structure the base from which unemployment statistics are derived, without drawing public attention to the fact?

The Prime Minister: I am happy to assure the hon. Gentleman that I have found no significant evidence of it.

Q3. **Mrs. Huxley** asked the Prime Minister if he will list his official engagements for Thursday 15 November.

The Prime Minister: I refer the hon. Lady to the reply that I gave some moments ago.

Mrs. Huxley: Will the Prime Minister confirm that the Cabinet is unable to agree on the Department of Energy's plans for the disposal of nuclear waste?

The Prime Minister: That is not so. My Cabinet took a unanimous decision. [HON. MEMBERS: "Hear, hear."]

Q4. **Mr. Allgrove** asked the Prime Minister if he will list his official engagements for Thursday 15 November.

The Prime Minister: I refer the hon. Gentleman to the reply that I gave some moments ago.

Mr. Allgrove: Will the Prime Minister find the time today to consider why, despite all the money spent on the new anti-missile missile, it was scrapped as obsolete the day before the first one came off the production line?

The Prime Minister: Our policy has not been as effective as we'd hoped – [*Interruption.*] – as we'd hoped, and clearly we got it wrong. [*Laughter.*]

The Leader of the Opposition (Mr. George Hedley): So when will the Prime Minister request the resignation of the Minister responsible?

The Prime Minister: The right hon. Gentleman well knows that I will ask for my right hon. Friend's resignation when he makes a mistake that could have been seen at the time, not with the benefit of hindsight.

Many Hon. Members *rose and cheered* –

Mr. Speaker: Order.

Mr. Chapman: On a point of order, Mr. Speaker.

Mr. Speaker: I will take points of order in their usual place.

Q5. **Mr. Gill** asked the Prime Minister if he will list his official engagements for Thursday 15 November.

The Prime Minister: I refer my hon. Friend to the reply that I gave some moments ago.

Mr. Gill: Will my right hon. Friend assure the House that the Government is not and has not been tapping hon. Members' telephones?

The Prime Minister: Much as I respect and value the opinion of this House, I must confess to having no desire to listen to the words of hon. Members for any longer than I actually have to. [*Laughter.*]

The Leader of the Opposition: Is the Prime Minister really saying that the hon. Member for Aintree (Mr. Halifax) has not had his phone – [*Interruption.*] – has not had his

PPS, a member of my own Administration, I can't think where he got such a daft idea.' With hindsight I realised that this reply may sound foolish, but I had no reason at all to suspect the truth. Humphrey tried to interrupt me but I didn't listen. After all, how could I have known that I didn't know?

'Can you imagine?' I said, brushing Humphrey aside, metaphorically that is. 'Why should we want to listen in on an MP? Boring, ignorant, self-opinionated windbags, I do my best *not* to listen to them. And Hugh's only a PPS, I mean, *I* have enough trouble finding out what's going on at the Ministry of Defence, what could *he* know? It's my idea of Hell. That's how God will punish me if I've led a wicked life – he'll make me sit and listen to tapes of MPs talking.'

I must admit I was pretty pleased with myself. Humphrey was not amused. 'So I gather you denied that Mr Halifax has been bugged?'

'Yes,' I said. 'It was the one question today to which I could give a simple, clear, straightforward, honest answer.'

At which point Humphrey ranted for some considerable while. And I simply couldn't understand him, try as I might.

[*Fortunately, Sir Humphrey made a note of his comments in his private diary that very day – Ed.*]

I explained to the Prime Minister that unfortunately, although the answer was indeed simple, clear and straightforward, there was some difficulty in justifiably assigning to it the fourth of the epithets he had applied to the statement [*honest – Ed.*] inasmuch as the precise correlation between the information he had communicated and the facts insofar as they can be determined and demonstrated is such as to cause epistemological problems of sufficient magnitude to lay upon the logical and semantic resources of the English language a heavier burden than they can reasonably be requested to bear. [*Appleby Papers TK/3787/SW*]

Opposite: Prime Minister's Question Time from Hansard.

Thursday 15 NOVEMBER

I explained to the
Prime Minister that
unfortunately, although
the answer was indeed
simple, clear and
straightforward, there
was some difficulty in
justifiably assigning to
it the fourth of the
epithets he had applied
to the statement
inasmuch as the precise
correlation between the
information he had

[*Hacker's diary continues – Ed.*]

I realised that he was wrapping up whatever he was trying to say in the hope that it would be less hurtful or embarrassing or something. But I had to ask for a translation.

He nerved himself up for his reply. He looked at the floor, the ceiling, out of the window – and finally his eyes met mine. 'You told a lie,' he said.

I couldn't believe my ears. 'A lie?'

'A lie,' he repeated.

'What do you mean, a lie?' I simply couldn't understand what he could be referring to.

'I mean, Prime Minister . . .' he hesitated, apparently searching for a way to explain himself, '. . . you . . . lied!'

I didn't know what he was talking about. I stared at him blankly. He tried again. 'Um . . . I know that this is a difficult concept to get across to a politician, but . . . you did not tell the truth.'

Could he mean, I asked myself, that we *are* bugging Hugh Halifax? I didn't know the answer, so I asked him.

He nodded. 'We were.'

'We *were*?' I was appalled. 'When did we stop?'

Humphrey glanced at his wristwatch. 'Seventeen minutes ago.'

I was hurt, and upset that my integrity had been impugned in this manner. 'You can't call that lying,' I complained.

'I see.' Humphrey inclined his head to one side and stared at me hopefully, like a Bearded Collie that is eager to learn. 'What would you call the opposite of telling the truth?'

'There was no intent. I didn't mean to deceive them. I would never knowingly mislead the House.'

[*Hacker, in his state of outraged innocence, had clearly forgotten that he had proudly admitted to misleading the House several times that day. Nonetheless, it is almost certainly true that he would never intentionally have lied to the House, for fear of the consequences. Indeed, for reasons that are quite unclear to the historian, lying appears to be the one offence that the House does not forgive, trivial though it is in comparison to the many great calamities that our politicians inflict upon us – Ed.*]

'Nonetheless,' said Humphrey, 'you did tell them an untruth.'

'But it's not my fault!' He couldn't seem to understand. 'I didn't know he was being bugged.'

Bernard coughed quietly to attract my attention. 'Prime Minister,' he explained sympathetically, 'it's not enough to say you didn't know. You are deemed to have known. You are ultimately responsible.'

Now I was getting angry. 'So why the hell wasn't I told?'

Bernard looked at Humphrey. They were both pretty embarrassed. 'The Home Secretary', mumbled Humphrey, 'might not have felt the need to inform you.'

'Why?'

'Perhaps because he was advised that you didn't need to know.'

This is ludicrous. 'But I *did* need to know,' I pointed out.

At this point *Bernard* took refuge in Civil Service gibberish. He's spending too much time with Humphrey. I haven't the foggiest notion of what he was trying to say.

SIR BERNARD WOOLLEY RECALLS:[1]

I recall what I said only too well. Briefly I explained that the fact that Hacker needed to know was not known at the time that the now known need to know was known and therefore those who needed to advise and inform the Home Secretary perhaps felt that the information that he needed as to whether or not to inform the highest authority of the known information was not yet known and therefore there was no authority for the authority to be informed because the need to know was not at this time known. Or needed.

I should have thought that my explanation was crystal clear but, alas! not to Hacker. Perhaps he couldn't assimilate what I was saying because he was in such a blue funk.

[*Hacker's diary continues – Ed.*]

I needed a translation. I turned to Humphrey, of all people! He provided it.

'Perhaps the Home Secretary didn't know either. And we assumed that, if you were asked a question in the House, you would stall, or you'd say you had no knowledge, or that you would look into it. We didn't know, we couldn't *possibly* have known, Prime Minister, that you would take the novel step of actually answering a question.'

I could see his point. But I'd evaded and stalled on the previous four questions, I had to give a straight answer to this one. And this seemed safe.

Humphrey was sympathetic. 'Yes, but we couldn't know you'd answer it. And that in the House you would actually deny all bugging.'

'Obviously I would, if I didn't know and I were asked.'

Humphrey said: 'We didn't know you would be asked when you didn't know.'

An idiotic argument. I explained that I was *bound* to be asked when I didn't know if I didn't know. But he didn't seem to understand. Sometimes old Humphrey's a bit slow-witted. It's lucky he's not in politics.

[1] In conversation with the Editors.

Humphrey continued trying to justify his totally unjustifiable position. And in an impatient tone that I did not altogether care for. 'Prime Minister, it was thought it was better for you not to know. Mr Halifax is a member of your government team and as such it was felt that it might be better not to create distrust. We only tell you if you should be aware.'

'When's that?' I asked.

'Well . . . you should *now* be aware because you've just denied it.'

'It would have been somewhat better if I'd been aware *before* I denied it.'

Humphrey didn't see it that way. 'On the contrary, if you'd been aware *before* you denied it, you *wouldn't* have denied it!'

'But', I exclaimed passionately, 'I needed to know!'

'That is not the criterion.' Humphrey was stubbornly insistent that he was right. 'We don't tell you about bugging when you need to know, we only tell you when you *know* you need to know.'

'Or when you need to know that you need to know,' said Bernard.

'Or when *we* know that you need to know,' said Humphrey.

'You see,' added Bernard helpfully, 'at times it is needed for you to need not to know.'

'*That's enough*!' I shouted. Startled, they fell silent at once, staring at me, puzzled. 'Why?' I shouted at Humphrey. 'Why did you decide that I shouldn't know?'

'I didn't,' he said, sounding rather offended.

I was baffled. 'Then who did?'

'Nobody.'

I was getting desperate. 'Then why didn't I know?'

'Because nobody decided to tell you,' Humphrey said.

'That's the same thing, dammit!'

Humphrey had now resorted to his icy-calm-I'm-dealing-with-a-dangerous-lunatic voice. 'No, Prime Minister, it's not. To decide to conceal information from you is a serious burden for any official to shoulder, but to decide not to reveal information to you is routine procedure.'

I told Humphrey that I wanted to know everything.

'Everything, Prime Minister?'

'Everything!'

'Very well.' He consulted one of his files. 'Stationery deliveries this week to the Cabinet Office comprise four gross packets of size two paperclips, 600 reams of A4 cut bank typing paper, nine dozen felt-tipped . . .'

165

He was being silly. 'Important things!' I snarled.

'So who should decide what is important?' he asked with deceptive innocence.

'I should,' I said, and then realised that I was about to be given a list of stationery supplies again. 'No, you should,' I said, and then realised the pitfalls *there*. There seemed to be no answer. Angrily, I asked him to tell me, very simply, how he could possibly excuse this cock-up.

'As you said in the House,' he replied smoothly, 'clearly we got it wrong.'

Imitation is the sincerest form of flattery, but this was flattery that I could do without. 'I got it wrong' is an inadequate excuse for dropping the Prime Minister in the shit.

'I am merely a humble servant,' continued the least humble servant whom I've ever encountered. 'A lowly official. It was the Home Secretary's decision.'

Was it indeed? I might have guessed. He's never liked me. 'Can you think of any reason why I shouldn't ask him to resign?'

Impudently he replied, 'With respect, Prime Minister, perhaps you should not ask him to resign until he makes a mistake that could have been seen at the time, not with the benefit of hindsight. Besides, the trouble today has arisen as a result of your own error of judgement in making this denial.'

I was shocked by his brazen impertinence. 'What?' I said. I was literally speechless. [*We refrain from further comment – Ed.*]

'You should not have denied something about which you were not informed,' he lectured me self-righteously.

I couldn't believe my ears. 'But it's your fault!' I shouted. 'You've just admitted keeping secrets from the Prime Minister.'

Now he was indignant. 'Not at all. The system works perfectly well as long as the Prime Minister tells the Civil Service anything he intends to say before he says it. But if precipitately he says something without first clearing it with his officials he only has himself to blame. You should never say anything in public without clearing it. With respect, Prime Minister, you must learn discretion.'

I've never heard such an incredibly circular argument. 'But I didn't *know*, Humphrey, that there was anything to be discreet *about*!'

'In government, Prime Minister, there is always something to be discreet about.'

A new question suddenly occurred to me. I can't think why I never thought of it before. 'But Humphrey . . . why *were* we bugging Hugh

Halifax? Was he talking to the Russian Embassy?'

'No,' said Humphrey. 'The French Embassy. Which is much more serious.'

'Why?'

'The Russians already know what we're doing,' said Bernard.

But the French are our allies, whatever we think of them – and who doesn't!

[*It is well for the readers to remember that the Foreign Office has three national groups that it loves:*

a) *The Arabs*
b) *The Germans*
c) *The Americans*

And three nationalities that it hates:

a) *The Russians*
b) *The Israelis*
c) *The French*

It hates the French most of all. This is why talking directly to the French is regarded as prima facie an act of treason by the FO[1] – Ed.]

'Who authorised it?' I asked. 'Which officials authorised this bugging?'

'The Foreign Office. I just said!' He hadn't just said! And I'd never realised they had the power to authorise buggings. I suppose they can, since they control MI6, but they can't officially authorise surveillance since MI6 does not officially exist. I suppose Foreign Office official officials unofficially authorised MI6's unofficial officials.

Humphrey wanted to bring the discussion to a close. 'Prime Minister, the less said the better, wouldn't you agree?'

I was confused. 'About what?'

'About everything.'

[*Sir Humphrey's wish to say no more about the Hugh Halifax bugging was not to be fulfilled. Shortly afterwards he received a letter from a House of Commons committee, asking him to appear before it to discuss the matter. Sir Humphrey sent the letter to Jim Hacker, with a note asking for Hacker's advice on how to handle it. Hacker sent the following reply, which was released under the Thirty Year Rule – Ed.*]

---

[1] This also explains why the Suez invasion was such a diplomatic trauma for the Foreign Office: the Cabinet sided with the French and Israelis against the Arabs and Americans.

1O DOWNING STREET

THE PRIME MINISTER

November 21

Dear Humphrey,

You can hardly refuse to appear before a Committee of the House. And obviously you must tell them everything that you must tell them.[1] I'm sure you will find something appropriate to say.

yours truly

Jim

---

[1] Sir Humphrey would understand this to mean everything that the Committee could find out from some other source.

SIR BERNARD WOOLLEY RECALLS:[1]

Sir Humphrey called me into his office and showed me the Prime Minister's letter. Of course it offered no answer. Sir Humphrey was concerned with how a loyal public servant should reply if the Committee were to ask him if the Prime Minister had ever authorised the tapping of an MP's telephone. And it was highly likely that the question would indeed be asked.

I suggested that he say it was not a question for him, but for the Prime Minister, the Home Secretary or the Foreign Office.

'Or the British Telecom Service Engineer's Department?' he enquired sardonically.

Clearly I had not given him the answer he wished to hear. So I suggested the usual safety-net catch-all reply: that it's a security matter, and therefore I'm not at liberty to divulge, confirm or deny, et cetera.

Humphrey sighed. 'Bernard, do you think I am unaware of these options?'

Naturally he was aware of them. But he explained that it was a trap: if he dodged the question about the Prime Minister authorising telephone tapping, the follow-up question was bound to be: *Why will you not give the same clear denial that the Prime Minister gave the House yesterday*? To which there was no safe answer.

I made a suggestion to Humphrey: 'You could say that the Prime Minister knows more about it than you do.'

'Then they'd *know* I was lying,' said Humphrey. This was unarguable.

I'm ashamed to admit that, in my eagerness to help, I even suggested that Humphrey simply deny the accusation. Like Hacker had done.

Humphrey, to his credit, was rather shocked. 'You mean lie?'

'No one can prove it's a lie,' I said.

Humphrey appeared to be very disappointed in me. 'So anything is true, so long as one can disprove it? You're talking like a politician, Bernard.'

Indeed I was. And I must tell you that if Humphrey had been *sure* that his statement could not have been disproved, he too would have talked like a politician and denied that the phone had been tapped. My suggestion was bad not because it was misleading but because it was dangerous.

Still, after that reproof from on high I felt disinclined to offer any further suggestions.

At that uncomfortable moment the phone rang. It was the BBC. But it wasn't about the phone tapping. Of all things, they wanted to interview old Humphrey for a Radio 3 documentary on the structure of government. He seemed quite ridiculously pleased. He wanted to accept! Now it was my turn to be shocked. A Civil Servant giving a public interview? How *could* he? And he seemed to have no qualms.

I felt obliged to remind him of the risk. 'They might want you to say things.'

[1] In conversation with the Editors.

'That's quite normal on radio.' A facetious, evasive and misleading reply. He knew that it was against all the traditions of the Service to speak on the radio. For a start, one might make a slip and find oneself saying something interesting. Or even controversial.

But times were changing. Civil Servants were beginning to come out of the closet (is that the phrase?). He claimed that he had an obligaton to do it because of his duty to put the record straight. I, for my part, was not aware that the record was crooked.

'It's not for oneself!' He was protesting too much, methinks! 'I have no inclination to become a celebrity. That's just petty vanity. But one can be *too* self-effacing.'

I didn't see how. I told him that my understanding of the Civil Service was that we were supposed to be faceless.

'They don't show your face on radio.'

I was tiring of this self-serving, dishonest claptrap. I could well see how he would fall for such a dangerously seductive offer as a discussion programme on Radio 3, but I really did feel he ought to know better. 'Anonymity,' I reminded him. 'Service. Discretion.'

Embarrassed, he poured himself a glass of Tio Pepe [*It must have been after 6.00 pm – Ed.*]. 'Bernard, they said that if I couldn't do it, Arnold[1] has said that he would.'

'Perhaps that would be better,' I said. Humphrey's eyebrows shot up. But I wasn't being rude. It's just that Sir Arnold was retired, and could therefore not reveal anything much any more, certainly not about current events. Furthermore, he was now President of the Campaign for Freedom of Information and fully committed to opening up government – so long as it was in the national interest!

Humphrey had never got over his jealousy of Arnold, and he yearned for public recognition. But he would rather die than admit it. I'll never forget his lame excuse: 'For myself, Bernard, I'd rather not do this interview, *of course*. But I think one's sense of duty compels one to ensure that Arnold is not held up as an example of a top Civil Servant.'

I pointed out to Humphrey that he would need the Prime Minister's permission. He was momentarily concerned about this. But I took pleasure in adding that in my view there'd be no problem with the Prime Minister because, as it was for Radio 3, no one would be listening anyway.

[*It must have been very galling for Permanent Secretaries at this period of British history. A meritocracy of brilliant men who occupied forty-two of the most powerful jobs in the country, although highly paid and festooned with honours, were nonetheless deeply deserving of sympathy – for by tradition and to their own advantage, they were*

---

[1] Sir Arnold Robinson, Sir Humphrey's predecessor as Secretary of the Cabinet.

virtually unknown. To most British people a Permanent Secretary was the opposite of a 'temp', at best a senior clerical assistant. This is perhaps the reason that Sir Humphrey was quite unable to resist the invitation to speak on the radio, a boost that his ego undoubtedly needed – Ed.]

[*Hacker's diary continues – Ed.*]

November 26th
Humphrey popped in to see me this morning, looking incredibly tense and nervy. At first I thought some new crisis was about to hit me, but then I remembered it was the day of his radio interview.

I told him not to worry, and he pompously denied that he was anxious. 'I have some experience in dealing with difficult questions.'

'Yes,' I agreed, 'but if you're too evasive or confusing on radio they just edit you out. You actually have to say something.'

He looked blank. 'Say something?' He didn't understand.

'Something simple and interesting,' I explained.

His hand started shaking. 'Simple and interesting,' he repeated, then licked his dry lips. 'Well . . . er, if you have any advice . . . especially if the questions are aggressive.'

I explained that dealing with an aggressive question is like dealing with fast bowling – unless it's deadly accurate you can use its own momentum to help you score. 'The more aggressive the questions are, the better. They'll put the listeners on your side.'

'But nonetheless I may have to answer them.'

'Why?' I asked. 'You've never answered my questions.'

'That's different, Prime Minister,' he replied. 'I may be asked some perceptive questions.'

I glared at him, 'Humphrey,' I asked rhetorically, 'why are you doing this interview? To explain the Civil Service point of view, presumably. So you must do what I do – go in with something to say, and say it. Simply ask yourself whatever question you want to reply to.'

'Fearlessly and honestly,' agreed Bernard encouragingly, who had clearly taken to heart the lessons I'd given him a few months ago.

'Or', I continued, 'if you want more control you say, "That's really two separate questions." Then, fearlessly and honestly, ask yourself *two* questions you want to answer, and answer them.'

Humphrey dried his wet palms on his handkerchief. 'Their researcher mentioned that a lot of people want to know about why so much power is centralised in my hands.'

'A lot of people?' I tried not to smile. 'Most people have never heard of you, Humphrey.'

He didn't look awfully encouraged by that insight.

'Perhaps they mean a lot of Radio 3 listeners,' Bernard wondered.

'That's a contradiction in terms,' I said amiably. 'But if they do ask that question, what should he reply, Bernard?'

'Name six of them,' answered Bernard promptly. He's a good student.

'That's right,' I said. 'Because then you've got him. He'll never think of more than two, see?'

Humphrey smiled for the first time. 'I see, Prime Minister. Bernard, how did you know that?'

Bernard said, 'The Prime Minister taught me a few tricks of the trade after my unfortunate talk with those reporters last August – the time I inadvertently said that when it came to official secrets the Prime Minister was above the law.'

'I see.' He turned to me. 'Any other tricks, Prime Minister?'

I turned to Bernard. 'Yes,' he said. 'Attack one word in the question. You know: "*Frequently*? What do you mean, *frequently*?" Or you can attack the interviewer: "You obviously haven't read the White Paper." Or you can ask a question back: "That's a very good question. Now let me ask you one: when did you last visit a decentralised government department, such as the Vehicle Licensing Centre in Swansea?" And if you're desperate you can always use security as an excuse for not answering.'

'Well *done*, Bernard!' I congratulated him. 'You'll go far.'

But something else had just come to Humphrey's mind. 'That reminds me, Prime Minister – I'm afraid that I must appear soon before the Committee to answer questions on the alleged bugging of Hugh Halifax MP.'

I knew that. Bernard had already told me. 'You'll just have to confirm what I said in the House.'

He feigned incomprehension. 'But that would be lying.'

I shrugged. 'No one would know.'

'Oh, what a tangled web we weave . . .' He's so mealy-mouthed!

'Come off it Humphrey,' I snapped.

He had assumed his butter-wouldn't-melt-in-my-mouth choirboy face. 'I'm sorry, Prime Minister, I cannot tell a lie.'

I couldn't believe that he could do this to me. 'But Humphrey!' I found to my horror that I was pleading with him! 'If you don't, it will look as if *I* was lying.'

He pursed his lips and remained silent. Clearly he didn't feel that was his problem. I lost my temper. 'Humphrey!' I thundered. 'You have a loyalty!'

'To the truth,' he agreed primly.

I was up from my chair now, pacing up and down the full length of the Cabinet Room. 'But . . .' I was lost for words. 'But . . . you can't just go in there and shop me in front of all the press and the Opposition. When it wasn't even my fault. You must back me up. You must!'

He refused to meet my eye. 'You make it very hard for me, Prime Minister,' was his totally unsatisfactory response.

'Humphrey,' I said firmly, 'I am ordering you to confirm what I said in the House.'

He stared at me insolently. 'Very well, Prime Minister, I will tell them that you have ordered me to confirm it.'

That was hardly what I meant! 'Humphrey, I order you not to tell them I ordered you.'

He was implacable. 'Then I shall have to tell them you have ordered me not to tell them you ordered me.'

I glowered at him. I was bloody furious. He was icy and superior as only he can be. 'I'm sorry, Prime Minister, I cannot become involved in some shabby cover-up.'

Treacherous, disloyal bastard.

[*Sir Humphrey drove from Number 10 Downing Street directly to Broadcasting House, where he gave his first-ever radio interview. Only one copy of the recording now exists, not at the BBC itself but in Sir Humphrey Appleby's own private archive. With the kind permission of Lady Appleby, his widow, we gained access to the strongroom of the Midland Bank in Haslemere, and we made a transcript of the recording, the relevant portion of which we print below – Ed.*]

Sir Humphrey: Whereas there must inevitably be some element of shared responsibility for the governance of Britain as between the legislators on the one hand and the adminstrators on the other, the precise allocation of cause to consequence, or agency to eventuality, in any particular instance is invariably so complex as to be ultimately invalid, if not irresponsible.

[*It seems that Sir Humphrey was not able to keep his answers either simple or interesting, as Hacker had correctly advised him – Ed.*]

Interviewer: Yes. If I could press you for a more precise answer or a concrete example, how much blame can the Civil Service take for the present level of unemployment?

Sir Humphrey: Well, of course, unemployment is a single name applied by the media to what is in effect a wide range of socio-economic phenomena whose most politically viable manifestation happens to be . . .

Interviewer (interrupting): But to be precise, how much blame . . .?

Sir Humphrey: One moment. Happens to be a current frequency of weekly registrations on the national unemployment register which is deemed to be above what has historically been held to be an acceptable level. But even separating out the component causes, let alone allocating the responsibility for them, is a task of such analytical delicacy as not to be susceptible of compression within the narrow confines of a popular radio programme such as this.

[*Sir Humphrey Appleby's notion that a Radio 3 talks programme was popular suggests a very slight acquaintance with the listening figures. Alternatively, Sir Humphrey may have used the word popular to suggest that it was heard by those outside the top ranks of the Civil Service. One wonders, if that was a popular programme, what an unpopular programme would have been like – Ed.*]

Interviewer: Sir Humphrey Appleby, thank you very much.

[*At this point, when the interview apparently ended, it is possible to hear the bored but polite voice of the Producer – Ed.*]

Producer (over studio intercom): Thank you very much, Sir Humphrey. Absolutely splendid.

[*And now the conversation continues, the tape still running even after the interview is finished – Ed.*]

Sir Humphrey: Was that all right?

Interviewer: Couldn't you have said a little more? At least about unemployment?

Sir Humphrey: Such as?

Interviewer: Well, the truth.

Sir Humphrey laughs.

Interviewer: Why do you laugh?

Sir Humphrey: My dear chap, no one tells the truth about unemployment.

Interviewer: Why not?

Sir Humphrey: Because everyone knows you could halve it in a few weeks.

Interviewer: How?

Sir Humphrey: Cut off all social security to any claimant who refused two job offers. There is genuine unemployment in the north, but the south of England is awash with layabouts, many of them graduates, living off the dole and housing benefit plus quite a lot of cash they pick up without telling anyone.

Interviewer: You mean moonlighting.

Sir Humphrey: Well, it's cheating really. They'd need to earn nearly £200 a week to be better off working full time. But there are thousands upon thousands of unfilled vacancies and most employers tell you they're short-staffed. Offer the unemployed a street-sweeping job and a dishwashing job, and they'd be off the register before you can say 'parasite'. Frankly, this country can have as much unemployment as it's prepared to pay for in social security. And no politicians have the guts to do anything about it.

Interviewer: I wish you'd said that before.

Sir Humphrey: I'm sure you do.

[*The tape ends at this point. Sir Bernard Woolley recalls*[1] *the tape's progress – Ed.*]

The following day Sir Humphrey had asked me to obtain a cassette player, so that he could listen to a cassette that the BBC had sent to him. He was rather excited, because he felt that he had given a thought-provoking, dynamic and thoroughly exciting interview, albeit couched in his usual low-key language.

I had borrowed a ghettoblaster from one of the Garden Room Girls [*the upper-crust members of the typing pool in the basement of Number Ten – Ed.*]. Sir Humphrey had not heard the word ghettoblaster, and enquired if it was used in the demolition industry. How true – the demolition of hearing!

There had been a note attached to the cassette. [*We reproduce it overleaf – Ed.*]

[1] In conversation with the Editors.

Sir Humphrey Appleby
Cabinet Office
70 Whitehall
London SW1   November 27th

Dear Sir Humphrey,

Here is a copy of the off-the-record part of your radio
interview. We found it particularly interesting. I will
contact you shortly.

Yours sincerely,

Crawford James

Crawford James
(Producer, Talks)

The letter struck me as suspicious, for several reasons. Firstly, it seemed to be less than straightforward. What could he mean by 'particularly interesting'? Secondly, I have always had an instinctive distrust of people whose Christian names and surnames are reversible. But when I expressed surprise that his interview could be described as interesting, Sir Humphrey took umbrage – though I don't know why, because his stated intention had been to say nothing, as always.

I had doubted his ability to say nothing on the radio, and the letter had prepared me for a surprise. But not for a surprise of the magnitude that I then encountered. For we switched on the ghettoblaster and I heard a voice that sounded horribly like Humphrey's saying, 'My dear chap, no one tells the truth about unemployment.'

'Why not?' came the question.

'Because', said Humphrey's voice, 'everyone knows you could halve it in a few weeks.'

I looked at Humphrey in horror. He looked at me, poleaxed.

'How?' continued the inexorable tape recording.

'Cut off all social security to any claimant who refused two job offers.'

Humphrey lunged at the ghettoblaster. I think he was trying to switch it off but he pressed *fast forward* by mistake. His voice mickey-moused forward at high speed until he let go of the switch – at which point we heard the fatal words: 'And no politicians have the guts to do anything about it.'

I leaned forward and switched it off myself. We gazed at each other for a long time, in total silence. For the first time I was aware of the distant hum of traffic on the Mall.

Finally I spoke. I had to be sure. 'Sir Humphrey,' I asked quietly, 'that was you, wasn't it?'

'Yes, Bernard.'

'Not Mike Yarwood?'[1]

A faint ray of hope crossed his haggard visage. 'Do you think I could say it was?'

I shook my head gloomily. 'No, they could prove it was you,' I said. I could hardly believe that he had said those things. I asked if there was more. He nodded mutely.

'As damaging as we just heard?'

He nodded again. He seemed unable to speak. But I waited patiently and eventually he croaked, with the voice of a broken man: 'More damaging. I believe I referred to parasites.'

I was incredulous. I asked him how he could have been so indiscreet. He explained pathetically that the interview was over – so he thought! – and that they were just chatting harmlessly. Harmlessly!

'It was off the record,' he said.

'Maybe – but it's on the tape,' I remarked.

[1] A well-known impressionist of the 1980s.

Suddenly, uttering an anguished cry of 'My God!', Humphrey smote his forehead and leapt to his feet. 'Oh my God, oh my God!' he moaned desperately. 'I've just realised. It's blackmail!' And he grasped the letter and shoved it into my hand.

I re-read the ominous document. It certainly looked like blackmail. My suspicions appeared to have been well-founded.

Humphrey stared at me, hollow-eyed, his tie crooked, his hair – usually so immaculately brushed and neatly parted – standing up on end as if he had been awoken at 3.41 am by the ghost of Stanley Baldwin.

'What do they want of me?' he moaned.

I pondered the question carefully. What did the BBC want of Humphrey? What did it want of anyone? This was one of the abiding mysteries of the twentieth century, not to be solved at such short notice by such a one as I.

I tried to think politically, always difficult for someone like myself who has spent a lifetime in the Civil Service. Perhaps, I wondered, the BBC wanted the licence up fifty per cent? Or maybe it was a *private* blackmail by the Producer/Talks, to ensure that the Producer *didn't* talk.

Humphrey was crumbling before my eyes. A piteous sight. He sank into a Chippendale armchair and leaned forward, his head in his hands. 'Doesn't he know I'm a poor man?' he cried.

I wondered. It occurred to me that the Producer/Talks may not have read that Sir Humphrey lived in Haslemere in abject poverty on seventy-five thousand a year.

'What'll I do?' Sir Humphrey, wide-eyed and terrified, was staring ruin in the face.

'Keep your mouth shut in future,' I advised him.

'I mean *now!*' he snapped, staring *me* in the face instead.

I didn't see what he could do, except wait and hope. Wait to see what they demanded. Hope that they hadn't yet distributed cassettes to every national newspaper. I had private visions and horrid imaginings of horrific headlines. CABINET SECRETARY CALLS UNEMPLOYED PARASITES, or GOVERNMENT HAS NO GUTS, SAYS SIR HUMPHREY.

I shared my visions with him. He sat there, stunned, begging me not to breathe a word about it to anyone.

I was perfectly willing not to spread it around Whitehall generally, even though I could have dined out on it for months. But Humphrey's 'anyone' appeared to include the Prime Minister, and I was forced to point out that my duty to him was paramount.

Humphrey tried to regain his authority. He stood up, and faced me squarely. 'Bernard, I am ordering you!'

'Very good, Sir Humphrey,' I replied. 'I shall tell him that you have ordered me not to tell him.'

Hoist by his own petard, he acknowledged defeat, sat down, leaned back and asked the ceiling what he was going to do.

Although he did not appear to be addressing me, hesitantly I offered the only suggestion that I could think of: that he put out a press statement expressing sympathy for the unemployed. After all, he was likely to be joining them at any moment.

[*Hacker's diary continues – Ed.*]

November 28th
I was sitting in the Cabinet Room, all alone, thinking, when Bernard interrupted me.

I asked him what he wanted.

'Excuse me a moment, Prime Minister, but as you don't appear to be doing anything I wondered if I might have a word.'

I gave him an unwelcome stare. 'As a matter of fact,' I replied curtly, 'I am busy. I'm wondering whether to tell the Cabinet about this bugging business. Do I tell them what I told the House, or do I tell them the truth?'

Bernard did not hesitate. 'Prime Minister, may I venture to suggest that perhaps you should behave to the Cabinet as you would expect them to behave to you?'

'You're absolutely right,' I told Bernard. 'I'll tell them what I told the House.'

I returned to the mass of papers on the table and was just starting to read an eighty-page briefing about possible replacements for the anti-missile missile when I heard Bernard cough. He was still there, obviously wanting to get something off his chest.

'What's the matter now, Bernard?'

'Yes, there is a matter, that you need to know.'

Suddenly I was on the alert. 'Need to know?'

I didn't quite gather what he said next. Why is it that both Bernard and Humphrey are pathologically incapable of making themselves clear whenever we're talking about 'need to know' matters? They seem bent on telling me things in such a way that they haven't actually told me at all.

SIR BERNARD WOOLLEY RECALLS:[1]
I was certainly not intending to be oblique in my speech, though I was fairly highly strung. I have looked up my own diaries. All I said was that Hacker needed to know, particularly because Sir Humphrey had particularly asked me to be discreet about the particulars of this particular matter. I reminded

---

[1] In conversation with the Editors.

Hacker that he [Hacker] knew that Humphrey was very particular, particularly about what Hacker needed to know and what Humphrey needed Hacker to know, which he thought he didn't. Need Hacker to know, that is.

I should have thought that was perfectly clear.

[*Hacker's diary continues – Ed.*]

It appeared that my Private Secretary was talking about Sir Humphrey's radio broadcast. 'Was it boring?'

'Initially, yes,' said Bernard. 'But then it livened up immensely as he became more and more indiscreet.'

I could hardly believe my ears. 'Humphrey? Indiscreet? On the air?'

'Well, he thought the broadcast was over, so he was just chatting. Unofficially. But the tape was still running.'

I began to have a sinking feeling in my stomach. And my heart was literally in my mouth. [*If so, Hacker had a uniquely mobile anatomy – Ed.*] 'He fell for that old dodge?'

Bernard nodded.

'You *always* treat an open microphone as a live one. Doesn't he know that?'

Bernard tried to defend him. 'I don't think he's done a lot of broadcasting, Prime Minister.'

'It sounds as if he's done too much,' I complained. 'Have you heard the tape?'

'A copy, yes.'

'What did he say?'

'Something about it being possible to halve unemployment tomorrow, only the government hasn't got the guts.'

I was so horrified that I wasn't even angry. I just sat and stared.

Bernard tried to explain. 'He didn't know it was being recorded.'

The hideous implications were racing through my head. If the BBC kept the original, which Bernard seemed to believe as they'd sent Humphrey 'a copy', it meant that the story would be all over the papers tomorrow. Yet Bernard didn't seem at all concerned. He simply remarked that Humphrey had not given much thought to the newspapers – yet. He was more worried about the blackmail threat.

Blackmail threat? This was news to me.

'There was an accompanying letter, saying the sender would be in touch shortly. They sent the cassette to Sir Humphrey – which means they have kept the original reel-to-reel tape.'

I had visions of private pirate copies of the tape all over Broadcasting House by tomorrow. 'Bernard!' I said decisively, 'you must do something.'

'Actually, Prime Minister, I've done it already.'

I was not wholly surprised. He was so calm that I'd known that he had it under control somehow.

'I was at Oxford with the producer. When I rang the BBC he reminded me of this. I had not remembered him at all, but it appears that we had mutual friends and he had vivid memories of one of my speeches at the Union – I spoke eloquently in favour of the *status quo* one night. Apparently he was the unobtrusive little chap who used to record the debates. Anyway, it transpires that he never had the slightest intention of releasing the tape. So I got him to give it to me.'

Whereupon Bernard produced a spool of tape from his pocket.

'Is that the original?' Bernard nodded. 'There are no other copies?' He nodded again. 'And does Humphrey know you've got it?' Bernard shook his head. A slow smile of deep content spread across my face. And Bernard's.

'Shall I tell him?' he asked innocently.

'Why?' I enquired.

'I think . . .' Bernard was stepping carefully '. . . that he'd like to know.'

'I'm sure he would,' I countered. 'But does he need to know?'

'Ah,' replied Bernard. There was a gleam in his eye. He thought for a moment. Then he said – and I know because I got him to repeat it – 'You mean *somebody* needs to know, but if you now know then Sir Humphrey doesn't need to know and you need to know Sir Humphrey doesn't know, and he doesn't need to know you know or that you know he doesn't need to know?'

I stared at Bernard, marvelling at the uselessness of an education in logic. 'I couldn't have put it less clearly myself,' I said.

Bernard asked me if I'd like to hear the tape. Of course I was dying to – but then I got a great idea. 'I think it deserves a wider audience, don't you? I think Humphrey should hear it too. Ask him to join us, would you, Bernard?'

He didn't need to be asked twice. He hurried to the phone. 'Tell Sir Humphrey the Prime Minister wants him . . . straight away!'

He hung up and scurried out of the room gleefully to fetch the tape-recorder. On his return, as he threaded the tape from reel to reel, he reminded me that he had told me all this in confidence. It was unnecessary – I always respect confidences.

By now he was grinning from ear to ear. I tried to arrange my face into a solemn expression and told Bernard that this was a very serious matter.

'Yes Prime Minister,' he said, the corners of his mouth twitching.

There was a knock. Humphrey's head appeared round the door. 'You sent for me, Prime Minister?'

'Ah yes. Come in, Humphrey, come in. How did the broadcast go?'

He's not a bad liar. 'Very well. Very well.'

'Good, good,' I murmured amiably. 'Do you remember what you said?'

Sir Humphrey appeared to have only the vaguest recollections. 'Oh, nothing in particular,' he drawled. 'I think I pointed out some of the difficulties in allocating responsibilities as between politicians and civil servants.'

'But were you discreet?'

He cleared his throat. 'Why do you ask?'

'Were you or weren't you?'

A slight pause. 'Yes.'

'Yes you were or yes you weren't?'

'Yes.'

'Humphrey!'

He challenged me. 'Wouldn't you expect me to be discreet?'

'Yes, I would,' I said.

'There you are then,' he retorted, neatly begging the question.

'I see,' I said. 'Then that's all right.' And I treated him to one of my piercing stares.

He wriggled about in his chair, crossed his legs, uncrossed them, and cleared his throat again. 'Why do you ask, Prime Minister?' His voice sounded higher-pitched than usual.

'Because the BBC has just sent me a tape.' He flinched. I showed him the tape-recorder, set up on the table near the door. He hadn't seen it when he came in.

He swallowed. 'A tape? What tape?'

I pretended unconcern. 'Just a tape, Humphrey. Of you. I thought it might be fun for us to listen to your broadcast together.' And I walked towards the tape-recorder.

'No.' He stood up. 'No. No.'

I turned, as if surprised. 'Why not?'

'It . . . it wasn't at all interesting.'

I chuckled. 'Humphrey, you carry modesty and self-effacement too far. Not interesting? The Cabinet Secretary talking to the nation about government?'

His eyes were shifty. 'Well, not very interesting.'

'You mean,' I suggested, 'that you were *too* discreet?'

He was silent. He knew I knew. And I knew he knew I knew. And Bernard knew I knew he knew I knew. [*Hacker was spending too much time with Bernard Woolley – Ed*.] I switched on the tape.

I must say that even I was unprepared for the astounding remarks I heard. Sir Humphrey saying that no one tells the truth, that unemployment could be halved in a few weeks, talk of layabouts, moonlighting, and parasites.

I switched off the tape. And I stared at him in silence.

Never have I seen a more woebegone figure than the Secretary of the Cabinet and the Head of the Home Civil Service. He stared at me, unable – apparently – even to excuse himself. So I just waited. And finally he blurted out: 'Prime Minister, I'm terribly sorry, I had no idea, they didn't tell me. You see, we'd finished the broadcast and . . .'

I held up my hand for silence. 'Humphrey! The irresponsibility! Is there any more?'

'No,' said Humphrey.

'Yes,' said Bernard.

I said, 'We'd better hear it.'

'No,' said Humphrey.

Bernard restarted the tape. 'Frankly,' said Humphrey's cheerful, complacent voice, 'this country can have as much unemployment as it's prepared to pay for in social security. And no politicians have the guts to do anything about it.'

The tape stopped. Silence reigned supreme. I couldn't believe that Humphrey had been foolish enough to talk like that in public, even though *I* knew that it would never be broadcast.

'How could you say that?' I asked finally.

'I . . . I . . . it was Mike Yarwood,' he explained in a strangled voice.

'Was it?' I asked.

'No,' said Bernard.

I wandered from the table over to the window. The afternoon November sky was black and heavy with rain. 'I really don't know how to handle this,' I mused. 'I shall have to take advice.'

'Advice?' whispered Sir Humphrey.

'Yes,' I said, turning the knife in the wound. 'I think I'd better play it to the Cabinet. Get their reaction.'

He seemed on the verge of falling to his knees. But 'Oh please' was all he could say.

'Or the Privy Council,' I suggested.

'Oh please,' he begged.

'Or Her Majesty,' I said lightly.

'Oh God!' he groaned, and collapsed into a chair again.

I walked across the room and stood over him. 'Suppose this were to get into the papers? How much damage do you think it would do me? And the government?'

Humphrey, of course, still believed that it *would* get into the papers. 'I shall say I was wrong. That I've checked the figures and it's not true.'

'But it *is* true!' I hissed.

'But I can say it's not. Nobody can prove it. It's never been tried.'

I pretended shock. 'You would deny the truth? In public?'

'Yes Prime Minister. For you!' For me indeed!

He had other ideas. 'We could issue a clarification to the press.'

I indicated the tape. 'I think your views are quite clear.'

'Prime Minister, in government a clarification is not to make things clear, it is put you in the clear.'

'I don't think even a wizard such as yourself could do that here,' I said. 'But I'm touched that you would be willing to lie for me – and I'll take a raincheck on that. And now I've got something to tell you.' And I put him out of his misery. 'Bernard, give Humphrey the tape. Humphrey, this is the original. The master.'

It took him a moment or two to assimilate the news. 'You mean . . .'

'There are no other copies,' I reassured him. 'It has been retrieved from the BBC.'

'How? By whom?'

Bernard flashed a desperate, wide-eyed *remember your promise* look at me. But he needn't have worried.

'Intelligence,' I said calmly.

Bernard visibly relaxed.

'So – you mean it's all right?' asked Humphrey, hopeful but very subdued.

I didn't want to let him right off the hook. I had an important trade-off to offer. 'It depends what you mean by all right,' I said.

'Nobody will ever know?' That's what *he* meant. But I thought about his question, as he waited on tenterhooks.

'I suppose', I answered eventually, 'that depends on whether I choose to tell them. I mean, I could just hand you the tape . . . or I could hold on to it while I consider the security and disciplinary implications. I certainly can't become involved in some shabby cover-up.'

He was waiting for the verdict of the court. So I offered him my deal, casually. 'Oh Humphrey, one other thing. When do you appear before the Committee?'

'Tomorrow, Prime Minister.'

'And have you decided yet what to tell them? About my authorising the tapping of MPs' phones?'

'Oh. Yes. Yes. I've . . . er . . .' he tried to focus on his vague memories of that other problem, the tape recording having temporarily driven all else from his mind. 'I've been thinking about it a lot. Very hard.'

I asked him for his conclusions. They were not wholly surprising. 'I have concluded, Prime Minister, that in the interests of National Security the only honourable course is to support your statement in the House.'

I prompted him. 'You'll say that Hugh Halifax's phone was never bugged?'

'I'll say that I have no evidence that – '

I stopped him mid-sentence. 'No, Humphrey. You'll say that the Government has never authorised any tapping of MPs' phones.'

He breathed deeply. 'And I'll say that the Government has never authorised any tapping of MPs' phones.'

I smiled. He whispered: 'What happens if they ever find out the truth?'

I couldn't even see a problem there. 'You'll have to say that nobody told you. Because you didn't need to know. Agreed?'

He nodded. I handed him the tape. 'Is that settled then?'

'Yes Prime Minister,' he muttered, and clasped the spools of tape close to his heart.

7
The Patron of the Arts

December 3rd

'Do you think perhaps . . .' asked Bernard hesitantly, 'I mean, would it have been wiser? . . . you know, with hindsight, was it a mistake?'

'Yes Bernard,' I said.

We were discussing the British Theatre Awards, a really unimportant, self-serving, narcissistic gathering, and not one on which the time of the Prime Minister should be wasted.

But Malcolm, my press officer, Bernard and I had spent the best part of an hour wondering how to handle the hideous predicament in which I find myself.

The irony is, I certainly didn't have to agree to present these awards. Malcolm recommended it! He is denying that now, of course. 'With respect, Prime Minister, I didn't actually recommend it. I just said that the British Theatre Awards dinner was being televised live and that as the guest of honour you'd be seen by twelve million people in a context of glamour, fun and entertainment. And that you'd be associated with all the star actors and actresses who give pleasure to millions.'

'And you don't call that a recommendation?' I was incredulous. 'It was worth ten points in the opinion polls, the way you described it.'

Malcolm nodded mournfully. But Bernard was confused. 'Isn't it a bad idea to be associated with actors? I mean, their job is pretending to be what they're not. And if you're seen with them, well, people might realise . . .'

He stopped short. Might *realise*? I stared at him, daring him to continue. 'Go on, Bernard,' I invited him with menace.

He hesitated. 'Er, I mean, not *realise* exactly . . . might suspect, might think that you were . . . I mean, I don't mean they'd think you were *entertaining*, obviously not, I mean, they might see you were pretending . . . Um, what was it you wanted to speak to Malcolm about?' he finished desperately.

The problem would have been clear to anyone except an ivory-tower career Civil Servant like Bernard. Malcolm had assured me that it would be a non-controversial occasion: there would be no other politicians there, and actors and actresses are usually nice to politicians because they live on flattery and some of them dish it out as eagerly as they receive it.

But nobody had thought it through. Accusingly, I tapped the file in front of me. 'What about this?' I asked.

Malcolm was embarrassed. 'I'm sorry, Prime Minister, but we didn't know about that when we accepted the invitation.'

All I can say is, he *should* have known. He should have found out. That's what he's paid for. 'You knew the government was being criticised for not spending enough on the arts?'

He shrugged. 'All governments are always criticised for not spending enough on the arts.'

Bernard hastened to agree. 'It's the standard way for arts journalists to suck up to actors and directors. That's how they get back on speaking terms after they've given them bad reviews.'

'But you knew – or should have known – what the situation would be,' I insisted.

Malcolm stubbornly refused to concede the point. 'No, Prime Minister, we didn't know how small the Arts Council grant increase was going to be. How could we? It was only finalised yesterday.'

He was right. And it was my fault, though I didn't admit it – I had insisted on no leaks. Hoist by my own petard *again*. Yesterday the news broke that there'd be virtually no increase in grant for the National Theatre. And, by a hideous coincidence, the Chief Associate Director of the National Theatre is Chairman of the Awards Dinner, making the speech that introduces me, which will inevitably be full of snide remarks and sarcastic jokes, and which is bound to portray me as a mean-spirited Philistine. Live on TV, in front of twelve million people.

'What about when I make my speech?' I asked hopelessly. 'The audience will be totally hostile. There may even be boos.'

'There's always lots of boos,' said Malcolm. I was appalled. Was he serious? 'But we don't have to pay for it,' he continued reassuringly. I suddenly realised he meant booze, not boos.

'Booo!' I hooted in explanation, and added a 'Sssss' for good measure.

Bernard was amazed. 'Do actors boo?' he asked, wide-eyed. 'I thought audiences did that.'

187

'It's an audience full of actors,' I reminded him. 'It's their only chance in the year to do any booing, to get their own back on all the people who boo them.'

Bernard made a suggestion. 'Why don't you go back to the Arts Minister and ask for an increase in the grant? Or, better still, send him along to the dinner instead of you. That way they'll all blame him. That's what junior ministers are for, isn't it?'

On the face of it, it was a smart idea. But on reflection I realised it wouldn't work. 'He'd just blame the Treasury.'

'You could talk to the Treasury,' countered Bernard.

I've been doing that. That's the problem. For six weeks I've been telling them to cut spending!

'It's still better to send the Arts Minister,' insisted Bernard.

'Is it?' I didn't believe it. 'Can't you see the headlines? JIM CHICKENS OUT. PRIME MINISTER RUNS AWAY FROM CRITICS.'

'They wouldn't say that if you had a major crisis to deal with.'

I turned to Malcolm. 'Any major crises coming up, Malcolm?'

Sadly, he shook his head. 'Not really, Prime Minister.'

Incredible, that the lack of a crisis should be bad news for us! I racked my brains, but I couldn't think of one either. 'Any distant crisis we could bring forward?' Malcolm and Bernard shook their heads hopelessly.

I tried to approach the problem positively. 'What sort of crisis would justify cancellation?'

Bernard could think of plenty. 'The pound plunging, small war in the South Atlantic, nuclear power station catching fire . . .'

I stopped him. 'Bernard,' I explained gently, 'I don't think any of those would help improve my image either.'

'No, but they'd justify you staying away,' he said, completely forgetting that the whole idea was – if not to improve my image – at least to prevent it from deteriorating further.

Bernard had a sudden inspiration. 'I know! How about the death of a Cabinet collague.'

'That would certainly do it! Is one imminent?' I asked, trying not to appear too hopeful.

'No,' said Bernard cheerfully, glad to have solved what was, to him, an academic problem. 'But that would justify your absence without damaging your image, wouldn't it?'

Malcolm agreed. 'He's right. But we can hardly hope for that to fall on the right day. At least not by accident,' he added darkly.

Was he hinting? I sincerely hope not. I could see that I really had no option, not at such short notice. 'I'll have to go,' I decided. 'I'll keep a stiff upper lip. Grin and bear it.'

Bernard said, 'You can't actually grin with a stiff upper lip because . . .' And he demonstrated. 'You see, stiff lips won't stretch horizontally . . .'

I might have hit him but he was saved by the bell – the telephone bell. Sir Humphrey was outside, ever anxious to discuss the agenda for Cabinet.

I welcomed him. 'Ah Humphrey, never mind that agenda, I need help.'

'You do!' Instantly I fixed my beady eye on him. 'You do?' I wasn't sure if he was asking or agreeing.

'I've got to make a speech,' I began. 'And I think it could be very embarrassing.'

'Oh Prime Minister, your speeches are nothing like as embarrassing as they used to be. In fact . . .'

These Civil Servants really are appallingly patronising. 'No, Humphrey. I didn't say my speech would be embarrassing, I said the occasion would be.'

'Indeed? Why?'

I explained as impartially as I could. 'It'll be to an audience of hostile, narcissistic, posturing, self-righteous theatrical drunks.'

'The House of Commons, you mean.'

I explained, in words of one syllable, that I meant the British Theatre Awards at the Dorchester.[1] Being the guest of honour is not much of an honour if they don't honour the guest.

Humphrey got the point at once. 'The small Arts Council grant, you mean? Well, it's very hard to influence the Chief Associate Director of the National Theatre, as I know only too well. I'm on the Board of Governors.'

I hadn't realised that. So I asked him what I do about it? How do I make the theatrical community feel that I'm really one of them?

'Surely,' murmured Humphrey acidly, 'you don't want them to see *you* as a narcissistic, posturing, self-righteous theatrical drunk?'

'Not that it would be very difficult,' said Bernard. I suppose he was alluding to my histrionic talents. After all, great statesmen have to be great actors. [*Hacker begs an important question here – Ed.*] Nonetheless, the programme will be live on TV, and I can hardly risk a hostile reception.

[1] Hotel.

Humphrey clearly felt that it was inevitable. 'With respect, Prime Minister, if one is going to walk into the lions' den, one should not start by taking away the lions' dinner.'

'So what is your advice?'

'Give them more of their dinner back. Increase the grant to the Arts Council. An extra two million or so would make a significant difference.'

'Two million? That would make it a fairly expensive dinner.'

Humphrey smiled. 'Well, it is the Dorchester.'

This was hardly an impartial recommendation. As a Governor of that subversive body [*The National Theatre, not the Dorchester Hotel – Ed.*] he has a vested interest. And a conflict of interest too! Well, he may want to support that bloody place! But I don't owe them anything. They keep putting on plays attacking me. They set *The Comedy of Errors* in Ten Downing Street. And, I reminded him, they did a modern-dress *Richard II*, making him into a foolish, vainglorious national leader who got booted out for incompetence. 'Don't deny it, Humphrey! I know who they were getting at.'

'I was only going to suggest, Prime Minister, that it was better than setting *Macbeth* in Number Ten.'

A feeble excuse. The truth is, they hate me there. 'They did a whole play attacking our nuclear policy,' I reminded him. 'A farce.'

'The policy?'

'The *play*, Humphrey!' He knew very well what I meant. I asked him why they did it, and why he wasn't concerned.

'It's very healthy, Prime Minister.'

'Healthy?' I couldn't see how.

'Practically nobody goes to political plays.' He sat back and crossed his legs urbanely. 'And half of those that go don't understand them. And half of those who understand them don't agree with them. And the seven who are left would have voted against the government anyway. Meanwhile, it lets people let off steam, and you look like a democratic statesman – with a good sense of humour! – for subsidising your critics.'

I still didn't see that the pros outweighed the cons. 'If they want to criticise me they should pay for it themselves. From the Box Office.'

Humphrey couldn't see that logic. 'Prime Minister, they'd never make enough money. Plays criticising the government make the second most boring theatrical evenings ever invented.'

I was curious. 'What are the most boring?'

'Plays praising the government.'

Personally I should have thought that they'd be much more interesting. And I still couldn't see why a theatre should insult me and then expect me to give it more money. But Humphrey explained that this is what artists always do. 'Undignified, isn't it? They advance towards the government on their knees, shaking their fists.'

'And beating me over the head with a begging bowl.'

'Um, Prime Minister,' said Bernard, 'they can't beat you over the head if they're on their knees. Not unless you're on your knees too, or unless they've got very long arms.'

I waited patiently. This pedantic wittering is the price I have to pay for Bernard's undoubted efficiency. Unfortunately it's this obsessive attention to detail that makes him both irritating and essential. I waited till he stopped talking, then I turned back to Malcolm.

'Isn't it true that there are no votes for me in giving money to the Arts?'

'Yes . . . but there's a lot of terrible publicity if you take it away.'

He's right. It's so unfair.

Humphrey spoke up for his vested interest again. 'It's not really unfair, Prime Minister. The arts lobby is part of the educated middle class. It's one of the few ways they can get their income tax back. Mortgage tax relief, university grants for their children, lump-sum pensions . . . and cheap subsidised seats at the theatre, the opera and the concert. You shouldn't begrudge it to them.'

I ticked him off. 'Humphrey, you're getting off the point.'

'Ah,' he replied gravely, 'what was the point?'

Unfortunately I couldn't remember. Bernard had to remind me. 'How to stop the Chief Associate Director of the National Theatre criticising you in his speech on Sunday.'

'That's *right*!' I turned emphatically to Humphrey. 'And since you know him, I suggest you have a quick word with him. You might point out that the knighthood which he might expect in the course of time is within the gift of the Prime Minister.'

Humphrey wasn't impressed with this plan. 'Frankly, Prime Minister, he told me he couldn't care less about a knighthood.'

Humphrey's being silly. Everyone says that about a knighthood until it's actually dangled before them.

[*Sir Humphrey Appleby did indeed have lunch with Simon Monk of the National Theatre. They met in the restaurant front-of-house, where it could be guaranteed that their meeting would be completely discreet and unobserved owing to the unique food offered by that estab-*

lishment. The luncheon is referred to in Simon Monk's best-selling autobiography Sound and Fury – *Ed.*]

We met in the theatre restaurant. Sir Humphrey Appleby had telephoned me previously, wanting to meet in a place where we wouldn't be overheard by people at the next table. Naturally I suggested our restaurant, where it was unlikely that there would be any people at the next table.

Sir Humphrey told me that the Prime Minister was paranoid again, about plays that attacked him. I asked Humphrey to tell Hacker that no one has ever submitted a play defending him, but Humphrey wasn't sure that that would help.

Hacker's in politics. He's fair game. It seemed to me that hostile plays are just one of the crosses he had to bear. To his credit, Humphrey wasn't a bit concerned either. 'He can bear any number of crosses,' he said with a sly grin, 'so long as they're in the right place on the ballot paper.'

Actually, I couldn't have cared less about Hacker's problems. He doesn't spare a thought for mine. All I wanted to know was what that year's Art Council grant was going to be. The Council needed the extra £30 million that it had applied for.

But Humphrey was enigmatic. 'My dear Simon! I couldn't disclose the figure in advance. Least of all to one of the Directors of the National Theatre.'

I didn't expect him to disclose it, not in so many words. So I picked up the bowl of Grissini breadsticks that was on the table and offered them to him. 'Have some of these,' I offered.

Humphrey carefully took three Grissini, and offered them to me.

I was appalled. 'Only *three*?'

I couldn't believe it! But Humphrey nodded gloomily. 'I'm afraid it's the new diet. Three breadsticks is the absolute maximum.'

'Is that gross breadsticks or net breadsticks?' I asked.

'Net breadsticks.'

I had to ask the next question, but I dreaded the answer. 'Then how much are we going to get at the National?'

Solemnly Humphrey broke approximately one quarter off one of the breadsticks and handed it to me.

'Only a quarter? But that's disastrous! How do they expect us to manage on a quarter of a million?' [*It should be noted that the amount in question was a* raise *of a quarter of a million – Ed.*]

Sir Humphrey looked innocent. 'I don't know where you got that figure from.' He loves playing his little games.

I begged him to help. The problem was serious – and genuine. A quarter of a million was not merely less than we had told the *press* was the absolute minimum to stave off disaster – it was lower even than the *real* minimum required to stave off disaster.

Humphrey said that he could help no further. Even though he's on the Board of the Theatre he explained his first allegiance is to the Government and the Prime Minister. But this turned out to be another of his little games, for he continued: 'Let me make it quite clear that I am here to represent the Prime Minister's interests. Now, certain things would gravely embarrass him. I must urge you on his behalf not to contemplate them.'

I got my notepad out. Things were looking up. 'Good,' I said. 'What are they?'

He smiled. 'Well, you will be making the speech introducing him at the Awards dinner. It would be a courtesy to submit a draft to Number Ten in advance.'

'For approval?' I was surprised.

'Let us say . . . for information.' I saw the point. 'The Prime Minister is extremely anxious that your speech should not refer to the modesty of the grant increase. There are certain words he wants you to avoid: *Miserly, Philistine, Barbarism, Skinflint, Killjoy.*' I was writing as fast as I could. Humphrey speaks fast. 'He also wants you to omit all reference to how much other countries spend on the arts.'

I asked him for the figures. He immediately produced a sheet of paper. 'There you are. To make sure you don't mention them by accident.'

'I certainly won't mention them by accident,' I confirmed.

'Most important of all,' concluded Sir Humphrey, 'the Prime Minister wants absolutely no comparison between the extra money your theatre needs and certain sums the Goverent spent last year on certain projects.'

He was being more oblique than usual. I asked him to be more specific.

'Well, suppose the sum you need is four million. Purely as an example, you understand. The Prime Minister earnestly hopes you will not draw attention to the fact that the Government spent five million on radar equipment for a fighter plane that had already been scrapped. Or that the Department of Energy has been able to afford to stockpile a thousand years' supply of filing tabs. Or that another department has stocked up with a millions tins of Vim. Not to mention a billion pounds written off the Nimrod early warning aircraft system.'

'Anything else we can do?' I asked, writing furiously.

'Those are things you can't do,' he reminded me hypocritically. 'What you *could* do is . . . perhaps arrange for the Prime Minister to get an award of some sort? And let him know in advance?'

This was a tall order. An award for Hacker? What on earth for? Philistine of the Year was the only title I could think of. I pointed out that he never even goes to the theatre.

To my surprise, Sir Humphrey defended him. 'He can't really, he's frightened of giving the cartoonists and gossip columnists too much ammunition. He couldn't go to *A Month in the Country* because it would start rumours about a general election, he couldn't go to *The Rivals* because there have been so many Cabinet Ministers after his job, and he couldn't go to *The School for Scandal* for fear of reminding the electorate that the Secretary of State for Education was found in bed with that primary school headmistress.'

I almost felt sorry for Hacker.

'And as for that Ibsen you did, *An Enemy of the People* . . .' I'd got the point. 'So if you could give him some flattering honorary title, that would improve his image and appeal to his sense of self-importance . . .'

What on earth did Humphrey have in mind? Actor of the Year? For the most polished performance, disguising one backstage catastrophe after another? I suggested it.

'Very droll,' chuckled Humphrey. 'No, I think Comic Performance of the Year might be more appropriate.'

I topped him. 'Tragic Performance of the Year!'

'Both!' said Humphrey, and we fell around.

[*Hacker's diary continues – Ed.*]

December 4th

A meeting with Nick Everitt, the Arts Minister. He was in a bit of a state. He's been got at, he's losing his nerve! He was party to the decision about the Arts Council grant – oh no he wasn't, I forgot he's not in the Cabinet, but it's a free country, he could have resigned if he didn't want to support it! Anyway, it's a Government decision, a collective decision, he's part of the Government and he's got to accept it whether it was his decision or not. That's democracy.

'Jim,' he said, 'I think there's going to be terrible trouble when they find out how small the grant increase is.'

'We'll just have to brazen it out,' I said. 'Won't you?'

He didn't look too happy, peering out nervously through his big rectangular glasses. Young, earnest, and a regular visitor to Glyndebourne, he didn't like being accused of Philistinism. 'I do think we'll have to try and find a bit more.'

I told him we'd been through it all before. He shook his head. 'We haven't really taken the employment argument on board.'

I sighed. The employment of actors cannot be allowed to dictate our fiscal policy, however famous and vocal they are. I told Nick that they'd just have to get other jobs, outside the theatre.

'They can't. Actors are unemployable outside the theatre. A lot of them are unemployable in it.'

He's one hundred per cent wrong about that. Annie tells me that half the mini-cab drivers she meets are out-of-work actors.

Nick had a different explanation. 'Most mini-cab drivers *say* they're out of work actors. It's more glamorous than describing yourself as a "moonlighting nightwatchman".'

Bernard raised a forefinger and looked in my direction. Apparently he felt he had a useful contribution to make to the discussion. 'Er, nightwatchmen can't moonlight. It's a moonlight job to start with. If they drove minicabs they'd be sunlighting.'

Nick went through all the arguments that the Treasury had already rejected. 'The theatre brings in tourists,' he declaimed with passion.

'Fine.' I stayed cool. 'Then the British Tourist Authority should subsidise it.'

'But they won't,' he complained. 'That's the trouble. They say they've got better ways of attracting them.'

'So,' I summed up, 'you want us to subsidise a bad way of attracting tourists.' He tried to interrupt. 'No, Nick, we waste too much on the Arts anyway.'

He flinched. Then he tried the old chestnut about how the arts are educational. Maybe – but why should I give public money to people who use it for the very uneducational purposes of attacking me?

'We'd have to spend the money anyway,' said Nick, trying his final ploy. 'It's only a concealed way of preserving old buildings.'

I couldn't see what he meant. 'All those theatres and art galleries and museums and opera houses are listed buildings,' he pleaded. 'We'd have to maintain them anyway. And they're totally useless otherwise. So we put in central heating and a curator and roll it into the grant to make it look as if we're supporting the Arts.'

Half true; but not persuasive enough. I have a simpler solution. We'll sell them.

December 5th

This Arts Council crisis is becoming a bloody nuisance. Tonight we had a drinks and buffet party at Number Ten. A couple of hundred guests, many of them theatricals – we always do this to attract good publicity but tonight's do was organised many weeks ago and, had we known, we would have invited a more respectful bunch: backbench MPs, for instance, who never argue with me on social occasions and usually confine themselves to getting harmlessly pissed. It's a change from Annie's Bar.[1]

As a matter of fact, I've often thought that we should breathalyse

[1] One of the many House of Commons bars.

MPs – not when they're driving but when they're legislating. I would guess that well over fifty per cent are over the legal limit by seven pm. Just think of the permanent damage they do to the nation with their impaired judgement and poor reflexes.

Anyway, we had drunken theatricals to contend with tonight. And, which was worse, sober ones! Annie, who didn't realise what was at stake, congratulated me on taking such trouble over all those 'lovely theatre people' even though they're not important.

I explained that they were very important. Not for their votes, which are too few to count, but for their influence.

She was surprised that they have influence.

'Annie,' I explained patiently, 'show business people have a hotline to the media. Once you've drunk a couple of pints in *East-Enders* the press want your opinion on everything: Britain's schools, the Health Service, law and order . . . right through to the European Monetary System. They get far more exposure than my Cabinet.'

There's no sense in it, of course. But editors want people to read their papers, so if an article starts with a picture of Dirty Den[1] they read it. But who is going to read an article because of a photo of the Secretary of State for Trade and Industry?

Annie said, 'So all these actors turn into your supporters after a couple of drinks at Number Ten?'

'Some do,' I told her. 'But not enough. That's why we dish out a couple of CBEs or Knighthoods every year. Keeps them all hoping. And they're less likely to knock the Government next time they're on Wogan.'[2]

[*Simon Monk was, by a fateful chance, one of the guests at this party. His autobiography records his quiet conversation with Sir Humphrey, who had been anxiously waiting at the top of the grand circular staircase, watching out for Monk's arrival – Ed.*]

Sir Humphrey took me aside, into a sort of panelled lobby outside the main state reception rooms. He faced away from a few bystanders and spoke softly in my ear. He wanted me to talk to Hacker that night. In fact, he implied that I'd been invited to the party – several weeks ago – for that very purpose. The date of the grant announcement was known months back.

'But isn't it better to wait till the figure is published?' I asked, not really relishing a confrontation with Hacker that night.

[1] Den Watts, a character in *EastEnders*, a soap opera which had prominence in the latter part of the 20th century.
[2] Well-known TV talk show of the 1980s on which the host, Terry Wogan, talked and the guests listened.

Sir Humphrey was astonished. 'What on earth for?'

'If I try to lobby him before, he won't say anything, will he?'

Sir Humphrey explained. 'Of course he won't say anything. You don't want him to say anything. You want him to *do* something.'

I began to argue. Then I realised that I was getting free advice from the most skilful political operator in the land. 'If you wait,' he muttered into my ear, 'the figure will be published and everyone will be committed to it. They'll have to stick with it to save their faces. It you want to change government decisions you have to do it before anybody knows they're being made.'

It's a good principle. But, I asked, 'isn't that rather difficult in practice?'

'Yes,' Humphrey answered. 'That's what the Civil Service is for.'

'To change Government decisions?' I realised that I was a complete innocent.

'Yes,' he smiled. 'Well, only the bad ones. But that's most of them, of course.'

I asked Sir Humphrey what he wanted me to do. Quite simply, he wanted me to help emphasise to Hacker that a small grant might cause him great embarrassment . . . at the Awards Dinner on Sunday.

SIR BERNARD WOOLLEY RECALLS:[1]

Everyone was politicking furiously. Humphrey got Simon Monk into one corner. And a bunch of actors and actresses got the Prime Minister into another. And Hacker did his utmost to persuade the thespians that he was a theatre lover. Without much success, I fear.

'Do you really believe in the British theatre, Prime Minister?' said a deeply sceptical young actress, whose roots were showing, metaphorically and literally.

'Of course. Absolutely.'

'Why?'

Hacker said something to the effect of 'Well, er, it's, er, it's one of the great glories of England.'

'You mean Shakespeare?' said a smooth old fellow, apparently being helpful.

'Yes,' said Hacker gratefully. 'Absolutely. Shakespeare.'

'Who else?' asked the old smoothie. He had a very plummy voice. I'd seen him at the RSC. Can't remember his name. I liked him though.

'Who *else*?' repeated Hacker, desperately stalling while he gave himself time to think. 'Well, er, Shakespeare of course. And er, er, Sheridan. Oscar Wilde. Bernard Shaw. All great English playwrights.'

'They were all Irish,' said the aggressive young actress.

Hacker tried to charm her with a smile, a fairly hopeless task. 'Yes, I know that, but well, Irish, English, it was all the same thing in those days, wasn't it?'

---

[1] In conversation with the Editors.

'Bernard Shaw died in 1950,' said a slim young man on the edge of the group, who was apparently studying a Gainsborough on the wall with such intensity that he didn't even turn to look at the Prime Minister.

'Oh I'm so sorry,' replied Hacker inappropriately.

A large middle-aged actress with a beautiful smile and a husky deep voice, born of thirty years of gin and Benson and Hedges, smiled warmly at him and asked if he went to the theatre a lot.

Hacker hedged. 'Well, of course, I'd love to – but you know how it is in this job.'

The plummy old actor spoke up again, quoting the Prime Minister back at himself. 'Don't you think the Prime Minister ought to go. If it's one of the great glories of England?'

The Prime Minister's explanation was less than tactful. 'Oh yes,' he said. 'But the Minister for the Arts goes. His job, really.'

'Why?' asked the plummy actor.

'Well, the Prime Minister can't do everything himself. Have to delegate the work.'

The throaty actress appeared to take offence. 'Going to the theatre is work?'

'Yes. No,' said Hacker indecisively. 'But I don't want to trespass on another minister's territory.'

'Does that mean,' enquired the sceptical young actress with a smile, 'that you can't feel ill without clearing it with the Minister of Health?'

'Exactly,' said Hacker, then realised what he'd said. '*Not* exactly', he added, trying but failing to clarify his position.

The slim young man on the edge of the group turned and asked him if he ever went to the theatre when he'd been in opposition. Hacker started to explain that, even then, it had not been within his purview.

'So when you say you believe in the theatre,' said the young man, 'it's like saying you believe in God. You mean you believe it exists.'

Hacker denied this hotly. I think he should have been wiser to admit the truth, for he was fooling nobody.

'What was the last play you went to?' asked the young actress, contempt written all over her face. These people show no respect at all, you know.

'*Went* to?' repeated the Prime Minister, as if he sat at home all day and *read* plays. 'Last play?' he repeated, panicked, playing for time. 'Ah. Well. Probably *Hamlet*.'

'Whose?' asked the plummy old fellow.

'Shakespeare's,' said the Prime Minister with confidence.

'No, who played Hamlet?' asked the slim young man on the edge of the group. 'Henry Irving?'[1]

'Yes,' said Hacker, 'I think that might have been his name.'

---

[1] Sir Henry Irving was a famous nineteenth-century actor and the first knight of the first nights.

The acting fraternity gazed at each other, unable to grasp that the Prime Minister neither knew nor cared what went on in their temples of art and culture.

I saw Sir Humphrey detach himself from Simon Monk. So I detached myself from Hacker and the actors, and took the Cabinet Secretary aside for a private word.

I explained that the Prime Minister was not enjoying himself.

'He's not supposed to,' retorted Humphrey. 'Cocktail parties at Number Ten are just a gruesome duty.'

'But people are asking him questions,' I said.

'He should be used to that.'

'But they weren't tabled in advance. So he isn't briefed.'

'But he's not on the record. Does it matter?'

I explained that all of the people at the party were going to think that he was a Philistine.

'Good Heavens!' said Humphrey.

Joking apart, I emphasised that in my opinion he should be rescued. Humphrey said he would handle it.

As we approached Hacker in the theatrical crowd we passed Annie, the Prime Minister's wife, talking to a very small and dapper musician who'd recently been appointed Principal Guest Conductor of one of the five London symphony orchestras. Annie may have had too much to drink.

'I'm interested in hi-fidelity too,' she said. 'My husband is a high-fidelity husband.'

'That's nice,' said the conductor, who was famous for being exactly the opposite.

'In a way,' she said conspiratorially, and giggled. 'High fidelity but low frequency.'

The conductor, who clearly found Mrs Hacker extremely attractive, seemed unsure how to reply. 'You mean, sort of Bang and Olufsen?'

'Well, Olufsen anyway,' said Mrs Hacker.

[*Hacker's diary continues – Ed.*]

I was doing well with the acting fraternity. To be honest, I really didn't know much about the theatre, but I'm sure they didn't notice, they're all so self-centred.

They all knew the Arts Council grant was to be announced any day now, and of course they all pressured me like hell. But I'm pretty used to being lobbied by vested interests, and I reminded them that there were numerous other calls on the public purse that some people might consider even *more* important.

It is, of course, a basic rule for self-interested pressure groups that you present the case for your own financial gain as if the public interest is all you care about. Teachers present demands for their own pay rises as being for the good of education. Even as they go out on strike their leaders argue that they're doing it for the sake of the children they're sending home. Miners, if we are to believe them, go on strike so that old people can have cheaper coal, Health service workers – from doctors to porters – close down hospitals so as to save the health service for the wretched patients who can't get any treatment in the meantime.

So obviously these very pleasant entertainers, who need the love and applause of thousands of total strangers, and who therefore put on plays because dressing up and showing off in public is fun and makes them feel good, also present their demands for subsidy under the guise of the public interest – education, usually.

So I countered by pointing out that much more money is desperately needed for genuine educational purposes, trusting that they would not mention that I was not in any case giving the money to those with a prior call. Not to mention hospitals, kidney machines . . .

'Tanks and rockets', said one of the actresses, 'is what you spend the money on.'

'H-bombs,' chimed in another.

Perfectly true. But we could hardly defend ourselves from the Russians with a performance of *Henry V*. I said so. They weren't amused.

Humphrey arrived at my side and it was with some relief that I escaped from that little group.

'This isn't a drinks party, it's a siege,' I complained bitterly.

Humphrey merely commented that people are very concerned about the arts. He's wrong. *These* people are very concerned – the nation doesn't give a damn. If they did, they'd spend their own money on the Arts. Why should the Government's money be spent on other people's pleasure, I asked him.

'Nobody could call it pleasure,' said Humphrey rather shocked. He's a true Calvinist at heart. 'The point is that we have a great heritage to support. Pictures hardly anyone wants to see, music hardly anyone wants to hear, plays hardly anyone wants to watch. We can't let them die just because no one's interested.'

I was curious. 'Why not?'

'It's like the Church of England, Prime Minister. People don't go to church, but they feel better because it's there. The Arts are just the same. As long as they're going on you can feel part of a civilised nation.'

All very well in its way, but he's totally unpolitical and unrealistic. 'There are no votes in the Arts,' I reminded him. 'Nobody's *interested*!'

Stubbornly he refused to concede the point. 'Nobody's interested in the Social Science Research Council. Or the Milk Marketing Board. Or the Advisory Committee on Dental Establishments. Or the Dumping At Sea Representation Panel. But Government still pays money to support them.'

'Don't they do a lot of good?' I asked.

'Of course they don't. They hardly do anything at all.'

'Then,' I proposed, 'let's abolish them.'

Now he was panicked. This was not the turn that he had expected the conversation to take. 'No, no, Prime Minister. They are symbols. You don't fund them for doing work. You fund them to show what you approve of. Most government expenditure is symbolic. The Arts Council is a symbol.'

I told him it was no good. My mind was made up. He promptly suggested that I have a word with the Chief Associate Director of the National Theatre, who by chance had also been invited to this drinks do. I didn't want to face another salvo, but Humphrey told me that he's been trying to persuade this fellow Simon Monk to make the right sort of speech at the Awards Dinner.

'That's very good of you, Humphrey' I said gratefully.

'Not at all. But you might have more success than I.' So Humphrey's persuasion had not borne fruit.

Well, before I had time to collect my thoughts I was face to face with this theatrical wizard. He was actually perfectly polite and seemed a little ill at ease. Small, thinning hair and without the beard that I'd so often seen in the newspapers, he could almost have been a politician.

I was ill at ease too. 'So you'll be introducing me at this Awards Dinner thing?' I began.

'That's right,' he replied, and fell silent. We half-smiled nervously at each other for what seemed like an eternity. It became clear that if I didn't speak the conversation might never resume.

'Any idea of the sort of thing you'll be saying?'

'I suppose it all depends really.'

'On – er – on . . .?' I enquired.

'On the size of the grant.'

Just what I'd been warned. And I knew he had no idea what it was to be. [*The Prime Minister was not aware of the discussion with Sir Humphrey about breadsticks in the NT Restaurant – Ed*.] So I told him the grant was still under discussion.

'Of course,' he agreed. 'But if it turns out to be generous it would give me a chance to say something about the way this Government has got its priorities right. Believing in Britain's heritage, and what Britain stands for.'

I hinted that he could say something of that sort anyway, even if I couldn't persuade the Arts Minister to cough up, but he indicated that this would be difficult.

'Surely you wouldn't want to make it a political occasion?' I said in a voice of disapproval.

'Not for myself, no. But I have a duty to the profession.' He's good! 'And to the Arts,' he continued. 'My colleagues would expect me to voice their feelings.'

I tried to make *him* understand about money for inner cities, schools, hospitals, kidney machines. He acknowledged my problem and said he proposed to solve it by making a funny speech about the government.

This was grim news indeed. Humorous attacks are the most difficult to deal with. The one thing I can't afford is to look as though I'm a bad sport or have no sense of humour – the British public never forgive you for that.

[*The following morning the Prime Minister received a letter from Simon Monk. Sir Humphrey Appleby preserved it in the Cabinet Office files, and we reproduce it opposite. It contained a serious threat – Ed.*]

NATIONAL
THEATRE

Patron H.M. The Queen

December 6th

Dear Mr. Hacker,

I enclose a draft of a part of my speech, for your amusement. It will make good television, don't you think, in a
light-hearted way? Of course, I hope I don't have to say all
this, as I would rather not embarrass you. But I do hope you
understand that if we <u>don't</u> get a substantial rise the National
Theatre will collapse - and there will be a huge empty building
on the South Bank, a decaying monument to this country's
barbarism.

Yours sincerely

Simon Monk

enc.

The Olivier Theatre
The Lyttelton Theatre
The Cottesloe Theatre

Ladies & gentlemen, I thought that tonight you might be amused by some of the <u>other</u> ways the government has spent your money.

The money it can't afford for the arts.

Did you know that in one year a London borough spent a million pounds on hotels for families while they had 4000 empty council houses?

Did you know that another council spends £100 per week on a toenail cutting administrator? And that one city in the UK was still employing four gas lamp lighters eight years after the last gas lamp was removed? That cost a quarter of a million!

Not to mention the Council that spent £730 to have two square yards of shrubbery weeded. And the government office block that's scheduled for demolition two weeks before it's completed.

And finally, do you know where all the British Local Authorities held their conference on spending cuts? The Café Royal! [1]

[1] An expensive and elegant restaurant in Regent Street, London.

[*Hacker's diary continues – Ed.*]

December 6th

I got a vile, threatening letter from that man Monk this morning. Not only was it full of examples of local authority waste, it threatened that the NT would shut down if I didn't hoick the grant up. This would be cataclysmic news for me, the press would kill me!

I called Dorothy to discuss his draft speech. Her view of it was that the TV viewers wouldn't make the distinction between wastage by local or national government – it's all public money, the taxpayer pays the rate-support grant. And therefore they would agree with Monk that if money is wasted like that it would be inexcusable to risk the closure of the NT on financial grounds.

I decided she was right. The fact is, the National Theatre is going to call my bluff.

'What is your bluff?' she asked.

'My bluff is: I'm willing to risk the National Theatre's bluff.'

'What's their bluff?'

'Their bluff is that they think I'm bluffing, whereas . . .'

'Whereas you are!' she said.

I realised that I no longer knew who was bluffing whom. Dorothy thought it was obvious. I couldn't see it. [*Perhaps it was a case of blind man's bluff. Or bland minds' bluff – Ed.*]

My cassette recorder was on the desk, because I was about to dictate some notes for my memoirs and a couple of personal letters. Bernard offered to clarify the situation for me. He then spoke for several minutes but I was none the wiser. So I asked him to repeat his clarification into my cassette.

'Prime Minister,' he said, 'you think that the National Theatre thinks that you are bluffing and the National Theatre thinks that you think that they are bluffing, whereas your bluff is to make the National Theatre think that you are bluffing when you're not bluffing, or if you *are* bluffing, your bluff is to make them think you're *not* bluffing. And their bluff must be that they're bluffing, because if they're not bluffing they're not bluffing.'

I thanked him and resumed the intelligent part of conversation with Dorothy. She asked me what my policy actually *is*? Am I willing to risk their closure if I don't increase the grant?

I replied, flustered. 'I have already stated my policy. I think. All I can do is go on restating it until . . . until . . .'

'Until you know what it is?' Bernard enquired, unhelpfully.

'The point is, this situation is now a real hot potato. If I don't do something it could become a banana skin.'

Bernard intervened. 'Excuse me, Prime Minister, a hot potato can't become a banana skin. If you don't do anything a hot potato merely becomes a cold potato.'

I wonder if Bernard ever realises how close to death he sometimes comes.

December 7th

Dorothy came to me with a plan. Not a good plan, not a great plan – but a plan of sheer genius!

In a nutshell, she recommends calling their bluff. She says I should sell the National Theatre building. And the National Film Theatre. The South Bank is a prime site, overlooking St Paul's and Big Ben.

The site, she proposed, should be sold to a property developer. Her information is that it is worth about £35 million pounds on the market. This money could be put into an Arts Trust Fund, producing – at an average of ten per cent per annum – £3.5 million a year.

This £3.5 million of interest earned from the Trust Fund would finance the National Theatre. Not the theatre *itself*, because we would have sold it, but the company – which is all that matters.

Apparently the current National Theatre *building* absorbs about half of the company's grant, i.e. out of a grant of £7 million about £3.5 million goes into the upkeep of that building. Dorothy contends that this is a waste of money, money that could actually be spent on productions. After all Simon Monk was complaining last week that they shouldn't have to spend their grant that way – 'the theatre is about plays and actors, not bricks and mortar'.

So where would they put on plays? Answer: there are plenty of theatres in London. And all over the country. The National Theatre could rent them, like any other producer.

The scheme is perfect. The company might even have to go on tour and become genuinely national – whereas at the moment it only serves a few Londoners and a lot of tourists. Much more money than ever before could be injected into National Theatre productions while still giving the Government that net profit of thirty million, which could then be invested to produce three million a year for the British Theatre as a whole.

I was exultant. 'No one could accuse me of being a Philistine any more!'

She smiled. 'Not unless they knew you.'

December 9th

The night of the Awards dinner. Confidently I arrived at the Dorchester in my dinner jacket, with Annie on my arm, actively looking forward to the encounter. If there was to be a knock-down drag-out fight tonight, I felt I stood a good chance of emerging as the champ.

Knowing that much of the audience for my speech would be experienced performers, I'd taken some extra trouble. I had rehearsed in front of the mirror. Dorothy had watched my recent TV appearance and had some advice for me.

'Always use full gestures. If you only gesture from the elbow up you look like an Armenian carpet salesman.'

On the whole, it could be better to look like an Armenian carpet salesman than an actor. Or even a politician. But since I now see myself as a statesman, only the most statesmanlike gestures are permitted. Punchy, powerful gestures – but always *preceding* the sentence, Annie tells me, never after! Gestures afterwards look weak and ineffectual.

Of course, before the speech there was the small matter of a final negotiation with Mr Monk. If all went well, I wouldn't have to say anything controversial, which would be the best outcome of all. I always remember the advice given to me by an elderly peer years ago when I first entered the Cabinet: 'If you want to get into the Cabinet, learn how to speak. If you want to stay in the Cabinet, learn how to keep your mouth shut.'

In the ante-room before the dinner Humphrey got me together with Simon Monk. He'd now heard the news about the grant. I gave him a big smile and a sincere handshake [*or was it the other way round? – Ed.*].

He did not smile at me. 'This is very bad news about the grant, Prime Minister.'

'Surely not?' I said innocently. 'It's gone up.'

'Nothing like enough.'

'Enough to make it unnecessary for you to recommend closure, tonight?'

'I'm afraid not.' He was sombre, but confident.

I helped myself to a handful of peanuts. 'Because next year,' I continued indistinctly, 'I think we can really do something significant. You remember you complained that £3 million of your grant goes on the upkeep of the building?'

'Yes?'

'I have a plan that would relieve you of that.'

He brightened considerably. 'Really? That would be marvellous.'

'Yes,' I enthused, 'wouldn't it? And it would make the National Theatre really national too.'

Instantly he was on his guard. 'How do you mean?'

'I'm thinking of selling it,' I explained cheerfully.

He was aghast! He stood there, his mouth open, staring at me as though I were Attila the Hun. So I took the opportunity to explain that that's how we save three million on upkeep.

He finally found his voice. 'Prime Minister! That's impossible.'

'No it's not, it's easy.' I assured him. 'We've had a terrific offer for the site.' And we had, too.

Humphrey intervened, apparently shell-shocked. He had been quietly confident that I would submit to Simon's closure bluff. 'But Prime Minister – the National Theatre must have a home.'

I explained that it would have. They could have offices anywhere – Brixton or Toxteth, for instance. Or Middlesbrough.

Simon asked about theatres, about scene-building workshops.

Rent them, I explained, like everyone else. As it is, most of the workshops at the NT are closed down because of bad management and high cost.

'Be like the others,' I exhorted him. 'Perform in the West End. Or the Old Vic. And provincial theatres. Become strolling players again, not Civil Servants. Didn't you once say that the theatre was about plays and actors, not bricks and mortar?'

And, while he was reeling on the ropes, I followed up with the knockout blow. I suggested Dorothy's *second* plan – she came up with it this morning. If anyone complained that the National Theatre needed a *permanent* home, we would designate *all* the regional theatres in the UK the National Theatre. For instance, the Haymarket Theatre in Leicester would become the *National Theatre in Leicester*; the Crucible would be called the *National Theatre in Sheffield*; the Citizens could be subtitled *National Theatre in Glasgow* . . . and so forth. 'You,' I explained to Simon, 'would just run the London branch of the National Theatre.'

It would be a perfectly true description. I reminded him that they are all run exactly the same way, with Artistic Directors and Administrators appointed by local boards of governors, financed by a combination of Arts Council grants, local authority grants and box office income. Why should the London branch of the National Theatre be the only branch entitled to that elevated title? And we could use the £35 million, or the £3 million annual income, to help them all. 'That would be terribly popular with the profession, don't you think?'

Humphrey, who had not heard this plan either, was virtually speechless. His eyes were popping out of his head. 'Prime Minister, it's barbaric!' he gasped.

'Spending money on actors and writers instead of buildings?'

'Yes,' he spluttered. 'No,' he added as, wide-eyed, he realised what he was saying.

'Anyway,' I concluded, 'it's only one of the options. I might decide against it. Or I might not. I could outline it in my speech. It all depends, really.'

Simon spoke at last. 'On what?'

I smiled benignly at him. 'To change the subject completely, Simon, have you decided what to say in your speech yet?'

He was sweating. 'Not finally.' He knew he was beaten.

'You see,' I explained, 'thinking it over, I wasn't sure that those examples of government waste were awfully funny. But of course, it's your decision.' I waited. He eyed me balefully. 'I'm sure you understand,' I said, and walked away from them both.

Well, either way I was the winner. But I didn't know which way it would go until the last moment. We ate the usual rubber chicken dinner with croquette potatoes – I've never ever eaten croquette potatoes *anywhere* except at formal dinners – I gave the loyal toast, the smokers were told they could smoke, and in no time it was time for the awards. Monk was introduced by the pompous ringing tones of the Toastmaster: 'Prime Minister and Mrs Hacker, My Lords, ladies and gentleman, pray silence for the Chief Associate Director of the National Theatre, Mr Simon Monk.'

He rose to a round of warm applause. 'Ladies and gentlemen,' he said, 'you will have read this morning of the grant to the Arts Council and to the National Theatre. I know that many of us are disappointed by the amount.'

Low hostile murmurs reverberated around the Banqueting Suite. Several 'hear hear's'. Lots of approving bangs on the table-tops. Simon Monk stopped and looked at me. I stared back. Little pink anger spots appeared on his cheeks and he looked back at his speech.

'Of course we would all like it to be larger. But apparently this is a time of national stringency and we all have to think in terms of national needs. There are many calls on the public purse . . .' One of my favourite phrases, that! '. . . Education, inner cities, health, kidney machines.'

I nodded sagely. Another murmur went round the room, this time of disappointment. Simon Monk, it was clear, was not going to attack me. And, in fact, at that moment he removed a couple of pages from his speech and slipped them into his pocket. Very wise. Perhaps he knew the old adage: 'Never speak when you are angry. If you do you'll make the best speech you'll ever regret.'

Simon's speech was unexpectedly brief. All that was left of it was 'I suppose we should be glad that any increase has been possible. And grateful to our Guest of Honour whose personal intervention has made even this small increase possible.'

I beamed at him. The cameras were on me, I knew. 'Ladies and gentlemen,' said Monk, holding up his glass, 'I give you our Guest of Honour, the patron of the arts, the Prime Minister.'

He sat down to a smattering of unenthusiastic applause. Little did his audience know, but he'd made the smart move and the only possible speech.

I let him see me remove the appropriate pages from *my* script. And I whispered to Humphrey: 'Excellent speech, wasn't it?'

He seemed as angry as the theatricals. 'Yes Prime Minister,' he said, through clenched teeth! But then, old Humphrey's always been a bit theatrical himself.

8
The National
Education Service

December 11th

From the arts to education – real education. The party has serious problems with the local authorities and our education system.

But today was fascinating for other reasons. Before I got to the petty problems of British schools I spent the day on the world stage dealing in a statesmanlike way with matters that affect the future, indeed the very existence, of mankind. Or personkind, as some of our more dedicated so-called educationalists would have it.

After Christmas I'm due to visit the USA, which will certainly be good for my standing in the opinion polls. I'm going to try to follow this with a spring trip to Moscow, which will demonstrate to the voters that I'm the man to bring world peace to them.

Of course that may be beyond me in the short term – we will need several more working funerals for that. But it'll still be excellent for the image.

So this morning I was working on my speech for my special appearance at the UN while I'm in New York. My first draft was quite good, I thought. I'd based it on the UN Charter itself. The Foreign Office sent me over a copy, with a note attached explaining that the preamble to the Charter was known as the Unconditional Surrender of the English language.[1]

---

[1] The first sentence of the preamble runs as follows:

WE THE PEOPLES
OF THE UNITED NATIONS
DETERMINED

  to save succeeding generations from the scourge of war, which twice in our life-time has brought untold sorrow to mankind, and

  to reaffirm faith in fundamental human rights, in the dignity and worth of the human person, in the equal rights of men and women and of nations large and small, and

  to establish conditions under which justice and respect for the obligations arising from treaties and other sources of international law can be maintained, and

  to promote social progress and better standards of life in larger freedom,

The first draft of my speech referred to the British belief in peace, freedom and justice. It talked of the impossibility of *justice* while the vast majority of member states of the UN have prisoners of conscience; of the impossibility of *freedom* while most of the member states have one-party government (appealing though the idea is if you happen to lead the one party); and of the low chance of world peace when almost everyone votes blindly in special-interest blocks instead of with us. [*It is interesting to note that Hacker, after all this time in government, remained a moralist at heart, even though he was seldom able to see his moral positions through into practical politics – Ed.*]

The FO took one look at my speech. They only got it on Saturday. Today they effectively vetoed it. Dick Wharton[1] phoned me and said that, for God's sake, I mustn't say any of it.

'Because it's wrong?' I asked.

'Because it's right,' he replied.

I told him I didn't want to mouth platitudes or clichés ever again. [*To 'mouth platitudes' is itself a cliché – Ed.*] I reiterated that I wished to say something about peace and freedom. Dick Wharton said that if I insisted I could speak about peace at the UN, but not freedom – it's too controversial. I told him I didn't mind controversy. Controversy gets better headlines.

Over lunch I prepared for PQs[2] in my room at the House. The PQ Secretary expected questions from the anti-nuclear lobby about the rumour in the press today about the latest US missiles. It seems that there's a fear of Soviet infiltration at the place where most of our guided-missile microchips are manufactured.

'Is that California?' I asked Bernard. 'Silicon Valley?'

'Taiwan,' he replied.

I was staggered. 'Taiwan??'

---

[1] Permanent Secretary of the FCO.
[2] Parliamentary Questions.

AND FOR THESE ENDS

to practice tolerance and live together in peace with one another as good neighbours, and

to unite our strength to maintain international peace and security, and to ensure, by the acceptance of principles and the institution of methods, that armed force shall not be used, save in the common interest, and

to employ international machinery for the promotion of the economic and social advancement of all peoples,

HAVE RESOLVED TO COMBINE OUR EFFORTS TO ACCOMPLISH THESE AIMS.

Bernard nodded. 'It appears that we have paid for about fifteen million faulty microchips.'

'What is meant by faulty?' I asked carefully.

He shrugged hopelessly. 'No one knows exactly, Prime Minister. We don't dare ask. Maybe the missiles simply wouldn't work. Maybe they'd blow up in the face of whoever pushes the button.'

'My God!' I said. I was horrified. I asked what else might happen. Bernard shrugged. 'Maybe they'd boomerang. Go all the way round the world and land back on us.'

I stared at him in silence, my boggling mind trying to assimilate the full implications of this horror.

Bernard spoke again. 'Maybe it would be better to avoid full and frank disclosure of this matter.'

Malcolm Warren,[1] whom Bernard had included in the meeting, nodded vigorously, in full agreement.

A sudden thought struck me, a thought even more horrific than that of boomeranging missiles. My mouth went dry with panic. 'When did we buy these?' I asked, petrified.

Bernard reassured me. 'Before you took office, Prime Minister. So there's nothing to worry about.'

Thank God! It's certainly fortunate that I wasn't responsible. But I am now, now that I know! And 'nothing to worry about' is a curious way to talk of guided missiles that might do their own thing. 'Nothing to worry about?' I repeated incredulously.

'No. I mean, nothing to worry about *personally*,' he said. 'Unless they boomerang on Whitehall,' he added pensively.

'And what doesn't?' muttered Malcolm. He's so gloomy!

I asked who was responsible. 'The MOD,'[2] said Bernard. 'And the Pentagon. The issue seems to be lack of control over the defence industries.'

'The issue', said Malcolm, 'appears to be lack of control over the missiles.'

'The issue', *I* said, 'seems to be the low level of imagination in the MOD.'

'Might be better to avoid disclosing that too,' suggested Malcolm.

In the event, the PQs went off smoothly and, as always, I left the Chamber immediately afterwards. The Chief Whip and the Party Chairman were ushered in to my room at the House. I ordered Bernard to stay and listen.

[1] The Press Secretary.
[2] Ministry of Defence.

He was reluctant. 'Isn't this a party matter, Prime Minister? A meeting with the Party Chairman and the Chief Whip?'

'It's also a government matter,' I told him firmly. 'It concerns our education policy.'

Bernard is a stickler for detail. 'The government's? Or the party's?'

'It's the same thing, Bernard!' I was getting testy with him.

Neil, the Party Chairman, who's looking rather overweight and breathless, foolishly interfered. 'With respect, Prime Minister, they're not the same thing.'

Jeffrey[1] joined in. 'That's why we want the meeting.'

Bernard tried to slide out of the room again. 'Well, it seems to be a party matter, so if you'll excuse me . . .'

'Sit!' I commanded him. He sat. He's quite obedient really, and impeccably trained. 'You would try the patience of a saint, Bernard,' I told him. 'Now stay!'

He stayed. I turned to Neil and Jeffrey and asked what the problem was.

'Education,' said Neil succinctly.

I was feeling belligerent. 'What the hell do you think I can do about it?'

'You're the Prime Minister,' said Jeffrey. I knew that already. But so what? The Prime Minister has no direct control over education. I can't control the curriculum, the exams, the appointment of Head Teachers – nothing! But the voters are holding me responsible for everything that's going wrong.

'You do have influence,' said Neil.

'And I'm utterly fed up with it,' I remarked. 'I thought that when I became Prime Minister I'd have power. And what have I got? *Influence*! Bloody influence, that's all! I have no power over the police, the rates, EEC directives, the European Court, the British courts, the judges, NATO, the falling pound . . . What *have* I the power to do?'

Neil eyed me beadily. 'You have the power to lose us the next election.'

'Which you will,' said Jeffrey nodding solemnly. 'Unless we do something about education.'

I wonder if they overstate the seriousness of it. Maybe not. I told them I was listening.

'The voters', said the Party Chairman, beads of sweat appearing on

---

[1] Jeffrey Pearson, the Chief Whip.

his forehead, 'want something done about low academic attainment, the non-competitive ethos . . .'

'You mean the three Rs,' I said, cutting him short. I got the point.

He nodded gloomily. 'Kids are being taught about Marxism, sexism, pacificism, feminism, racism, heterosexism . . .'

Bernard chimed in. 'It's all the isms. They're causing schisms.' I think he was trying to get me to tell him to go. But I wouldn't!

I'd not heard of heterosexism. Neil explained that it's the idea that children are being taught not to be irrationally prejudiced in favour of heterosexuality. 'This has come up before,' I remarked. 'But I see the problem. We don't want prejudice.'

Neil exploded. 'Prejudice!' he shouted. 'You can't describe it as prejudice to teach kids to be normal.' His face had turned a curious mauve colour. I thought he was going to have a heart attack. I wasn't very bothered, to tell you the truth – I was thoroughly fed up at his suggestion that *I* might lose the next election. He's the bloody party chairman, and all he ever does is criticise me. I may be out of a job after the election – but *he* may only have to wait till I reshuffle.

He was still ranting on about 'normal'. I silenced him. 'It all depends, Neil,' I explained, 'on how you define normal. I'm certainly not against homosexual teachers *per se*. And I'm not against sex education. Now calm down.'

He tried. He took a deep breath. 'I'm not against teaching kids the facts of life in the classroom. But not homosexual technique. Nor heterosexual technique, come to that.'

'Where should they learn it then?' I asked curiously.

'Behind the bike sheds,' said Neil firmly. 'Like we did!'

This was a whole new insight into Neil. 'Did you?' I asked with interest.

Jeffrey, our Chief Whip, was not remotely interested in Neil's adolescence. 'Never mind about the sexual technique. Some of our schools are teaching more Hindi than English.'

This was even trickier. Perhaps it's lucky that I have no power over education. *I* agree that English is more important than Hindi. But I can't say it in public – I'll be accused of racism. Only last week, while I was receiving a deputation from the Ethnic Awareness Council, I looked at my watch while a black woman delegate was speaking. I was immediately accused of racist body language. And sexist body language. And I only did it because I was bored rigid!

Still, I'd got their message and I didn't see what I could do. So I asked them to be specific.

'Get Patrick[1] to get a grip on the Education Department.'

'You know it can't be done,' I replied. 'They've got Patrick completely housetrained.'

'Then sack him.'

'I can't have another Cabinet convulsion. Not yet.'

'Then,' said the Party Chairman, 'invite the Leader of the Opposition's wife round to Number Ten.'

'Why? What could she do?' I was puzzled.

Neil's face was a little less puce but no less grim. 'She can start measuring up for carpets and curtains.'

[*Hacker turned to Sir Humphrey Appleby for advice, believing that Sir Humphrey would be a believer in excellence for its own sake. But Sir Humphrey had his own hidden agenda, as this note in his private diary makes clear – Ed.*]

B.W.[2] had a private word with me. He told me the Prime Minister has a problem with Education. I've known that for years. But it's a bit late for him to do anything about that now, especially as he's got to Number 10 without any.

But apparently I was mistaken. The Prime Minister was not concerned about his own education (or lack of it). That would be too much to hope for. No, it was the education *system* that was on his mind – and in my view it's a bit too late to do anything about that either.

He thinks, Bernard told me, that Education is going to lose him the next election. This is indeed a possibility, but it is my view that worse things could befall the nation.

Furthermore, there is nothing to worry about. Our education system does all that most parents require of it. It keeps the children out of mischief while they're at work. Most of them, anyway.

It must be conceded that it does not, as Woolley pointed out, train their minds or prepare them for a working life. But then some of our local authorities would be most unhappy if it did.

When Bernard quoted the Party Chairman's paper, which suggests that the whole comprehensive system is breaking down, I sent him away with a flea in his ear. He's clearly been got at by the enemy – the Prime Minister's Chief Policy Adviser[3] to be precise. I will not put up with Bernard Woolley standing in my office telling me that as comprehensive education was an experiment, it ought to be validated. Of course it should – but on no account should it be invalidated.

[1] Patrick Snodgrass, the Secretary of State for Education.
[2] Bernard Woolley.
[3] Dorothy Wainwright.

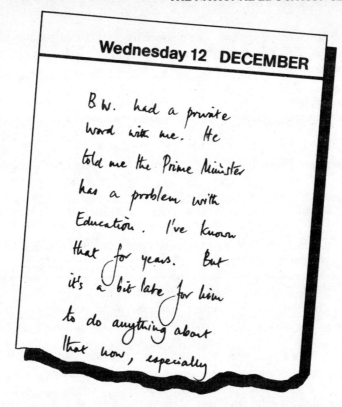

Wednesday 12 DECEMBER

B.W. had a private word with me. He told me the Prime Minister has a problem with Education. I've known that for years. But it's a bit late for him to do anything about that now, especially

Comprehensive education was not introduced with the idea of improving educational standards. It was to get rid of class distinction. But the impression has been allowed to develop, quite wrongly, that the intention was to remove class distinction *among children.*

Nobody at the DES,[1] however, ever mentions children. They never have. Comprehensives were introduced so as to get rid of class distinction in the teaching profession. It was to improve the living standards of teachers, not the educational standards of children, and to bring the NUT[2] teachers in primary and secondary-modern schools up to the salary levels of their rivals in the National Association of Schoolmasters who previously taught in the Grammar Schools.

When there is a Labour government the Department's official line is *Comprehensives abolish the class system.* When there is a Conservative government the Department says: *Comprehensives are the cheapest way of providing mass education.* Thus the DES takes the view that selective education is divisive (if you're Labour) or expensive (if you're Conservative).

[1] Department of Education and Science.
[2] National Union of Teachers.

It is in the interest of the Civil Service to preserve this *status quo*. This enables the DES and the Government as a whole to have a happy relationship with the NUT. And it doesn't affect us personally because we educate our children independently.[1]

B.W. stubbornly insisted that the government wants change. Sometimes he is really dense. The teaching unions do not want change – and whereas we only have to cope with any government for four or five years, the teaching unions are there for ever.

Furthermore, Woolley seems to be under the impression that it is our job to get the unions to accept government policy. It is in this very fundamental sense that he has been got at and brainwashed by the enemy. Mrs Wainwright may believe that this course is in the government's interest; she may even have persuaded the Prime Minister; but she is wrong!

Our objectives in the Civil Service are harmony and consistency, conciliation and continuity. Laudable aims, as anybody will agree. And since governments change policy all the time, and the unions never change their policy at all, common sense requires in practice that it is the government that should be brought into line with the unions. And that is what the DES is there for – to get the government to accept the policies of the teachers' unions.

Bernard Woolley remained doubtful, I am sorry to say. He merely reiterated that his master, the Prime Minister, is deeply worried that he is responsible for something he can't change.

I'm sure he is. I call it Responsibility Without Power – the prerogative of the eunuch throughout the ages.

[*Hacker's diary continues – Ed.*]

December 13th

At my usual early morning meeting with Humphrey, right after breakfast, he raised the education question.

'I understand, Prime Minister, that you're worried about the Local Education Authorities?'

'No,' I told him, 'I'm worried about the Department of Education and Science.'

He was visibly surprised. 'In my opinion, the DES does an excellent job.'

He can't possibly believe that! *Nobody* could believe that. 'I don't believe you believe that,' I said.

'You don't?'

'Sorry, no.' Now he was insulted, I realised. I suppose I'd inadver-

---

[1] Privately.

tently called him a liar. Still, I was committed. 'Don't you believe that I don't believe you believe that?'

He was adamant and emphatic. 'I believe that you don't believe that I believe that, but I must ask you to believe that although you don't believe that I believe it, I believe it.'

I felt I had to accept that, especially as it took me quite a while to work out what he'd said. 'Be that as it may,' I continued, 'look what's happening to education in this country.'

Dorothy had armed me with actual questions from school exam papers. *Which do you prefer – atom bombs or charity?* And a maths question – even maths is becoming political: *If it costs £5 billion a year to maintain Britain's nuclear defences and £75 a year to feed a starving African child, how many African children could be saved from starvation by abandoning nuclear defence?*

Humphrey answered the second question immediately. 'That's easy. None. The MOD would spend it all on conventional weapons. But the question is simply asking for £5 billion divided by £75.'

'Do you deny', I remonstrated with him, 'that kids aren't even being taught basic arithmetic?

'No,' he replied carefully. 'But the LEAs[1] would doubtless argue that they don't need it – the kids all have pocket calculators.'

'But they need to know how it's done,' I reminded him forcefully. 'We all learned basic arithmetic, didn't we?'

Humphrey then asked me a whole bunch of stupid and irrelevant questions designed to prove to me that a strict academic education had no value! Humphrey, of all people! I couldn't believe it. He had the most traditional strict academic upbringing of anyone I've ever met. Anyway, I brushed his smokescreen – for that was what it was – aside.

SIR BERNARD WOOLLEY RECALLS:[2]
I read this portion of Hacker's diary with the greatest amusement. The questions to which he refers were neither stupid nor irrelevant.

When the Prime Minister asserted that we had all learned basic arithmetic Sir Humphrey immediately asked him: 'What is three thousand nine-hundred and fifty-seven divided by seventy-three?'

Hacker prevaricated, then said that he would need a pencil and paper for that. I offered him both but to no one's surprise he refused them, remarking simply that he could certainly have done that sum when he left school.

'And now you'd use a calculator?' enquired Humphrey. The point was

---

[1] Local Education Authorities.
[2] In conversation with the Editors.

well taken. But Hacker denied that Sir Humphrey had made any useful point at all. Instead, he remarked peevishly that hardly anyone knew any Latin any more either.

'Tempora mutantur, et nos mutamur in illis,' replied Sir Humphrey appropriately.

There was a slight pause as Hacker stared vacantly at him. Finally he was obliged to humiliate himself again by asking him for a translation.

'The times change and we change with the times,' I said.

'Precisely,' said the Prime Minister, as if the quotation proved his point – whereas any fool could see it helped Sir Humphrey's side of the argument.

Humphrey provocatively continued to speak in Latin. 'Si tacuisses, philosophus mansisses,' he said.

Hacker was suspicious. He asked what *that* meant. Sir Humphrey obliged. 'If you'd kept your mouth shut we might have thought you were clever.'

Hacker looked apoplectic. I thought he was going to suffer a coronary then and there. Sir Humphrey hastily explained. 'Not you, Prime Minister. That's the translation.'

Hacker then berated Sir Humphrey for denying the value of an academic education, whereupon Sir Humphrey replied – rather too insultingly in my view – that he could see no use for it if he personally couldn't even use it in conversation with the Prime Minister of Great Britain.

There is no doubt in my mind that Sir Humphrey, with his arrogance and determination to win the argument for its own sake, lost sight of his own policy objectives. By provoking and humiliating Hacker he ensured that Hacker would not drop the matter – a serious miscalculation.

[*Hacker's diary continues – Ed.*]

Humphrey was basically refusing to admit that our educational system was a disaster. I told him: 'Children are being taught subversive nonsense. There is total indiscipline in the classroom.'

Humphrey simply wouldn't acknowledge the truth. He kept making cheap debating points. For instance: 'If there's total indiscipline in the classrooms, they won't even know they're being taught subversive nonsense. And they certainly won't learn any. Anyway, no self-respecting child believes a word the teacher tells him.'

I was getting seriously angry at these facetious and unworthy answers. 'We're supposed to be educating them for a working life and three-quarters of the time they're bored stiff.'

'I should have thought being bored stiff for three-quarters of the time was excellent preparation for working life,' was the flip reply.

'Humphrey,' I said firmly, 'we raised the leaving age to sixteen to enable them to learn more. And they're learning less.'

Suddenly he answered me seriously. 'We didn't raise the leaving age to enable them to learn more. We raised it to keep teenagers off the job market and hold down the unemployment figures.'

He was right. But I didn't want to get into all that. I returned to the rest of the question. I asked him if he was trying to tell me that there's nothing wrong with our educational system.

'Of course I'm not, Prime Minister. It's a joke. It's always been a joke. As long as you leave it in the hands of local councillors it will stay a joke. Half of them are your enemies anyway. And the other half are the sort of friends that make you prefer your enemies.'

I finally saw where he was coming from in this discussion. He believes that education will never get any better so long as it's subject to all that tomfoolery in the town halls. He rightly observed that we'd never leave an important subject like defence to the local authorities – if we gave them £100 million each and told them to defend themselves we could stop worrying about the Russians, we'd have civil war in three weeks.

He claims that that's what we've done with education, that no one thinks education is serious the way defence is serious.

It's certainly true that no one takes *civil* defence seriously, and that's why it's left to the borough councils. But I assured Humphrey that I took education incredibly seriously – it could cost me the next election.

'Ah.' He smiled a superior smile. 'In my naïveté I thought you were concerned about the future of our children.'

Well, I am. These are not contradictory worries. After all, kids get the vote at eighteen.

Humphrey had a simple answer to the education screw-up: Centralise! Take the responsibility away from the local councils and put it under the Department of Education and Science. Then I could do something about it.

I wonder if he's right. It sounds too easy somehow. And yet . . . my hopes were raised.

'Humphrey,' I said, 'do you think I could? Actually grasp the nettle and take the bull by the horns?'

Bernard spoke for the first time. 'Prime Minister, you can't take the bull by the horns if you're grasping the nettle.'

I could hardly believe that this was Bernard's sole contribution to a discussion of such importance. I just sat there and goggled at him. He must have thought I didn't understand him, for he began to explain himself: 'I mean, if you grasped the nettle with one hand, you could take the bull by one horn with the other hand, but not by both horns because your hand wouldn't be big enough, and if you took a bull by only one horn it would be rather dangerous because . . .'

I found my voice. 'Bernard . . .' I said. And he stopped. Perhaps he just can't help it. Attention to detail is all very well, but *really*!

I told Humphrey he'd given me food for thought

'In that case,' he replied complacently, '*bon appétit.*'

December 14th

I'm off on a brief pre-Christmas tour of the North-West tomorrow. Dorothy gave me a schedule, which includes Prime Ministerial visits to factories and hospitals.

'Drumming up votes in the marginal constituencies,' I remarked jovially to Bernard.

'No, Prime Minister,' he said.

I didn't realise what he meant at first.

'I'm coming with you,' he explained carefully, 'so it's a government tour. But if it consists of canvassing in marginals it's a party event and I can't come – and, more to the point, the Treasury can't pay for it all.'

His pedantry can be useful! Dorothy immediately made it clear, for the record, that we are making a government visit to the North-West, and that it is a pure coincidence that all the stops are in marginals. Bernard was satisfied.

I was still preoccupied with education. I asked Dorothy what I could do about it. Quickly!

'Do you mean do, or appear to do?' she wanted to know.

Silly question. 'Appear to do, obviously. There's nothing I *can* do.'

She thought for a moment, then proposed that I made some television appearance associated with something good and successful in education.

I was pleased to hear there *was* such a thing. She delved into her briefcase and handed me a sheet of paper containing details of 'St Margaret's School business enterprise unit'. She thinks I should visit the school on my tour. Apparently it could be squeezed into the schedule.

The school has set up its own manufacturing and trading company. They make cheeseboards, paperweights, toast racks and so on. Then they market and sell them. Furthermore, in their maths and business studies classes they track the whole operation. They involve local businessmen, and parents help too.

It sounds great. And what's more, it costs the DES *nothing* – they make a profit.

I wondered if there was any downside. Bad publicity on the grounds that children are being taught to be grasping? But no – Dorothy tells me they give the money to local charities.

It's obviously a *must* for a North-West trip. I told Dorothy to give it enough time on the schedule for TV cameras to cover it properly. And, I added, 'give me a speech with a snappy twenty-second passage for the TV news. It should all help to win back a few seats.'

Bernard shifted uncomfortably in his chair. He cleared his throat. 'Um, Prime Minister . . .' he reminded me firmly.

'I mean, Bernard,' I said, changing my tone, 'it will give a lead to those responsible for the nation's education.'

'Of course, Prime Minister,' he said with a smile.

[*Hacker's tour of the North-West was a great success, and his visit to St Margaret's School was indeed reported on the national news. The film itself does not survive, but we are fortunate that a transcript was made and we reprint it overleaf, with the kind permission of Independent Television News – Ed.*]

Independent Television News Limited

THE ATTACHED TRANSCRIPT WAS TYPED FROM A RECORDING AND NOT COPIED
FROM AN ORIGINAL SCRIPT. BECAUSE OF THE RISK OF MISHEARING ITN
CANNOT VOUCH FOR ITS COMPLETE ACCURACY

'NEWS AT TEN'

TRANSMISSION: DECEMBER 17TH

ACTUALITY:

NEWSREADER (offscreen): And finally, this morning the Prime Minister
visited St Margaret's School, Widnes, on his north-western tour.

SHOTS OF JIM HACKER, WITH BERNARD WOOLLEY IN THE BACKGROUND,
SURROUNDED BY NUMEROUS PRESS REPORTERS, ENTERING A SCHOOL WOODWORK
SHOP WHERE BOYS AND GIRLS IN NEAT SCHOOL UNIFORMS ARE BUSY.

NEWSREADER (offscreen): The school has set up its own little
manufacturing business where the children make a variety of goods
in the school carpentry shop for sale in the local community.
The children do their own sales and marketing.

CUT TO:
JIM HACKER STANDING WITH A GROUP OF SCHOOLCHILDREN, WATCHING THEM
PACKING, LABELLING AND STACKING BOXES OF GOODS.

NEWSREADER (offscreen): And they use the experience they gain
from the enterprise as a basis for their maths and business
studies.

CUT TO:
WIDE ANGLE - THE SCHOOL HALL. PRIME MINISTER HACKER IS SEEN ON
THE DAIS. A SENIOR GIRL HANDS HIM A THREE-LEGGED STOOL. THEY
SHAKE HANDS. BULBS FLASH FOR PHOTOS.

- 1 -

NEWSREADER (offscreen): The Prime Minister was presented with an
example of the school's output.

CUT TO:
MEDIUM CLOSE-UP OF THE PRIME MINISTER, ADDRESSING THE SCHOOL.

HACKER: I must congratulate you all on the hard work, the
discipline and the success of your enterprise. You set an example
in British education which other schools would do well to follow.
We need more schools like St Margaret's. And I shall certainly
treasure your present - no Prime Ministers ever lose seats if they
can possibly help it.

CUT TO:
WIDE-ANGLE OF AUDIENCE IN SCHOOL HALL. LAUGHTER AND APPLAUSE.

CUT TO:
THE PRIME MINISTER, SMILING AND WAVING AS HE LEAVES THE PLATFORM.

- 2 -

[Hacker's diary continues – Ed.]

December 17th

I watched a very satisfying film report of my visit to Widnes on the News at Ten tonight. Annie and Dorothy, who'd stayed for dinner, watched it with me. We all agreed that it had gone pretty well, especially my joke at the end of my little speech.

Actually, Dorothy claimed it was *her* joke. She was being petty. If by *her joke* she meant that she *thought* of it, then I suppose she's right – but that's hardly relevant.

The coverage was much better than it had been on the BBC. The BBC didn't describe it as 'the Prime Minister touring the North-West', they said it was 'Jim Hacker visiting the marginal constituencies'.

Both versions are perfectly true, but in my opinion it shows that the BBC is biased against me. I tried to explain this to Annie, who couldn't see it.

'Why shouldn't they report the facts?' she asked.

I explained that they don't have to report *all* the facts. Furthermore, there's nothing wrong with visiting marginal constituencies, but they imply that there is.

Annie *still* didn't understand. 'You mean, it's all right to report the majority of the facts but not the facts of the majorities?'

That's the kind of smart-alec remark that really makes me angry. The point is, it's all part of a wider picture. The BBC did the same to me earlier on, in the Nine O'Clock News, when they reported our dispute with the French: 'Mr Hacker claimed that the action was permissible, but the French government stated it was a violation of the treaty.'

'Isn't that true?'

'Of course it's true!' I exploded. 'But it makes it sound like me, on my own, being put down by the whole of France. It makes me look as though I'm in the wrong.'

'But the French think you are.'

'That's not the bloody point!' I shouted. 'They could have said: "Monsieur Dubois claimed that the action was a violation of the treaty, but the British Government stated it was permissible." Then it would have sounded – quite correctly – as though all of us were putting some cheeky Frog in his place. But they don't say that! Oh no! They want to get me!'

Annie was apparently undisturbed by the BBC's manifest bias, hatred, intolerance and corruption. 'But what they said was still true,' she reiterated stubbornly.

My jaw seized up with fury and frustration. Through clenched teeth I snarled, 'It's *still* biased to say so!! The other's true too!!'

I didn't want to demean myself by losing my temper in front of Dorothy, who'd so far stayed very quiet. I took several deep breaths, then strolled calmly over to the drinks table and poured myself a very large Scotch.

Annie remained completely calm. 'Jim,' she said, 'I'm not interested in your paranoia, I'm interested in that school.'

Dorothy spoke up, relieved not to have to take sides in a family fight. 'Yes, it must be a good place if parents are queuing up to get their kids into it.'

'What a pity that they can't all get in,' said Annie, and poured coffee for us both. 'Why *can't* more parents send their children there?'

'No room,' I explained.

Dorothy corrected me. 'There is room actually, Jim. School numbers are falling.'

She's right, in one sense. 'But it would be poaching from other schools,' I pointed out.

Annie looked up. 'What's wrong with that?'

'It's obvious. The other schools would then be too short of pupils. They'd have to close.'

'Great,' said Annie. 'So then St Margaret's would take over their buildings.'

I tried to explain to Annie that they couldn't do that. It wouldn't be fair.

'Who to?' she wanted to know.

'To the teachers in the schools that had to close.'

'But the good ones would be taken on by the popular schools. They'd be needed.'

'What about the bad ones?' I argued. 'It wouldn't be fair on them.'

'What about being fair on the kids?' said Annie. 'Or are the bad teachers' jobs more important?'

I sipped my coffee, and put my feet up on the leather footstool. 'It's no good, Annie.' I was tolerant. 'Who's to say which are the bad teachers? It can't be done.'

'Why not?'

I couldn't really think of the reason, but I was sure there was one. Then, to my surprise, Dorothy asked the same question: 'Why not?'

This threw me. And to my surprise I found that I was really stuck.

Dorothy took up the argument. 'Suppose schools were like doctors,' she pondered, helping herself to a peppermint cream chocolate. 'After all, under the National Health Service you can go to whichever doctor you like, can't you?'

I nodded.

'And the doctor gets paid per patient,' she continued thoughtfully. 'So why don't we do the same with schools? A National Education Service. Parents choose the school they want, and the school gets paid per pupil.'

'There'd be an outcry,' I replied.

'From parents?' said Dorothy, knowing the answer full well.

'No,' I had to acknowledge. 'From the Department of Education.'

'I see.' And she smiled. Then she asked another question to which she already knew the answer. 'And who has the most votes, parents or the DES?'

That wasn't exactly the point. And she knew it! 'The DES would block it,' I reminded her.

And then she said something so revolutionary, so riveting and so ruthless that it shook me rigid. [*Hacker often displayed a talent, probably subconscious, for alliteration when excited – Ed.*]

'Fine,' said Dorothy. 'Get rid of them!'

It took me a moment to realise what she meant. I think I just stared blankly at her. Get rid of the Department of Education? I didn't really understand.

'Get rid of it!' she repeated. 'Abolish it. Remove it.'

I asked her what she meant, exactly.

'Eliminate it. Expunge it. Eradicate it,' she explained.

I was beginning to understand what she was driving at. But I asked her to explain further.

She looked slightly flummoxed. 'Um . . . I don't quite know how else to . . . well, let me put it this way.' She hesitated for a moment, considering her choice of words carefully. 'What I mean is,' she said finally, 'get rid of it.'

'Get rid of it?' I asked.

She confirmed that she meant that I should get rid of it.

'I couldn't do that,' I said. I was in a daze.

'Why?' she asked. 'What does it do?'

And, suddenly, I realised that I *could* do that! Local Authorities could administer everything that is needed. We could have a Board of National School Inspectors, and give all the rest of the DES's functions to the Department of the Environment. And I could send that house-trained idiot Patrick to the House of Lords.

'Golly!' I wondered in awe. 'What will Humphrey say?'

Dorothy smiled a beatific smile. 'Whatever he says,' she said happily, 'I want to be there when you tell him.'

'And witness a clash between the political will and the administrative will?'

She sat back thoughtfully. 'I think it will be a clash between the political will and the administrative won't.'

December 18th

I called Humphrey in first thing this morning. Dorothy was with me. I tried to disguise my excitement as I casually told him that I wanted to bounce a new idea off him.

The word 'new' usually alerts Humphrey that trouble's in store, but this time he seemed perfectly relaxed and actually chuckled when I told him that I've realised how to reform our education system.

So I let him have it. 'Humphrey, I'm going to let parents take their children away from schools. They will be able to move them to any school they want.'

He was unconcerned. 'You mean, after application, scrutiny, tribunal hearing and appeal procedures?'

It was my turn to chuckle. 'No, Humphrey. They could just move them. Whenever they want.'

'I'm sorry, Prime Minister, I don't follow you.' I could see that he genuinely didn't understand.

Dorothy spelled it out, abrasively. 'The government, Sir Humphrey, is going to let parents decide which school to send their children to.'

Suddenly he understood that we actually meant what we were saying. He exploded into protest. 'Prime Minister, you're not serious?'

I nodded benevolently. 'Yes I am.'

'But that's preposterous!'

'Why?' asked Dorothy.

He ignored her completely. 'You can't let parents make these choices. How on earth would parents know which schools are best?'

Coolly I appraised him. 'What school did you go to, Humphrey?'

'Winchester.'

'Was it good?' I asked politely.

'Excellent, of course.'

'Who chose it?'

'My parents, naturally.' I smiled at him. 'Prime Minister, that's quite different. My parents were discerning people. You can't expect *ordinary* people to know where to send their children.'

Dorothy was manifestly shocked at Humphrey's snobbery and élitism. 'Why on earth not?'

He shrugged. The answer was obvious to him. 'How could they tell?'

Dorothy, a mother herself, found the question only too easy to answer. 'They could tell if their kids could read and write and do sums. They could tell if the neighbours were happy with the school. They could tell if the exam results aren't good.'

Again he studiously ignored her. 'Examinations aren't everything, Prime Minister.'

Dorothy stood up, moved around the Cabinet table and sat down very close to me so that Humphrey could no longer avoid meeting her eyes. 'That is true, Humphrey – and those parents who don't want an academic education for their kids could choose progressive schools.'

I could see that, as far as Humphrey was concerned, Dorothy and I were talking ancient Chinese. He simply didn't understand us. Again he tried to explain his position, and he was becoming quite emotional. 'Parents are not qualified to make these choices. Teachers are the professionals. In fact, parents are the worst people to bring up children, they have no qualifications for it. We don't allow untrained teachers to teach. The same would apply to parents in an ideal world.'

I realised with stunning clarity, and for the very first time, how far Humphrey's dream of an ideal world differed from mine. 'You mean,' I asked slowly and quietly, 'parents should be stopped from having kids until they've been trained?'

He sighed impatiently. Apparently I'd missed the point. 'No, no. Having kids isn't the problem. They've all been trained to *have* kids, sex education classes have been standard for years now.'

'I see,' I said, and turned to Dorothy, who was wide-eyed in patent disbelief at our most senior Civil Servant and advocate of the Orwellian corporate state. 'Perhaps,' I suggested, 'we can improve on the sex education classes? Before people have children we could give them exams. Written and practical. Or both, perhaps? Then we could issue breeding licences.'

Humphrey wasn't a bit amused. He ticked me off. 'There's no need to be facetious, Prime Minister. I'm being serious. It's *looking after* children that parents are not qualified for. That's why they have no idea how to choose schools for them. It couldn't work.'

Dorothy leaned across in front of me, to catch his eye. 'Then how does the Health Service work? People choose their family doctor without having medical qualifications.'

'Ah,' said Humphrey, playing for time. 'Yes,' he said, flummoxed. 'That's different,' he concluded, as if he'd actually said something.

'Why?' asked Dorothy.

'Well, doctors are . . . I mean, patients aren't parents.'

'Really?' Dorothy was laughing openly at him. 'What gives you that idea?'

He was beginning to get extremely ratty. 'I mean, not *as such*. Anyway, as a matter of fact I think letting people choose doctors is a very bad idea. Very messy. Much tidier to allocate people to GPs. Much fairer. We could even cut the numbers in each doctor's practice, and everyone would stand an equal chance of getting the bad doctors.'

I was quietly amazed at Humphrey's – and the Civil Service's – concept of 'fair'.

Humphrey was now in full flow, passionate, emotional, scathing, committed like I have never seen. 'But we're not discussing the Health Service, Prime Minister, we're discussing education. And with respect, Prime Minister, I think you should know that the DES will react with some caution to this rather novel proposal.'

This was the language of war! Humphrey had all guns blazing. I've never heard such abusive language from him.

I stayed calm. 'So you think they'll block it?'

'I mean', he said, tight-lipped and angry,' that they will give it the most serious and urgent consideration, but will insist on a thorough and rigorous examination of all the proposals, allied to a detailed feasibility study and budget analysis before producing a consultative document for consideration by all interested bodies and seeking comments and recommendations to be incorporated in a brief for a series of working parties who will produce individual studies that will form the background for a more wide-ranging document considering whether or not the proposal should be taken forward to the next stage.'

He meant they'd block it! But it will be no problem. No problem at all. Because, as I told him, I have a solution to that. 'So I'll abolish the DES!' I mentioned casually.

He thought he'd mis-heard. 'I'm sorry?'

'We'll abolish it,' I repeated obligingly.

'Abolish it?' He couldn't grasp the meaning of the words.

'Why not?' Dorothy wanted to see if there were any reason.

'Why not?' he said, his voice rising to the pitch of a Basil Fawlty at the end of his tether. 'Abolish Education and Science? It would be the end of civilisation as we know it.'

I shook my head at him. He was quite hysterical. 'No, we'd only be abolishing the Department. Education and science will flourish.'

'Without a government department?' He was staring at us in horror, as though we were certifiably insane. 'Impossible!'

Dorothy seemed almost sorry for him. She tried to explain. 'Humphrey, government departments are tombstones. The Department of Industry marks the grave of industry. The Department of Employment marks the grave of employment. The Department of the Environment marks the grave of the environment. And the Department of Education marks where the corpse of British education is buried.'

He was staring the Goths and the Vandals in the face. He had no reply. So I asked him why we need the DES. What does it do? What's its role?

He tried to calm down and explain. 'I . . . I hardly know where to begin,' he began. 'It lays down guidelines, it centralises and channels money to the Local Education Authorities and the University Grants Committee. It sets standards.'

I asked him a string of questions. 'Does it lay down the curriculum?'

'No, but . . .'

'Does it select and change Head Teachers?'

'No, but . . .'

'Does it maintain school buildings?'

'No, but . . .'

'Does it set and mark exams?'

'No, but . . .'

'Does it select the children?'

'No, but . . .'

'Then *how*', I wanted to know, 'does the Secretary of State affect how *my* child does at *her* school?'

To Humphrey the answer was obvious. 'He supplies sixty per cent of the cash!'

So that's it. We were right. Dorothy pursued the cross-examination. 'Why can't the cash go straight from the Treasury to the schools? And straight to the University Grants Committee? Do we really need 2000 civil servants simply to funnel money from A to B?'

Almost in despair, he shook his head and cried: 'The DES also creates a legislative framework for education.'

What did he mean? There's hardly any legislation at all. What there is, the Department of the Environment could do – Environment deals with other local government matters.

Humphrey was fighting a desperate rearguard action. 'Prime Minister, you *can't* be serious. Who would assess forward planning and staffing variations, variations in pupil population, the density of schooling required in urban and rural areas . . . Who would make sure everything *ran properly*?'

'It doesn't run properly now,' I pointed out. 'Let's see if we can do better without the bureaucracy.'

'But who would plan for the future?'

I laughed. But I didn't just laugh, I laughed uproariously. Laughter overwhelmed me, for the first time since I'd been Prime Minister. Tears were rolling down my cheeks. 'Do you mean?' I finally gasped, breathless, weeping with laughter, 'that education in Britain today is what the Department of Education *planned*?'

'Yes, of course,' said Humphrey, and then went immediately and without hesitation straight into reverse. 'No, certainly not.'

Dorothy was getting bored with the meeting. She stood up. 'Two thousand five hundred private schools seem to solve these planning problems every day,' she commented curtly. 'They just respond to changing circumstances, supply and demand. Easy.'

I wanted to give Humphrey one last chance. 'Is there anything else the DES does?'

His eyes whizzed back and forth, as he thought furiously. 'Um . . . er . . . um.'

I stood up too. 'Fine,' I said. 'That's it. We don't need it, do we? Quod erat demonstrandum.'[1]

[*In her book* The Prime Minister's Ear, *Dorothy Wainwright made an interesting attempt to explain Sir Humphrey Appleby's complex attitude to state education. Her book is now out of print but we reprint a short extract below – Ed.*]

Sir Humphrey Appleby's paternalist attitude may not have been wholly cynical. He apparently believed that more central direction was the answer

[1] QED.

to all the nation's problems. It is probable that he viewed the main purpose of state education as a means of removing children from the undesirable influence of their semi-educated parents. And he doubtless felt that most parents regarded schools as somewhere that they could dump their children during working hours. In short, he truly believed that the man in Whitehall knew best. For at the root of this passionate dispute over education lay the fundamental tribal struggle between the Whitehall Man and Westminster Man.

It is not that Sir Humphrey was against giving the parents what was euphemistically known as a 'voice' in the running of a school. Indeed, he was unconcerned about parent governors because, so long as the parents as a whole were unable to remove their children from a school with which they were unhappy, the parent governors could safely be ignored. If a child was prevented from attending school by a dissatisfied parent, the Attendance Officer was soon on hand to threaten the parent with an appearance in court.

In the end, it was the more affluent middle classes who benefited from the system, the same middle classes who won the lion's share of all the benefits of the welfare state in not only education, but housing and medicine too. Inevitably benefits went to articulate people who could best advance their claims, who could move to the nicest residential areas with the best schools and doctors, who could claim mortgage tax relief, and who enjoyed subsidised art.

Sir Humphrey, however, clung to the only belief that he had left after thirty years in government: that if he had more control, he could make things better. Anything that was wrong with society was evidence, proof indeed, of not enough power. Sadly he remained unshakeably convinced right up till the very day of his death in St Dympna's Home for the Elderly Deranged.

[*The last entry of the year in Sir Humphrey's private diary records a meeting with Sir Arnold Robinson, his predecessor as Secretary of the Cabinet, at their old haunt: the Athenaeum Club – Ed.*]

Met Arnold for lunch at the Club. I told him of the truly appalling meeting with Hacker this morning.

Like me, he thought it was unthinkable. Once they start abolishing whole Departments, the very foundations of civilisation crumble. Indeed he's right. The barbarians are at the gates. This is the return of the Dark Ages.

I asked him if anything so shocking had ever been suggested while he was at 70 Whitehall.[1] Apparently not. Arnold had let them amalgamate Departments, of course, but that's quite a different matter: amalgamation means that you keep all the existing staff and put in an extra layer of co-ordinating management at the top.

[1] The Cabinet Office.

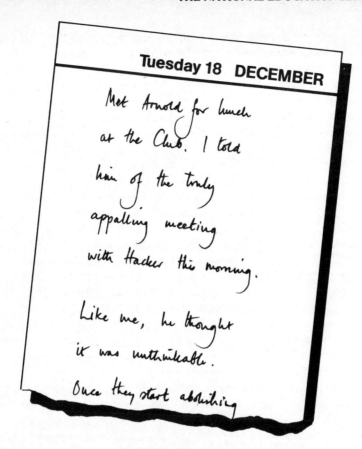

Tuesday 18 DECEMBER

Met Arnold for lunch at the Club. I told him of the truly appalling meeting with Hacker this morning.

Like me, he thought it was unthinkable.

Once they start abolishing

But he agreed that, come hell or high water, I have to stop the liquidation of the DES. He asked me if I'd tried discrediting the person who proposed it.

That is impossible in this case, of course. The Wainwright female is the culprit, and therefore Hacker's passing it off as his own idea.

Arnold had a couple of other tired old ideas:

1. *Discrediting the facts its based on.*

Not possible. It's a political idea, so obviously facts don't come into it.

2. *Massaging the figures.*

There are no figures involved.

I asked him what he really thought. Shamefully he peered over the side of his leather wing armchair to check that he wasn't being overheard, and then he leaned forward and whispered an appalling admission: that in his opinion it was actually quite a good idea.

I'd never even thought of that: for a mad moment I wondered if we ought to experiment with it, play along with it for the sake of the nation's children.

But this was not Arnold's intention and, seeing that I was wavering, he bolstered me up and gave me courage. 'Never mind about the nation's children! What about our colleagues in the Department of Education?'

I apologised for my lapse. It's just that I've been under great strain.

The fact is that the *only* people who will like this plan are parents and the children. Everyone who counts will be against it, namely:

i)   Teachers' Unions
ii) Local Authorities
iii) The Educational press
iv) The DES

We decided upon a temporary holding strategy:

1) The Unions can be counted on to disrupt the schools. And their leaders will go on television to say that it is the government who are causing the disruption.
2) The local authorities will threaten to turn the constituency parties against the government.
3) The DES will delay every stage of the process and leak anything and everything that embarrasses the government. Arnold will be able to help with that, at the Campaign for Freedom of Information.
4) The education press will print any damn fool story we feed them.

We relaxed and ordered a couple more brandies. There was one little problem: we hadn't decided what our argument would be. Arnold suggested that we say that this new proposal will destroy our educational system. But there was a problem: everyone knows it's destroyed already. So we decided that we will say [*by which Sir Arnold meant that the Press will say – Ed.*] that government interference has already destroyed the education system, and that this plan will make things even worse.

I was sceptical. I wondered if that would really do the trick. Arnold assured me that it always has in the past. He's right, of course, but this time the political pressure is much stronger.

We had no answer. Arnold stressed that I must find a *political* weapon with which to fight this battle. It is undoubtedly in the national interest to do so, even though I'd be in conflict with government policy.

'Government policy,' said Arnold thoughtfully, 'is almost always in conflict with the national interest. Our job is to see that the national interest triumphs. Governments are always grateful in the end.'

He may be right. But I have no political weapon in mind, and nor has he. And it's my job. I must somehow prove myself worthy of the high office to which I've been called.

[*But luck was on Sir Humphrey's side. A most unlikely event occurred that changed the course of history. When the Cabinet Secretary arrived at 70 Whitehall the following morning, with leaden step and a heavy heart and no strategy, Bernard Woolley was waiting anxiously to see him. Sir Bernard Woolley recalls*[1] *the momentous*

---

[1] In conversation with the Editors.

events of that morning, the turning point that never was – Ed.]

I was waiting for Sir Humphrey in his oak-panelled office. He was late. The Prime Minister had sent me to find him.

Humphrey asked for the agenda – which was all too simple. The Abolition of the DES.

He commented that it was going to be bloody! I agreed.

And on the way to the Cabinet Room I asked him for some advice on what I thought was an urgent but minor problem.

This was it: St Margaret's School in Widnes, the enterprise school which the Prime Minister had visited at the beginning of the week, where they'd given him that stool, had been in trouble with the law.

It had just come to light that the wood being used in the carpentry shop was stolen. In fact, stolen from the government, from a YTS[1] workshop. It was stolen by the previous year's pupils, who were working there.

Humphrey's reaction astonished me. He stopped dead, in the middle of the long dark corridor, stared at me, and then smiled what I can only describe as an ecstatic smile. 'How shocking!' he beamed. I gave him the file, which showed that the matter had been referred to the DES from the Department of Employment because the theft had come to light in a school. They didn't know whether to prosecute.

I apologised for bothering Sir Humphrey with such a minor matter. Little did I realise the significance of the report at that moment – though only five minutes later it was clear that I'd helped drop an atom bomb on Hacker's educational reforms.

[*Hacker's diary continues – Ed.*]

December 19th

A sad day. My greatest, most fundamental reform had to be abandoned. It's not that the DES is the most significant Department in Whitehall – but to me it had come to represent bureaucracy in its purest, least diluted form – a totally unnecessary Department, one that was not merely irrelevant but which was by its very existence an impediment to reform.

The meeting started well enough. 'Only one item on the agenda – abolition of the DES,' I began cheerfully.

I noticed Humphrey was in much better spirits than I had expected. 'If it's only one item, it's an agen*dum*,' he corrected me arrogantly as he sat down across the table from me.

Bernard leapt to my defence. 'I don't think the Prime Minister got

---

[1] Youth Training Scheme.

as far as the second declension,' he said. At least, I *think* he was leaping to my defence.

In any case, I felt extremely tolerant, even benign. 'I don't mind you scoring cheap debating points, Humphrey,' I said, 'since you've lost the battle of the DES.' Pride goeth before a fall!

'The DES will be very upset, Prime Minister,' replied Humphrey, who was worryingly relaxed, I noted.

'Does it matter,' I asked, 'since they'll have ceased to exist?'

Humphrey gave me every chance to back out and save face. But he withheld the crucial point of information that had come his way. I knew he was hiding some ace up his sleeve – but I didn't know it was the ace of trumps.

Meanwhile, we sparred. He told me that the process of abolishing the DES would take a year or two, and meanwhile they'd fight tooth and nail.

I asked what they could do to me. He was enigmatic, confining himself to veiled threats, such as 'They are a formidable Department.'

'I'm a formidable Prime Minister,' I retorted.

'Oh indeed,' agreed my Cabinet Secretary, 'but you might still need their co-operation.'

Actually, that idea struck me as intrinsically funny. The idea of the DES co-operating with the Government? Absurd. But as I sat there laughing, the axe fell!

'Fine,' said Humphrey. 'If you don't want their co-operation I'll tell them to go ahead with the prosecution.'

At first I thought I'd misheard. 'Prosecution? What prosecution?' I didn't know what he could mean. I looked at Bernard. Bernard stared intently at his shoelaces. I had no choice but to ask Humphrey what he was talking about?

He smiled again, so I knew I was in deep trouble. 'Well, it's hardly worth bothering you with, but that enterprise school where you were televised this week . . .' He paused, elegantly, to make me suffer.

'Yes?' I said.

'"An example of what's best in education,"' he quoted me saying.

'Yes?' I repeated, my heart in my mouth.

'"A model for other schools to follow."' I began to think he was going to re-enact my entire speech.

'Go on!' I snapped.

'Well . . . it's just that its profits were apparently the proceeds of theft.'

I didn't know what he meant. 'What do you mean, theft?'

'I mean', he explained pleasantly, 'removing goods without the knowledge or consent of the owner, with the intent of permanently depriving him of possession.'

'Yes, Humphrey.' I was getting pretty tight-lipped. 'I know what theft means. But what do *you* mean?'

Well, it all boiled down to this: the stool that they gave me in that presentation was made from stolen wood. It was nicked from the local YTS workshop by two of last year's pupils. A *pair* of nickers, as Bernard said, trying unsuccessfully to lighten the atmosphere.

The YTS want to prosecute. And the Department of Education can stop them – by returning the wood and hushing the whole thing up.

Humphrey said that the DES took a different view. Surprise, surprise!

I tried to tough it out. I said that the DES must obviously return the wood and forget the whole thing. It is their duty, I argued – otherwise I'll look ridiculous, having told millions of voters on TV that the school is an example to Britain.

'It is a *sort* of example,' conceded Humphrey maliciously.

'But it's not typical of enterprise schools,' I insisted.

He smiled a malevolent smile. 'It was enterprising.'

'They mustn't prosecute!' I commanded him, cutting the crap.

He looked surprised. 'Is that your instruction?' I nodded. He took a sharp intake of breath. 'Well, I hope that the Department of Education doesn't leak the fact that you're covering up for thieves.'

Blackmail, if ever I heard it. I changed my position immediately. 'You misunderstood, Humphrey,' I said grandly. 'It's *not* my instruction. Just tell them not to prosecute.'

'Ah,' said Humphrey thoughtfully. 'That would need their co-operation.'

Checkmate. Game, set and match. Snookered. I could just imagine the headlines: *PRIME MINISTER OF CRIME*! Or *JIM'S ENTERPRISING PUPILS*.

It was my turn to beg. 'Humphrey,' I said, 'you must persuade them to stop it.'

He was implacable. 'It's *rather* difficult', he drawled, 'to persuade people to co-operate when they're under a death sentence.'

I had no choice but to lie. 'Death sentence?' I queried, in a surprised voice.

'I thought you were about to abolish the Department.'

'Abolish it?' I said. 'Oh, *that*!' And I laughed as convincingly as I could. 'No, no, Humphrey, that was just a vague idea. I wasn't really serious. Can't you tell when I'm joking?'

'You're sure?'

'I'm sure I was joking.'

I left myself a loophole. But Humphrey spotted it instantly. 'And you're sure you're not going to abolish the DES?'

'Yes.'

'I have your assurance, Prime Minister?'

I took a deep breath. 'Yes,' I said quietly. My plans were turning to dust. Like all my plans. Suddenly I saw, with a real clarity that I'd never enjoyed before, that although I might win the occasional policy victory, or make some reforms, or be indulged with a few scraps from the table, nothing fundamental was ever *ever* going to change.

Humphrey was now in the best of humour. I heard his voice, as if in the distance. 'Prime Minister? Prime Minister? Are you all right?'

I focused on him. 'Yes.'

'Excellent. Then shall we continue with the agendum?'

'Agendum?' I smiled. All the fight had gone out of me. 'No, Humphrey, we have no agendum any more. Meeting declared closed. All right?'

'Yes Prime Minister.' He smiled at me with sympathy. He could see that at last I understood.